MW01485820

Praise for *Scaling Innovation*

"Like most new technologies before it, AI will upend old business models. This book is an essential read for successful AI founders."

—Clay Bavor,
Cofounder, Sierra

"*Scaling Innovation* shares the strategic frameworks and practical insights every leader needs to turn a great early idea into a scaling success story. The book brilliantly captures the strategies and principles behind how companies like Canva scaled effectively. For any entrepreneur or leader seeking a clear path to navigate the complexities of profitable growth, this book is a fantastic blueprint."

—David Burson,
Global Head of Revenue and Growth, Canva

"At Superhuman, we've lived the principles in this book—like beautifully simple pricing—and seen firsthand how they drive explosive growth. Not reading this book isn't just a mistake; it's a competitive disadvantage."

—Rahul Vohra,
Founder and CEO, Superhuman

"Brilliantly structured and deeply insightful. Ramanujam and Hartman expose the traps of one-dimensional scaling and provide practical strategies for turning great products into great businesses."

—Sridhar Narayanan,
Professor of Marketing,
Stanford Graduate School of Business

"A great product isn't enough—you need to prove its value. This book gives early-stage startups the tools to build value-based selling into their DNA, navigate tough negotiations, and confidently hold the line on price."

—Devin Bhushan,
CEO, Squint

"I've been a huge fan of *Monetizing Innovation*—I have handed a copy to every founder I met. *Scaling Innovation* takes it to the next level, showing how to turn great products into scalable, profitable businesses. I couldn't be more excited about this book and the impact it will have on founders everywhere."

—Zach Coelius,
Managing Partner, Coelius Capital

"An important lesson learned during the startup and growth phase at Segment was how much rigor you can apply to monetize and scale your innovation. It blew my mind that there was an entire field dedicated to pricing strategy, and we learned a lot from working with Madhavan and Simon-Kucher. This book encapsulates all those learnings and is a must read for founders."

—Peter Reinhardt,
CEO and Cofounder at Charm Industrial; Former CEO
and Cofounder of Segment

"*Forget the growth hacks and feel-good frameworks.* This is the real guide to building an enduring business."

—Naomi Ionita,
Venture Partner, Menlo Ventures,
Growth and Monetization Advisor

"The book's actionable frameworks and insights on monetization and scaling align closely with what drove Grailed's success and eventual acquisition by GOAT. It's a practical, no-nonsense toolkit for founders and leaders aiming to achieve impactful growth and transformative exits."

—Arun Gupta,
CEO and Founder, Grailed

"This book should be required reading for any founder in the early days of product-market fit—it will change how you think about pricing, packaging, and architecting growth."

—Leo Polovets,
General Partner, Susa Ventures and Humba Ventures

"Pricing and packaging have always been team sports, and if you have a viral product, there is unbelievable upside in optimizing it across the life cycle—but in the age of AI, the stakes are higher, the upside is bigger, and the decisions more complex. This book is essential for getting it right."

—Chris Farinacci,
Advisor, Investor, ex-Asana COO,
ex-Google Cloud CMO

SCALING
INNOVATION

FROM THE AUTHORS OF *MONETIZING INNOVATION*

MADHAVAN RAMANUJAM
EDDIE HARTMAN

SCALING
INNOVATION

HOW SMART COMPANIES
ARCHITECT
PROFITABLE GROWTH

FOREWORD BY BILL GURLEY

WILEY

Published by John Wiley & Sons, Inc., Hoboken, New Jersey.
Published simultaneously in Canada.

For general information on our other products and services or for technical support, please contact our Customer Care Department within the United States at (800) 762-2974, outside the United States at (317) 572-3993 or fax (317) 572-4002.

Wiley also publishes its books in a variety of electronic formats. Some content that appears in print may not be available in electronic formats. For more information about Wiley products, visit our web site at www.wiley.com.

Library of Congress Cataloging-in-Publication Data is Available:

ISBN 9781119633068 (Cloth)
ISBN 9781119633136 (ePub)
ISBN 9781119633105 (ePDF)

Cover Design: Wiley
Cover Image: © nuengrutai/stock.adobe.com

SKY10117549_061425

For Hema, Risha, Aarush, Ben, Darrow,
Langston, and Natalie

Contents

Foreword

The journey from an ambitious idea to a transformative business is never easy. It's filled with highs and lows, tough decisions, and moments of self-doubt. What separates those who succeed from those who don't isn't just hard work or luck; it's the ability to ask the right questions and make the right decisions at pivotal moments. *Scaling Innovation* is a guide for those moments, written for leaders who are determined to turn great ideas into enduring businesses.

At Benchmark, I've had the privilege of working with some of the most visionary founders in the world—people who dreamed big, took bold risks, and built businesses that reshaped their industries. Along the way, I've seen one consistent truth: Achieving real, sustained growth requires more than a great product. It takes a deep understanding of how to connect with your customers, deliver value, and build a scalable foundation for long-term success. This book captures that truth with a rare clarity and depth.

What makes *Scaling Innovation* stand out is its dual focus on the startup and scale-up phases—two stages that demand entirely different strategies. In the early days, it's all about landing and expanding, creating a pricing model that feels intuitive, communicating value in a way that resonates, and building the foundation for monetization that grows with your customers. Later, as you scale, the challenges shift. You might need to rethink your packaging, learn how to negotiate for fair value, navigate the inevitability of price increases, and prevent churn before it becomes a problem. The authors lay out these strategies in a way that's both practical and inspiring, offering insights that feel immediately actionable.

What I love most about this book is how it never loses sight of the human element of leadership. Growing a business is hard—it can feel lonely, overwhelming, and at times impossible. But this book feels like a trusted companion, reminding you that every tough decision has a framework, every challenge has a solution, and every step forward is an opportunity to learn and grow.

If you're a founder, an executive, or a leader at any stage of your journey, *Scaling Innovation* will equip you with the tools and mindset to achieve both market share and wallet share, not just for today, but for years to come. It's more than a guide—it's a roadmap for building something truly extraordinary.

—Bill Gurley
General Partner, Benchmark

Acknowledgments

Writing a book is never a solo endeavor, and this one is no exception. We are incredibly grateful to the remarkable individuals who helped bring this project to life through their insights, support, and dedication.

First, our heartfelt thanks to **Bill Gurley**, who graciously wrote the foreword and has been a steadfast supporter over the years. Your belief in this work means the world to us.

Our deepest gratitude to **Mark Billige** for his insights, guidance, and support, which were pivotal in laying the foundation of this book.

To **Josh Bloom**, our invaluable sparring partner, content collaborator, and meticulous proofreader—thank you for your sharp insights, endless patience, and unwavering commitment to improving this book.

A heartfelt thank—you to **Clay Bavor** for his invaluable feedback in sharpening the ideas and elevating the clarity of this book. A special shoutout for his insight to name each axiom individually—what started as 42 generic "Scaling Innovation Axioms" became a far more memorable and actionable set of ideas thanks to that simple but powerful suggestion. Grateful for his thoughtfulness and creative push.

A special thank—you to **Advait Halve**, who served as our internal editor and also contributed valuable content to key sections of the book. His thoughtful feedback and dedication were essential in refining the manuscript. Also thanks to **Sara Yamase, Michelle Verwest, Jan Haemer, Adam Echter, Peter Kuo,** and **Michael Einstein** for help drafting key sections and case studies.

We're deeply grateful to **Shikha Jain** for her thoughtful contributions to the chapter on promotions—her expertise helped elevate the content significantly.

We deeply appreciate **Matt Johnson** for helping us brainstorm the concept for this book and for his thoughtful feedback on key themes throughout the process.

We also want to express our gratitude to those who helped craft the compelling case studies:

- **Peter Reinhardt, Joe Morrissey, and Tido Carriero:** Thank you for your invaluable help in telling the Segment story and contributing to the writing.

- **David Burson and Cliff Obrecht:** Your contributions to the Canva story added richness and authenticity—thank you.

- **Tom Buiocchi:** Thank you for helping us tell the ServiceChannel story with such clarity and impact.

- **Jake Heller and Pablo Arredondo:** We're deeply grateful for your help with the CoCounsel story.

- **Laura Rillos and Drew Branden:** We're grateful for your time and insight in refining the Airbnb story.

- **Chris Farinacci and Dustin Moskovitz:** Thank you for sharing your time and expertise to help tell the Asana story.

- **Rahul Vora:** Your insights were instrumental in telling the Superhuman story and crafting the beautifully simple pricing chapter—thank you.

- **Arun Gupta:** Thank you for your thoughtful contributions to the Grailed story.

- **Hilary Schneider:** We're so grateful for your help in bringing the LifeLock story to life.

We were truly blessed to have an all-star team of reviewers. To all the reviewers of this book, thank you for your time, perspective, and honest feedback (in alphabetical order): Alex Osterwalder, Ali Ghodsi, Aparna Chennapragada, Arun Gupta, Chris Farinacci, Clay Bavor, Dara Ladjevardian, David Burson, Devin Bhushan, Hilarie Koplow-McAdams, Leo Polovets, Lenny Rachitsky, Naomi Ionita, Peter Reinhardt, Rahul Vohra, Sridhar Narayanan, Zach Coelius.

Finally, to all the friends, colleagues, and family members who supported this journey in ways big and small—thank you for your encouragement, patience, and belief in this project.

This book is a testament to your collective efforts, and we are profoundly grateful.

Madhavan and Eddie

Introduction: From a Great Product to a Great Business

W hat's the most important thing you have to do as a leader?

This is not a question with an obvious answer. Whether you are running a startup or leading a scale-up, you have a huge set of daily concerns. There might be a burning problem in HR or legal that needs your attention *right now*. You might go to sleep (or lie awake all night trying to sleep) sweating about a fight brewing with a competitor. You might be worried about making payroll. Then there is the crucial hire, the can't-miss launch date, the tricky investor meeting. Every fast-moving company has its pivotal moments. You may be thinking to yourself that one of these, maybe more than one of these, could make or break your company.

But you also know you have to prioritize. Your to-do list never gets any shorter. You are already operating on little sleep, working straight through the weekend, skipping holidays. You have to triage, you have to manage the time available to you. So what matters most?

One way to look at this question is to ask: *What are the leaders of fast-growing companies you admire known for?* Maybe it's the founder of a software company that started out solving one simple problem and grew the product into an essential workflow tool for an entire industry. Or a founder who turned a niche consumer product into a household name through smart positioning and relentless customer focus.

What sets successful founders apart isn't just that they had a big idea; it's that they architected growth around it and scaled without losing their edge. They built strong teams. They took on risk when it mattered. When their bets didn't pay off, they made hard calls—cutting projects or shifting resources without flinching. And when they saw something working, they doubled down.

But no one ever cut their way to greatness. What the best are known for—what truly sets them apart—is creating sustained, profitable growth that didn't just move the needle. It redefined their space.

If achieving profitable growth were easy, everyone would be doing it—and clearly, this is not the case. Very smart, capable people build companies that fail to achieve liftoff or that sputter and crash back to the ground far too soon. Why?

We wrote our first book, *Monetizing Innovation*, to help you build a great product. That term means something very specific to us. By our definition, "great" is not the same thing as flashy, cutting edge, or even exciting. (Boring can be beautiful.) For us, a product is great if and only if it does one thing: unlocks your customers' willingness to pay. It cannot just be something people want. It must be something people want *to pay for*. This is the elusive quality we defined called "product-market-price fit."

If you have succeeded in creating a product people want to pay for, great news. You are in a tremendously advantaged position, with the potential for real success. But as we all know, "potential" isn't the same thing as actual achievement. The list of promising ideas that never turned into powerful companies is a long one. You can be a visionary with a good team, a strong culture, and a large addressable market yet still fail to build a successful business if you are not thinking about profitable growth in the right way.

We, the authors, want to help you achieve your dream. If you see yourself building an organization that grows steadily larger and more significant, that expands year on year, that is known and respected, that makes an impact in your part of the globe—or around the world—we're right there with you. As two people who have devoted our careers to advising leaders of companies big and small, nothing gives us greater satisfaction than helping people take that journey.

And make no mistake: It *is* a journey. There is a tough road between "great fit" and "screaming market success." To climb that hill, you need a plan. That's where this book comes in.

This book is for founders. It's also for the brave people who pick up the reins from a founder: Sometimes the best person to continue a journey is not the one who started it. But mainly, it is for leaders, those with the courage to run divisions, departments, startups, and scale-ups. You are looked up to, and looked on as a rock star, but most people will never know how hard it is to succeed at what you do.

This book is about how to really grow—profitably. It is the result of studying hundreds of companies that qualify as true long-term successes. These businesses not only achieved their goals in the short run but sustained success for years or decades. When we lined them up and dug into them, a particular type of approach emerged over and over again. We call this pattern "architecting for profitable growth."

We've written this book to be a very specific outline of the profitable growth battle plan, split into two parts: one for your company as you are launching off the block and another for when you are truly out in open water. This approach is needed because you must take very different steps as a startup versus those you should pursue when you are scaling up. In fact, some scale-up tactics simply aren't available to a startup. For example, in your early days, you won't have the customer history required to optimize retention (discussed in Chapter 11)—and you certainly won't need to blow up your packaging (covered in Chapter 8) in response to shifts in the makeup of your target customers. All things have their time and place.

It's easy to be seduced by the notion that your product or service is so good that you can just wing it, that you can build a strong and growing base of customers by blind feel, improvising as you go. A lot of people do that, right? If you build a better mousetrap, they say, the world will beat a path to your door. And what about that phrase "a product so good, it sells itself"?

Well, no, it won't. These phrases come from survivor bias. We hear about the times this approach worked out, the few ships that made it back to shore, but not from the wrecks lining the ocean floor. Putting such grim matters aside, there's another reason to spend time getting your profitable growth strategy right: the better your offering, the more it deserves a truly high-performance growth engine. If you truly have captured lightning in a bottle, you had better be sure to realize its full potential. A fantastic product will make it much easier to win customers once you're in front of them, but first you must get there. That means you must create a powerful mechanism to attract the interest of prospects, convert them into paying customers, and make sure they keep coming back.

Sadly, that growth engine won't build itself. And if it did, what fun would that be? No: Even if you created the most compelling product in the world, even if you found the Fountain of Youth (and got the rights), you still have to conquer your market and develop a strategy for scaling your growth.

That's the job. Let's get to work.

The Build-Fail Axiom	Even the best product won't sell itself; architecting profitable growth is what defines the winners.

Part I

Beating the Barriers to Scaling

Chapter 1

A Tale of Three Companies

Putting your time, sweat, and money into a new venture always comes with risk. When a company clicks and you find yourself in that moment when a startup becomes a scale-up, or when a scale-up achieves truly sustainable, profitable growth, it can feel like more than just a bet that paid off. It can feel like magic. In that spirit, this chapter recounts three astounding fables, fairytales of the business world, that illustrate the fundamental truth about profitable growth.

Unfortunately for the subjects of these stories, these are not happily-ever-after stories. Collectively, these businesses lost more than $50 billion and they left thousands upon thousands unemployed.

Yet the stories those founders told to investors and their excited armies of recruits were extremely convincing. Listening to the founding teams describe their vision and the opportunity ahead, you would have heard arguments delivered with passion, been shown evidence of success in the market, and been walked through numbers that seemed to make sense.

Would you have spotted the fatal flaw in each company? And let's reverse the roles for a second. Say it was *your* business, with *your* name on the cover of the pitch deck. Imagine that it was your startup or scale-up headed toward disaster. Is there a single factor that, if identified and addressed, would have saved your company?

We believe there is. And it's surprisingly simple.

That single factor is this: Many leaders try to grow with what we term a "single-engine strategy." They found one source of power for their company and leaned in hard.

In this chapter, we see how this approach plays out. We consider three companies that exemplify single-engine thinking. By examining how each one took flight and ultimately fell to earth, we believe the "fatal flaw" in this approach—both its seductive promise and its fundamental problems—will become clear.

The First Fable: Acquisition at All Costs!

At almost the exact midpoint of the real estate–driven disaster economists call the Great Recession, two New Yorkers in their 20s, Adam and Miguel, had a meeting with their landlord about a lease.

They were both entrepreneurs, but they had never worked with each other before. On the surface, they were very different from one another. Miguel, a college graduate, founded an online language-instruction company that employed 25 people before he moved on. Adam, a college drop-out, had started a line of padded baby outfits that he originally called "Krawlers" (later "Egg Baby") and employed no one at all.

But after the two met at a party, they discovered a shared passion: creating a community. What they wanted from their landlord was permission to lease a vacant warehouse on Water Street, where they planned to provide a communal working space for young entrepreneurs like themselves. The name for their new venture would be Green Desk.

The idea was a hit. The warehouse became an office space. The office space was filled with thriving, young businesses. Other warehouse locations were interested, and the sky seemed the limit. And yet, this story ends with the two men losing $47 billion.

If you think you know everything about WeWork, the company Adam Neumann and Miguel McKelvey built out of their stake in Green Desk, you are not alone. When you lose that kind of money, it is bound to draw attention. Books have been written and movies have been made.

Yet the question of exactly why the business failed is still a subject of debate. Some claim that their business model was unviable. However, its fundamentals are no different from those of IWG plc, the well-regarded owner of brands such as Regus and Spaces. IWG is in its fourth decade of continuous operation and generated nearly £3 billion in revenue last period. Others will point to Neumann's shocking acts of self-dealing, some of which border on the comical: that he gave relatives high-paid jobs with titles like Chief Nurturer; that he made personal use of the company's $60 million Gulfstream G650 private jet; that he forced WeWork to give him zero-interest loans so that he could personally invest in property—and that he leased those same buildings back to the company. Yet in aggregate, these amounted to a fraction of 1% of the company's enterprise value. Deplorable? Yes. Capable of sinking a business worth nearly $50 billion? It does not seem likely.

We have an explanation that is both simple and supported by data: When your "single engine" of growth is adding new customers, at any cost, eventually you will run out of fuel.

Consider the facts: In 2010, WeWork occupied a single building. In 2015, it took on 50 locations; by 2017, it was 300, and two years later, 850. The company projected that in the next year, it would have 745,000 tenants. This is a shocking rate of expansion. In one target city, Seattle, there literally wasn't enough vacant office space to satisfy WeWork's goals.

To fuel his engine, which was sputtering under the strain, Neumann burned cash. He was already providing many tenants free beer, bottomless coffee, and complimentary Wi-Fi. What if he began handing out rent money as well?

And so, in many geographies, the company began paying tenants to occupy WeWork's own offices. This was not just a free taste. These were actual pinch-me-I-can't-believe-it deals that often spanned a year or more.

Yet there was a limit to the number of companies that needed office space, even if it was free. In 2017, an analyst showed that there weren't enough startups in existence to occupy all the real estate WeWork had taken on. But Neumann had an answer for this, too, proclaiming that the business had outgrown the confines of both its customer base and its name.

Shedding its skin, WeWork would now be "The We Company"—and its new market was, in a word, everyone. Fit adults would love the boxing, yoga, and mineral pools at Rise by We. Lonely adults would find companionship in the dorm-inspired living spaces at WeLive. Young children could enroll in Montessori schools called WeGrow, and older kids could matriculate at "college alternative" MissonU.

The music stopped during the leadup to the company's 2019 initial public offering. Among other things, the company's prospectus revealed that the firm had $4 billion of revenue against $47 billion in committed debt. Worth nearly $50 billion in January, the company's enterprise value would drop to $10 billion by October, the month it was scheduled to have its public debut. And this was before COVID-19; shares dropped from $527 in 2021 to 84 cents two years later, just before the company filed for bankruptcy.[1]

This was not the end of WeWork. The company tried to rebound under new management. But it was the end for Adam and Miguel. Neumann was forced out in the autumn of 2019, shortly after the company's prospectus revealed his unsustainable plans. McKelvey followed the year after. Neumann once said, in essence, that if you reach for the stars, "the money tends to follow." Reality requires more of a plan.

The Second Fable: Monetization Is Everything!

Another type of business that is flirting with trouble is one that makes a different mistake. Rather than pursuing customer acquisition exclusively as WeWork did, this sort of company focuses purely on building wallet share, *monetizing* the customers it has. Its dreams are all about how to charge customers as much as possible. It's another single-engine strategy that can be just as deadly.

To see what this looks like in motion, consider entrepreneur and vegan health enthusiast Doug Evans. He had found success in the extremely difficult and cutthroat area of retail food sales, starting the chain Organic Avenue in 2002. A decade in, he was ready for his next challenge. In 2013, he launched a company built around a single product and related services. The product was the Juicero Press, a Wi-Fi–connected device that would squeeze presliced servings of fruits and vegetables—purchased in packets also sold by the Juicero company—to make drinks that were supposed to be delicious and nutritious. The device was designed by "celebrity designer" Yves Béhar and was supposed to exert an impressive 4 tons of force during the squeezing process, thereby extracting the maximum amount of tasty goodness from the produce. Evans boasted that the power of the Juicero was "enough to lift two Teslas," and he compared his own obsession with producing quality juice drinks to Steve Jobs's obsession with the design of Apple computers.

As for the related services—well, those were less clear. Juicero's internet connection was supposedly designed to allow the machine to read the QR codes on the fruit and vegetable packets to make sure the produce hadn't passed its freshness date. Perhaps a secondary purpose was to make sure that the San Francisco–based company was viewed by investors and others in the business world as being a high-tech startup.

Juicero got off to a promising start. Doug Evans promised investors that he would be able to sell not just the juice-making machine but also delivery subscriptions for packets of fruits and vegetables. The idea was that Juicero customers would create a long-lasting stream of revenue that would take the innovation to scale, thereby making Evans and those who bought into his concept very wealthy. The premise was attractive enough to enable Evans to raise $120 million in venture capital funding. Flush with investor cash, Juicero built what was described as "a 111,000-square-foot food-processing factory, staffed by dozens of hourly workers, washing and slicing up fruits

11

A Tale of Three Companies

and vegetables in Los Angeles."[2] The company quickly reached several hundred millions in valuation—not quite unicorn territory, but within shouting distance of it.

Unfortunately, the investment concept turned out to be a lot more appealing than the business itself.

The Juicero Press was launched into the market with a steep price of $699. This was supposed to be a premium price for early adopters only, which the company expected to reduce two to three years later. However, sluggish sales forced Juicero to reduce the price to $399 only nine months after launch.

That was just the first problem. More serious was a tidal wave of bad publicity. A year after Juicero launched, *Bloomberg News* ran a story in which it reported that "after the product hit the market, some investors were surprised to discover a much cheaper alternative: *You can squeeze the Juicero bags with your bare hands.*" Two backers said the final device was bulkier than what was originally pitched and that they were puzzled to find that customers could achieve similar results without it.[3]

One reviewer of electronic gadgetry posted an online video in which he confirmed that the juice packets could easily be squeezed by hand, showing that the machine was absurdly overdesigned for its intended purpose.[4] Other critics pointed out that the value of a Wi-Fi connection so that the freshness of the produce packets could be verified was undercut by the fact that the packets already had expiration dates printed on them.

In short, Juicero was an absurdly expensive solution to a consumer problem that didn't really exist—a case of pursuing monetization without a sound rationale. Evans believed he could monetize customers through his high-priced machine and high-priced juice packets, all in the name of "democratizing juice."

Sadly, the company did not pay attention to what people wanted, let alone to what they wanted *to pay for*. As a result, it could never attract sufficient customers to its scheme—drawing instead critics who had a field day mocking Juicero as a product that only wealthy, out-of-touch denizens of Silicon Valley could love. Eighteen months after launch, the company announced that it was suspending the sale of its machines as well as the produce packets.

If WeWork's growth plan was unbalanced because it focused solely on customer acquisition, Juicero's plan was toppled by its single-engine focus on deep monetization. When that failed, Evans's company simply collapsed.

The Third Fable: Loyalty Above All Else!

A third type of company that is headed for trouble is a company led by executives who believe the path to scale comes only through deeply devoted customers.

In such cases, leaders often latch on to the supposed centrality of net promoter score (NPS). If you're not familiar with NPS, it's a business metric originally devised by Fred Reichheld, a director of the consulting firm of Bain & Company, and launched in a now-famous *Harvard Business Review* article in December 2003.[5] It's a way to measure a company's customer loyalty by using a single survey question: "How likely is it that you would recommend [company X] to a friend or colleague?" Customers are asked to respond on a scale of zero to 10. Those who are most enthusiastic about recommending the company, who choose a score of 9 or 10, are dubbed "promoters," Those who choose a score from zero to 6 are called "detractors." Subtract the percentage of detractors from the percentage of promoters and you have your net promoter score. Your NPS can be compared with NPS's from similar businesses, or with your own company's NPS as it changes over time, to determine the relative loyalty of your customers—and the health of your business.

NPS is an interesting business tool, and it has its uses. The problem lies in treating NPS as the *one* number you need to grow.

Don't misunderstand; we're not saying that customer loyalty isn't important. We consider retention very important to scaling innovation, and we devote significant space in this book to explaining how to measure it and increase it. We'll show how to connect it strategically to acquisition and monetization, and that is the point here: It's a mistake to focus on retention to the exclusion of everything else. Life, and business, is not that simple. Like acquisition and monetization, retention is just *one* of the things you need to enjoy sustainable growth.

The subject of our third tale, Shyp, illustrates what can happen when you mistakenly assume that retention is the one and only factor that determines your ability to scale innovation.

Shyp was founded by three partners—Joshua Scott, Jack Smith, and CEO Kevin Gibbon—and it was based on a simple business concept. In any city where Shyp operated, you could contact the company using its mobile app whenever you had something you wanted delivered. Upload a photo of the item to be shipped and the From and To addresses, and Shyp would pick it up, package it, and deliver it to a shipping company—all for a single fixed price.

Shyp got started in San Francisco in 2013, charging just $5 for its service. Customers liked its convenience and simplicity; thanks to Shyp, they no longer had to find a box of the right size for their item, figure out how to pack it, drive it to the nearest FedEx or post office, and wait in line. The fixed $5 charge was a reasonable price to pay for eliminating those hassles from their busy lives. Shyp became a hit. Investors bought into the concept, providing some $62 million in funding, and the company began to expand into other cities, including New York, Miami, Los Angeles, Chicago, and Philadelphia. Shyp boasted an estimated value of $250 million, seemingly well on its way to unicorn status.

So far, so good. But a convenient, affordable service that customers love doesn't automatically scale. That's what Shyp quickly discovered.

The single, low price point was one problem. As you can imagine, $5 might be a profitable price to charge for shipping a paperback book in 2013. But for any large, bulky, or unwieldy item—say, a set of golf clubs—the same price would probably be way too low to cover Shyp's own costs. And those costs would go up over time.

Another problem was Shyp's initial customer base, which was made up of individual consumers rather than businesses. This was a deliberate strategy based in part on the fact that Shyp wasn't yet equipped to handle large volumes of packages. "Starting with consumers not only allowed us to build a lot of operational systems but also gave people a chance to check out that early product," Gibbon says.[6] But since most ordinary people ship packages only occasionally, marketing to them didn't yield the consistent stream of repeat business that Shyp needed for long-term success.

Shyp's leadership team saw the company was in trouble and tried to pivot to a more realistic scaling plan. They introduced variable pricing that factored in the size and weight of the item—which improved their profit margins but alienated some customers who'd been attracted to Shyp by the promise of one-price-fits-all. They also shifted their marketing to focus on small businesses that had a steady flow of packages to ship. This was a smart change. But both adjustments ultimately proved to be too little, too late. In 2017, Shyp retrenched, abandoning operations in New York, Los Angeles, and Chicago. By March 2018, Kevin Gibbon had to announce that Shyp was closing down and laying off all its remaining employees.

What did Shyp do wrong? Like the other two companies we've looked at, Shyp made the mistake of focusing on just one element of business scaling. For Shyp, customer retention was viewed as the golden ticket to success. As CEO Gibbon proudly declared, "Consumers loved it. Small businesses loved it."[7] Once people tried Shyp, its convenience and affordability won them over. In other words, customer satisfaction—the characteristic measured by NPS—was high.

But retention alone is not enough to create scale. Shyp was focused on pleasing the customer in a way that was not economically feasible. It was, in effect, a company that simply couldn't or wouldn't say no to its customers. It committed itself to a fixed price that was unrealistically low, and it targeted individual customers who simply did not have the profit potential of business customers. Eventually Gibbon and his team recognized their mistake and tried to monetize. But the changes they made cost them the customers they'd already attracted, and, rather than saving the business, they accelerated the spiral of decline.

As Gibbon himself ruefully concluded, "What we didn't do is focus on having a sustainable business from day one."[8]

The One-Engine Trap Axiom	The single-engine strategy traps companies in narrow focus—on growth, monetization, or loyalty—at the expense of the balance needed for profitable growth.

CEO Questions

- In designing and executing your company's plan for scaling, have you knowingly or unknowingly pursued a *single-engine strategy*?

- Consider the way you've approached the challenge of customer acquisition. Have you treated it as one important component of an overarching strategic growth plan, or have you (consciously or unconsciously) behaved as if it is an end in itself, to be pursued at all costs?

- How have you tackled the challenge of monetization? To what extent have you examined what your potential customers really need, want, and will pay for? How does your monetization model fit into your overall plan for profitable growth?

- What is your company's approach to customer retention? Have you, perhaps unwittingly, become so focused on retention that you have lost sight of the need to ensure that your business model needs to be profitable and sustainable for the long term?

Chapter 2

Becoming a Profitable Growth Architect

L et's take a closer look at what we saw with the stories of the founders who led WeWork, Juicero, and Shyp.

Make no mistake: These were exceptional individuals. Some of them had prior success starting businesses. It's clear that each had a kind of magic to them.

But another thing they had in common was an unsustainable approach to growth, a *single-engine* strategy that failed their organizations in the long run. Adam Neumann and Miguel McKelvey saw new customer acquisition as WeWork's engine. From their perspective, growth was synonymous with rapid increases in the number of tenants. For Doug Evans, the engine was monetization. He did not want to catch every fish in the sea; instead, he wanted customers willing to pay a high price and readily accept additional charges. Finally, the Shyp founders believed their engine to be loyalty, trusting that word of mouth and fierce devotion from customers would drive growth.

In each case, this single-engine approach led to disaster. One wonders what would have happened if these founders had identified and corrected their bias of relying on a one-track growth approach before it was too late.

Identifying the Three Leadership Failure Archetypes

The founders we learned about may remind you of people you know. Their stories may call to mind strategies you contemplated or even adopted.

Companies like the ones in the last chapter are very common. Having studied hundreds of failed companies, we have seen these doomed approaches to growth over and over again.

What we have found is that single-engine strategies spring from certain types of leaders. The good news is that there are only three common types—what we term the three "leadership failure archetypes." They each have their defining characteristics. Their pattern of behavior can be seen clearly in their approach to scale: the metrics they track, how they build their organization—where they double down and what they neglect—and the "traps" they accidentally fall into. Over time, such individuals will kill the company they are trying to lead, unless they correct their approach. These three leadership failure archetypes are particularly dangerous because they seem sensible at first, with strategies that initially pay off. The initial success allows leaders to pursue their agendas for a long time before the damage becomes evident.

Leadership Failure Archetype #1: The Disruptor

The first type of leader believes that dominating their market is the clearest path to success. They want a land grab—to seize territory, wrest attention away from competitors, and become the go-to brand in their category. In this pursuit, no discount is too steep, no promotion too generous, and no cost of acquisition too high if it helps them capture a larger piece of the pie. We call this kind of leader "the Disruptor." Disruptors can generate impressive growth numbers in the short term and drive strong brand recognition. The downside is that these leaders may inadvertently undervalue their product, leading to a cycle of high churn and low margins as they focus on attracting new customers while neglecting existing ones.

In terms of key performance indicators (KPIs), Disruptors live and die by customer count, so if they are doing their job, the volume of new sales in each period will be high. However, this leadership archetype is prone to making product claims that do not pan out and other promises they cannot keep. This approach creates attrition, meaning gross dollar retention may be low. Net dollar retention may be low as well, particularly if there isn't sufficient attention to postsale monetization, which would otherwise have counterbalanced customer loss.

This lack of balance plays out in a Disruptor's organization, creating telltale indicators. Acquisition teams, meaning sales and marketing, are generally encouraged to do whatever it takes to land customers—even small ones; for this reason, they are prone to providing high discounts and likely to offer generous concessions. Since the priority on landing new customers results in entry-level offers that are very robust, there will be little left to upsell after the initial deal. This situation leaves customers to wonder why they should upgrade—if they think about it at all. Customer Success, or whatever group is responsible for upselling and expansion, may complain bitterly about this situation. However, no one is really listening to them, because they have been relegated to a backwater of the organization in which few people are recognized and from which fewer still are ever promoted. For these reasons, the group does not attract the best and the brightest; recruiting will say that it's not a priority for hiring—their emphasis is finding great sellers.

Due to this lopsided focus on market share while neglecting wallet share, the Disruptor is likely to steer the organization into two growth traps that will particularly threaten its long-term prospects.

Disruptor Growth Trap #1: "Landing Without Expanding"

A healthy company with a robust product portfolio may focus on creating an attractive entry-level offer to win customers or break into new markets, then gradually introducing them to additional packages and options to meet their evolving needs. However, when companies fall into the landing-without-expanding growth trap, the entry-level product loses its strategic purpose; what was the lure becomes the full offering. In an effort to be attractive to prospects, these companies give the farm away, often at a very low or unsustainable price. In their effort to appeal to every customer, these companies sacrifice long-term value, easily landing new customers but failing to expand and develop them into meaningful revenue sources. The extreme example is a one-size-fits-all or all-you-can-eat structure. If everything is included, you have a problem: You have no way to satisfy customers with different needs, expectations, and willingness to pay.

Companies that realize they have this problem try to course-correct and push higher-priced offerings to improve margins. However, if the entry-level product is priced to move, the next package up will often be much more expensive. And if the introductory offer has been stocked full of robust features, there is very little additional value left to entice customers into trading up for a higher price. Sales will consistently find upselling a difficult move to pull off. Furthermore, if the introductory package has high operating costs, such as support and maintenance needs, the expenses may be silently eating the company alive. Such expenses may not be evident in the initial selling and creep in only as the customer base expands. With a young startup, pain from tech debt can convert what seemed like a profitable product line into a looming balance sheet black hole.

The Free Farm Axiom	If you give away the farm in your entry-level offer, you leave nothing else to sell.

Disruptor Growth Trap #2: "Market Share Won Is Not Market Share Held"

The second trap that a Disruptor falls into is thinking that a single transaction with a buyer will naturally lead to others. Market share "won" is not the same as market share "conquered"; just because you take territory does not mean you will hold it. Catching the interest of a prospect and getting them to say "yes" once is what the Disruptor is after, but that is just the first step. Engagement, usage, and loyalty all require work. Acquiring a reliable customer—someone from whom you expect to see a positive lifetime value, not just today but tomorrow as well—is the true source of profitable growth. That kind of commitment is something you have to earn. You have to work your way into a customer's mind and wallet.

Bobby Pinero, CEO of Equals and the former head of Finance at Intercom, an AI-enabled customer service software company, tells a moving story about how a rabid pursuit of customer acquisition nearly crushed his growing startup.[2] When he and his cofounder launched their new company, they built on their experience at Intercom, speaking to every new customer, listening to the specific business needs that had brought them to their website, hand-holding the user through the onboarding, and requiring payment before continuing. The result was five months of stellar growth, measured in monthly recurring revenue. In its very first year, Equals attracted an eight-figure investment from a16z (also known as Andreesen Horowitz) among others.

"And then," Pinero says, "I broke everything."

It started with envy. By his account, his team knew that other companies in their sector—"the darlings of the software industry," in his words—had epic rates of customer growth. Pinero knew that his painstaking approach to building his user base would never allow the kind of adoption these other businesses were experiencing. And so he made a decision "with a ton of conviction—and I turned out to be wrong." Gone was the requirement for payment up front. Gone was the need to speak with each new customer. Prices were "slashed" and a "generous new free plan" was established.

At first, Pinero and his team thought they had cracked the code for profitable growth. "Within a month," he writes, "we 4x'd the number of companies using Equals on a daily and weekly basis." That is a stratospheric level of customer growth. The metrics looked solid—at least for a time—with the absolute number of onboards steadily increasing.

Then the cracks started to appear. Account retention dropped rapidly, offsetting early gains. Engagement, measured by the number of active companies, fell fast. The Equals team scrambled, launching additional products and features. None of it reversed the situation they found themselves in. Within six months, Pinero saw where the business was headed, and he did not like it one bit: "There was no path visible to drive faster revenue growth." In some ways, it was lucky he saw the fault lines appearing as quickly as he did. By the middle of that year, Equals had reinstated some of its previous standards. "Obviously, you don't want meaningless friction," Pinero writes, but you do need to ensure that those who buy your product or service really see the value and become committed to stick around. And he says, the right level of friction "forces us to focus on the customers who really matter." Moving away from a single-engine approach is not just a question of how you approach customers in the market, it is equally an important insight into how a profitable growth strategy should be managed inside your business.

Leadership Failure Archetype #2: The Money Maker

Unlike Disruptors, some leaders seek to squeeze as many dollars as possible from each buyer's wallet. Their mindset is rooted in optimizing every aspect of the customer interaction to drive financial outcomes. Although this approach can boost short-term revenue and establish a premium perception, it can limit the company's appeal to new prospects. It may also alienate customers who find themselves struggling to keep up with rising prices or straining to avoid new fees. By concentrating too much on monetization, such companies miss the opportunity to reach a broader audience and risk losing the customers they have.

The Money Maker's focus is solely on profitability. From a metrics perspective, net dollar retention will be strong, although new customer growth may be low.

When an organization is run by a Money Maker, expect to see discontent among members of the Sales or Marketing teams due to the high prices charged. Although it's not uncommon for Sales to complain of deals lost to lower-priced competitors, here the sentiment will be particularly strong. Both acquisition and renewal may be termed "a struggle." Furthermore, these teams may report that they are not convinced that the value is a match for the price. In some cases, this attitude can create a mercenary, low-empathy culture, where customers are to be squeezed for what they're worth.

Due to a single-minded focus on wallet share while ignoring market share, Money Makers are likely to steer their organizations into one of two growth traps.

Money Maker Growth Trap #1: "Nickel-and-Dimed to Death"

Even the ancient Greeks understood that there is such a thing as pushing a commercial relationship too far. In Aesop's 87th fable, "The Goose that Laid the Golden Eggs," a greedy man who has acquired a magical bird that lays eggs of pure gold butchers the animal in an attempt to find the treasure he's sure is inside. Of course, he finds there is no gold inside the goose— and now he has no hope of regaining the stream of gold he once had. One imagines that his investors were not very thrilled.

This lesson also applies to entrepreneurship. It is generally a good idea to monetize deeply, but as with anything in life, this can be taken too far. You do not want to squeeze your customers so hard that you wring the life out of them.

A business model that relentlessly tacks on small additional charges may produce significant revenue in the short run, but in doing so it may alienate its customers. Some buyers may put significant time and energy into reducing their costs, even gaming the system if possible. IBM, once a dominant player in its space, famously created a pricing scheme so complex that technology managers would take heroic measures to avoid triggering additional charges, going so far as to staff teams in the middle of the night when rates were lower or restricting use of vital software so as not to incur overages. The frustration this approach generated created an opening for

Becoming a Profitable Growth Architect

new entrants into the space IBM once dominated, including a fledgling company called Microsoft, contributing to decades of decline for Big Blue. This cautionary tale shows how overreliance on nickel-and-diming can alienate consumers and ultimately erode a company's dominance.

A classic case of a company that thrived by *avoiding* the pitfalls of nickel-and-diming is Stripe, a leader in payment processing. Stripe built its reputation on simple and transparent pricing. Rather than tacking on hidden fees or charging extra for basic features, Stripe adopted a flat-rate model that was clear and predictable for its users. This approach eliminated the frustration many businesses experienced with competitors who relied on opaque pricing structures and unexpected add-ons. By prioritizing fairness and transparency over short-term profits, Stripe earned the trust of both startups and enterprises, thereby solidifying its leadership position.

The Golden Goose Axiom	If you squeeze customers too hard, you may boost short-term revenue but you will most likely alienate them and destroy long-term value.

Money Maker Growth Trap #2: The "Premium Price Paradox"

Growth trap #2 stems from Money Makers setting prices that are too high for their markets and thereby unintentionally cutting themselves out of most buyers' consideration. It's a paradox because a high price generally signals quality, which triggers interest—and then a discount, promotion, or other concession can be used to close the deal. But in a premium price paradox growth trap, potential buyers do not even knock at a company's door. The company's reputation is that it's too expensive to be a realistic option.

Some professional services organizations have this issue, particularly lawyers. With few exceptions, law firms do not disclose their prices widely and have even been known to sue to keep their rates from being published. However, a secret they guard even more closely is that attorneys commonly discount their rates, a practice that has accelerated over the past few decades. According to the annual Thomson Reuters Peer Monitor report, the amount per hour actually realized by law firms is a fraction of what they term their "standard rate." Invoices are cut even further with "make-goods" and "give-backs," essentially rebates against the work done for a client. These cuts often do not show up on public reports, since the hours are effectively erased from the ledger.

Given the secrecy around rates, the public does not know how much a lawyer charges in the first place, and they certainly do not know about these deals. What they do know is what they have heard from friends and seen in the media: Lawyers are superexpensive. Major studies show that more than 70% of individuals with a significant legal problem would not seek the help of a lawyer, reporting that they believe an attorney's time to be out of reach for "people like me." This is a shocking result. The importance of a lawyer's counsel is so central to American life that it is enshrined in the Sixth Amendment of the US Constitution. Yet due to the premium price paradox, the overwhelming majority of Americans will never even consider reaching out to a lawyer.

The Look-Don't-Touch Axiom	Pricing too high may signal quality, but if it's out of reach, buyers won't even consider knocking at your door.

Leadership Failure Archetype #3: The Community Builder

A third type of leader believes that the best way to grow is by creating deep customer loyalty. We call this type of leader a "Community Builder" because of their emphasis on cementing an unshakable base of buyers. Generally, taking steps to ensure you have dedicated buyers is a virtue. However, this leadership failure archetype prioritizes nurturing the core customer group over other essential business activities and therefore winds up gaining neither wallet share nor new market share.

Community Builders often personally identify with their core custom-ers. Unlike Money Makers and even Disruptors, who understand that some amount of churn is a normal part of doing business, every lost customer hits the Community Builder like a blow. That's why the performance indicators they care most about are not customer count or sales growth but satisfaction measurements like the net promoter score; some will boast that they read every customer comment. Unwilling to risk a negative reaction from fans, the Community Builder may resist raising prices for years, irrationally fearing that even a slight increase will allow competitors to tempt customers away.

From an organizational perspective, a Community Builder may have a smaller Sales team than comparable organizations and may underinvest in paid forms of advertising, preferring organic sources and word of mouth. The Customer Success team will be listened to closely, but it may not be seen as a revenue-producing part of the organization, so when this team's performance is evaluated, the score won't incorporate measures like revenue from cross-selling or upselling. Meanwhile, R&D and Product teams are often crushed by stacks of customized product development tasks, the result of the Community Builder's tendency to say "yes" to every customer's request for new features, rather than building functionality with broad appeal.

While Community Builders can create high engagement and minimize churn, they often overlook the potential to reach new groups of buyers and reject opportunities to derive deeper revenue from their loyal fans. Without a strategy for capturing new customers or optimizing revenue, such leaders confine themselves to serving a limited market segment and fail to reach their full growth potential. This tendency is exemplified by the two growth traps described next.

Community Builder Growth Trap #1: "Protecting the Base, Ignoring the Frontier"

Community Builders generally work overtime to please their existing cus-tomers. It follows that what isn't interesting to their base isn't interesting to them. The situation becomes problematic when disinterest turns into outright neglect of emerging needs. Worse, overinvestment in their best customers may leave too few resources to invest in promising new areas. A lack of innovation can put the Community Builder's company behind rivals and new entrants. What once seemed futuristic may become a must-have, opening up a damaging competitive gap. Over time, these leaders may miss entire new markets.

This growth trap was first seriously analyzed in the breakthrough book, *The Innovator's Dilemma*, in which academic and consultant Clayton Christensen[3] explained that doubling down on existing customers while ignoring the acquisition of market share from new, emerging customer groups—particularly ones that seem less profitable—is a fatal flaw. Ceding this territory opens the door to hungrier competitors. It also expands the reach of incumbents who have placed a stronger emphasis on market share over unit profitability. By the time the company spots the wolf outside the door, it is generally too late.

While Community Builders are particularly vulnerable to this trap, it can ensnare nearly anyone. For example, the leaders of Google (Alphabet) started confronting this dilemma in 2024. The majority of the company's revenues came from businesses that pay for advertising slots, either on sites and apps it partners with or through its Google Ads network (formerly AdWords). As Google explains, "When we show ads, advertisers pay us either for the placement of an ad. . .or for how an ad actually performs—like when someone clicks on it."[4] The more searches that are performed, the more ads that are displayed, which equals more revenue. Therefore, the last thing Google wants is for people to conduct fewer searches.

Enter Generative AI with its promise to deliver exactly what you want the first time, at the level of detail that you want, with near-human—and sometimes superior-to-human—understanding of what you were hoping to get back. The threat this technology posed to Google's business model was crystal clear. Perfect results mean fewer searches, fewer ads displayed, and lower revenue.

Ironically, Google was an early powerhouse in AI and machine learning (ML). Just three years after its 1998 founding, Google was using these technologies to help correct users' spelling mistakes and, soon after, translate phrases into other languages. Google Research and its crown jewel, DeepMind, generated stunning advances, including breakthroughs in protein folding that are expected to lead to new drug technologies.

Google also developed an ask-and-answer technology, LaMDA, well before OpenAI's better-known ChatGPT. However, Google's management declined to release this technology to the public, citing its potential for misuse. Their reaction led some analysts to compare the business to Kodak, the film company that famously had been first in digital photography, then blew it. Kodak recognized the threat digital photography posed for its business and suppressed the technology for decades. By the time Kodak realized the world had moved on, it had lost its advantage and was unable to make up for lost time, ultimately declaring bankruptcy. Just how Google will deal with this existential threat is yet to be seen at the time of writing of this book.

The Loyalty Blind Spot Axiom	Focusing solely on pleasing existing customers blinds leaders to emerging needs, leaving innovation neglected and new markets untapped.

Community Builder Growth Trap #2: "Training Customers to Expect More for Less"

Community Builders are the ultimate people pleasers. As we've already discussed, a result of this is that they tend to jam as much value as possible into their offering, all while undercharging their customers. Over time, this method can cause the buying base to have a flawed conception of what a fair exchange is—the Community Builder has trained them, in effect, to expect too much from the company for too little.

Take Chargify, for instance. The company provided a leading billing and financial operations platform for business-to-business Software as a Service (SaaS) businesses. But things weren't always so rosy for Chargify. In fact, the firm almost failed shortly after its founding, all thanks to this growth trap. The company began by offering a generous freemium product, which was intended to be limited to customers with fewer than 50 paying accounts. Chargify provided full customer support to these free users, creating a large area of expense. Within a year, this rapidly growing cost pushed the company to the verge of bankruptcy. Forced to eliminate its free plan entirely to stay alive, Chargify infuriated users who had come to rely on the service and expected it would always stay free. Ironically, the severity of the problem, demanding quick action, saved the company: Providing this money-losing plan for multiple years might have killed the young company, as in the Shyp story. Instead, Chargify merged with leading revenue management firm SaaSOptics to become Maxio, receiving a $150 million investment from the well-respected venture capital firm Battery Ventures.

The Value Erosion Axiom	Overdelivering and undercharging trains customers to expect too much for too little, undermining the perception of fair value and long-term sustainability.

The Right Strategy for Profitable Growth

We understand why these leadership mindsets exist. If you place your focus squarely on one way to grow, you may believe you cannot pursue the others. Although you likely understand that both market share and wallet share are important to your business, if you are like most people, you may believe you're better at one side than the other—and this belief dictates your strategy. Some even believe that this divide is printed in our biology.

Becoming a Profitable Growth Architect

Studies in the natural sciences have shown that our interaction with agriculture gave some of us the DNA required to be farmers, selecting for attributes like patience and conscientiousness. Furthermore, much has been written about the hunter gene, which supposedly gives some of us a propensity to seek out new opportunities and seize them.

Whether there is an actual difference, psychological or genetic, between "hunters" and "farmers" is beyond the scope of this book. In the final analysis, it doesn't really matter—as a business leader, you know that just because something is outside of your comfort zone does not give you permission to ignore it. Of course, it's easier to focus on one side of the equation or the other, to either chase new territory or farm the terrain you have. But in reality, market share or wallet share is not a choice. The hard answer, and the right answer, is to go for both.

Separating leaders by their bias toward market share or wallet share, we can see clearly how the leadership failure archetypes emerge and the single-engine strategies they pursue. Refer to the 2×2 framework in Figure 2.1.

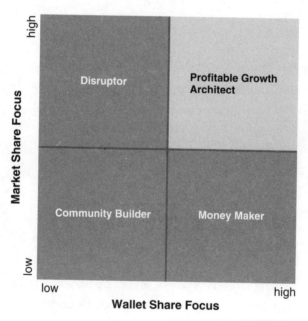

Figure 2.1 Leadership Archetypes

Scaling Innovation

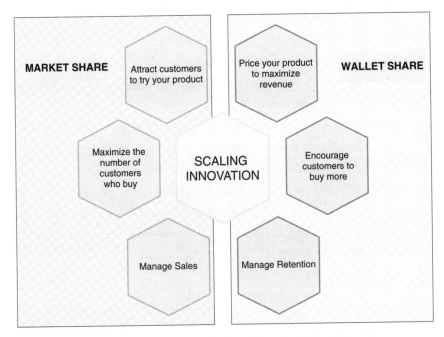

Figure 2.2 Profitable Growth = Market Share + Wallet Share

This framework is not a critique of disruption as a growth strategy, nor does it downplay the importance of monetization or retention. On the contrary, this framework underscores that focusing on any single lever is insufficient. *A robust company must balance efforts to grow both market share and wallet share simultaneously. This balanced approach is the key to achieving profitable growth and scaling innovation effectively.* This approach is captured in Figure 2.2.

Defining the Profitable Growth Architect

What defines the leadership mindset of a person who fits in the top-right quadrant in Figure 2.1, the home of Profitable Growth Architects?

These leaders have a clear game plan for both market share and share of wallet. They embrace the best qualities of the Disruptor, the Money

Maker, and even the Community Builder. But they do not believe success is as simple as doing what comes naturally to them; they are willing to put in the extra work.

Our use of the term "architect," with its connotations of foresight and planning, is a deliberate choice. If you have met one of the leadership failure archetypes, you may have seen that they truly believe that things will work out so long as they achieve the single goal they have in mind, often starting with the words "If I can just"—*if I can just* get more and more new customers flooding in, *if I can just* get buyers to open up their wallets as widely as possible, *if I can just* make sure those passionately devoted followers stay in love with us. The Profitable Growth Architect is thinking one step ahead: "If we increase our customer count, if we monetize more deeply, if we improve loyalty. . .what then?"

As architects of buildings have a blueprint, architects of profitable growth have a playbook. They develop a clear game plan for growth. This does not mean they give *equal effort* to wallet share and market share at every point in a company's life cycle. It does, however, mean that they pay *equal attention* to both sides of the equation.

Becoming a Profitable Growth Architect is a wildly attainable goal. That is not to say it is easy. At its core, it requires that you do not sacrifice one goal for the other. You must aspire to own your market without indulging in cheap shortcuts to get there, specifically undercharging and overpromising. You must plan to get fair and full value from your customers without forgetting the need to find more of them.

Doing this requires discipline. And it may mean you must flex muscles you do not normally use. However, the path to getting there is not a mystery. That's the focus of this book. We have organized the playbook into strategies that you need to adopt when you are a startup (Part IIA, "Startup Strategies") and strategies you need to adopt when you are a scale-up (Part IIB, "Scale-up Strategies").

Each of the strategies you're about to encounter—beginning with Chapter 3 and continuing through Chapter 11—is designed to help you think and act like a Profitable Growth Architect. Whether you naturally lean toward acquisition, monetization, or loyalty, the strategies in this playbook will stretch you. They'll challenge you to pursue growth that isn't just fast or flashy but balanced, scalable, and sustainable.

To help you orient yourself, we've summarized in Table 2.1 how each strategy in the next section reinforces the profitable growth mindset, helping leaders break free from single-engine traps and instead architect systems that drive both market share and wallet share.

These strategies comprise the toolkit of the Profitable Growth Architect. While each chapter can be read and applied on its own, they are most powerful when used together—forming a blueprint for durable growth in both reach and revenue.

The Twin Engines Axiom	A Profitable Growth Architect is one who gives equal attention—not necessarily equal effort—to both wallet share and market share, and builds a playbook for dominating both.

As you read on, remember the central question that defines the journey ahead:

Are you architecting for both market share and wallet share?

If so, you're not just scaling—you're building something built to last. You will have to work harder, but that's because you are creating something with real value, which will endure and which will deliver lasting returns to the people who believed in you—including yourself.

Table 2.1   Strategy Guide for Avoiding the Single-Engine Trap

Chapter	Strategy	How it Avoids the Single-Engine Trap	How it Fuels Market Share and Wallet Share
3. The Lure of Free	Use free offerings (freemium, trials) as acquisition tools with a path to monetization.	Avoids the Disruptor's trap of giving away too much without a plan to monetize and the Community Builder's trap of training customers to expect too much for too little.	Free offerings drive market share; optimal upsell paths to paid offerings convert to wallet share.
4. Choosing Your Pricing Model	Select a model that grows with customer value and is perceived to be fair.	Prevents overoptimization on revenue early (Money Maker trap) and avoids giving too much away to acquire (Disruptor trap).	Flexible models unlock access to more buyers (market share) and scale as value grows (wallet share).
5. Beautifully Simple Pricing	Remove friction and confusion from the buying process.	Avoids the traps of nickel-and-diming, the Premium Price Paradox (Money Maker), and the Community Builder's fear of charging fair prices.	Clarity and simplicity in pricing support faster adoption (market share) and increase conversions (wallet share).

(continued)

Table 2.1   *(continued)*

Chapter	Strategy	How it Avoids the Single-Engine Trap	How it Fuels Market Share and Wallet Share
6. Mastering Value Messaging	Clearly communicate why your offering is worth it.	Counters overpromising (Disruptor) and undercharging (Community Builder).	Boosts new customer acquisition (market share) while anchoring strong monetization (wallet share).
7. Discounting and Promotions	Use strategically, not reflexively, and if you give something, get something back.	Prevents unsustainable giveaway tactics to acquire (Disruptor trap) or giving too much to retain (Community Builder trap).	The strategic "gives" boost reach (market share), and the "gets" protect long-term margins (wallet share).
8. Redefining Offer Structure	Create packaging that meets different needs and segments.	Avoids one-size-fits-all trap, which makes expansion impossible.	Segmented packaging captures more users (market share) and creates upsell paths (wallet share).
9. Price Increases	Raise prices with purpose and fairness.	Counteracts fear-based stagnation (Community Builder trap).	Grows customer lifetime value (wallet share) while retaining customers (market share).

(continued)

Table 2.1 *(continued)*

Chapter	Strategy	How it Avoids the Single-Engine Trap	How it Fuels Market Share and Wallet Share
10. Big Deal Negotiation	Close large accounts without compromising value.	Avoids desperate land grabs (Disruptor) and underpricing for logos.	Wins high-visibility accounts (market share) and maximizes deal size (wallet share).
11. Stopping Churn	Build proactive measures to stop churn before it happens, and retain and grow customers.	Keeps leaders from ignoring loyalty—or overinvesting in the wrong retention efforts—and avoids the Disruptor trap of gaining market share but failing to retain it.	Holds onto market share already won, deepening customer value over time (wallet share), and acquires strategically (market share).

CEO Questions

- Is your company currently focusing primarily on market share or wallet share or both? Why? Have you chosen the focus that is most relevant to the current needs of your business?

- Examine the descriptions provided for the six growth traps. Have you fallen into any of them? If so, which ones? How do you plan to undo?

- What comes naturally to you—being a Disruptor, a Money Maker, or a Community Builder? What steps do you and your team plan to take to incorporate the best off from each of these archetypes and learn new skills to become a Profitable Growth Architect?

Part II

Nine Breakthrough Strategies for Architecting Profitable Growth

Part IIA

Startup Strategies

Chapter 3

The Lure of Free: When You Land, Be Sure to Expand

For the startup company seeking to scale innovation, the first question to answer is a basic one: *How can we attract customers to try our product?* After all, you can't acquire customers without first sparking their interest in your offering.

One of the most effective answers to this question is *the lure of free*. Merchants have long known that a free offer can attract curious individuals and convert them into customers. Social scientists have used experiments to demonstrate and quantify this power.

Behavioral economist Dan Ariely performed a simple experiment that highlights the lure of free. His team offered students a choice between a Lindt truffle, priced at 26 cents, and a Hershey's Kiss, priced at one cent. The result was an even split, with half choosing the truffle and half the Kiss. In a second trial, the team lowered each price by a penny, making the truffle 25 cents and the Kiss free. Now 90% chose the Kiss. The relative prices remained the same, but the introduction of the word "free" drastically shifted customer preference. The experiment demonstrated the powerful impact of *free* in shaping customer demand.

If you were in the business of giving away candy, the story could stop here. But for most companies, the challenge is to harness the power of free to generate sustainable, profitable revenue streams and thereby grow to scale. In this chapter, we explain how to do just that.

Let's start by recognizing that there are actually three different "flavors" of free: *freemium, free trial,* and *fully free.* You have probably encountered each of these. Here's how to tell them apart.

- *Freemium* is a model where a company offers customers a significant portion of its product or service for free forever. The goal is to impress customers so much with the free benefits that they upgrade to a premium version with additional paid benefits.
- *Free trial* offers customers full access to a product or service for a limited time—such as two weeks or a month. Once the trial ends, customers need to convert to the paid service.
- *Fully free* means customers don't pay for the full access of the product or service. This model is viable only with *third-party monetization*, typically through selling advertisements to businesses seeking access to your customers.

Now let's take a look at some examples of companies that have demonstrated how the lure of free—in one or more of these flavors—can be a powerful tool for customer acquisition.

Leveraging the Power of Free: Spotify and Beyond

Spotify, the music streaming service, has excelled at leveraging the power of free to attract a large base of profit-generating customers. Let's explore how the company achieved this.

Based in Sweden, Spotify arrived in the United States in 2011, two years after establishing itself in Europe. The music industry was undergoing a massive transformation. Sales of traditional music packages like CDs had plummeted, partly due to illegal online pirating services like Napster. Apple's iTunes, launched in 2003, worked with major record companies to create the first legal way to stream music online. At 99 cents per song, iTunes was both far more convenient and much more economical than buying physical CDs, which charged around $15 for a package that often included plenty of filler tunes alongside the few hits that music fans really wanted.

But there was still plenty of room for an innovative service that would take full advantage of the latest technology to make music even easier to access. Spotify jumped in to fill the gap. Its free music service offered unlimited access to a wide array of songs. Spotify also developed cleverly designed algorithms to generate recommendations for other artists that users were likely to enjoy based on their past selections.

Like the free Hershey's Kisses offered in Dan Ariely's experiment, the freemium version of Spotify attracted plenty of positive attention. Millions of music lovers quickly became hooked and spread the word about Spotify to friends and acquaintances. But giving away the service did not build a sustainable business. The challenge for Spotify was to convince users to upgrade from the freemium version of their service to a paid version. And here is where Spotify's acquisition strategy really shone.

Despite the fact that Spotify's freemium version offered very attractive value to millions of music lovers, the company wisely left itself plenty of space to monetize its popularity through service-enhancing features that were valuable enough to charge for. Those who opted for a premium subscription got a range of great benefits, including ad-free listening, a higher-resolution music stream, and easier options for offline and mobile listening—all features that music fans genuinely cared about and were willing to pay for.

For businesses like Spotify that seek to use their free offering as the primary tool to access paid customers, the conversion rate from free to paid is one of the most crucial metrics. The free-to-paid conversion rate varies widely from one sector to another as well as from one company to another, but typically it's in the low single digits for most businesses. By contrast, Spotify's public statements indicate a remarkable conversion rate north of 40% of monthly active users. As a result, by April 2020, Spotify boasted 133 million paid members worldwide, while maintaining a free listener pool

The Lure of Free: When You Land, Be Sure to Expand

roughly twice as large. By 2024, the paid subscriber number had surpassed 250 million.

Spotify serves as a prime example of leveraging the allure of free strategically to architect profitable growth by expanding both market share and wallet share.

Another example is the *New York Times*, which revitalized its business by adopting a digital-first strategy built around its freemium model. Through its freemium approach, it allows readers to access a limited number of articles each month at no cost. This free access serves as a powerful lure, showcasing the publication's journalism and encouraging casual readers to engage with its content. The restriction creates a sense of exclusivity and urgency—particularly when readers encounter paywalled articles they really want to read, prompting them to consider subscribing for unlimited access.

Adobe adopts a different approach, using free trials (instead of freemium) to give potential customers a taste of its powerful suite of software tools. Products like Photoshop, Illustrator, and Premiere Pro, part of Adobe Creative Cloud, are industry standards in creative fields. Adobe offers a full-access free trial—usually seven days—for its software. This trial includes every feature available in the paid subscription, allowing users to fully experience the product's potential.

This strategy works particularly well for Adobe because its tools often have a learning curve. By granting full access, Adobe ensures that users can experiment with the software and see firsthand how it meets their creative or professional needs. The trial period also acts as a gateway, offering tutorials and support to help users maximize their experience. Once users recognize the value of the tools during the trial, they are more likely to subscribe.

The appeal of free extends beyond media and software. Numerous industries have employed the lure of free effectively.

- *Automotive.* Tesla offered free charging to incentivize early adoption of its electric vehicles and the widely publicized seven-day free-return-with-no-questions-asked policy to entice customers to order.

- *Consumer goods.* Sephora uses free samples to attract new customers and drive additional sales.

- *Financial services.* Square provides a free credit card reader to acquire new customers.

- *Gaming.* Fortnite offers online games that are free to play while generating over $2 billion in revenue through in-game purchases of cosmetic items like skins and emotes.

- *Hardware.* Peloton offers a 30-day home trial program to entice potential buyers.

- *Industrial.* Caterpillar offers free trials or demonstrations of heavy machinery, allowing potential buyers to experience the performance and reliability of the equipment before committing to purchase.

- *Insurance.* Deal Shield provides a no-questions-asked 30-day guarantee for used-car insurance.

It's clear, then, that the lure of free can work to attract customers. But how and when is it a good business practice? How can you use the lure of free to get your company on the track to scaling innovation? Read on.

How to Design a Free Offering: What Best-in-Class Companies Do

To determine whether and how you can use a strategy based on the lure of free to architect profitable growth, follow this three-step system.

Step 1: Decide Whether Free Is an Appropriate Strategy for You

An effective free offer needs to drive four crucial benefits for your business:

1. *Acquisition.* The free offer should drive meaningful short-term acquisition of new users who otherwise would not have joined your customer base.

2. *Engagement.* The free offer should educate customers regarding the benefits of your product or service and encourage increasing usage.

3. *Paid conversion.* The free offer should have a clear migration path to convert customers from free to paid and support a longer-term monetization strategy.

4. *Revenue and profit.* The free offer should grow average revenue per paying customer over time via cross-sell and upsell opportunities, thereby enabling achievement of your financial goals and setting your business on the path to scale.

When one or more of these benefits can't be obtained through the lure of free, then a free offer is not appropriate. Here are some examples of specific situations in which a free offer strategy might *not* make sense:

- *One-time purchase.* No one is giving away a free version of Lasik eye surgery, since the benefits of the procedure are fully realized through a single use. For this reason, there's no migration path to convert users from free to paid.

- *Delayed value consumption.* An identity theft protection service like LifeLock offers benefits whose value may take months or years to realize, since it kicks in only when an identity breach occurs. Thus, a free offer of the core LifeLock service would not have the power to drive user engagement.

- *High cost for the customer.* If it's expensive for the customer to implement, configure, or learn to use your product or service, then few customers are likely to take advantage of your free offer, which means your customer acquisition cost is unlikely to be optimal.

- *High cost for the company.* A 3D printing service that physically produces custom prototypes can't realistically offer a free version of the product, since each print requires material, labor, and shipping. But do your due diligence: Even if your product is expensive, you may be able to create a freemium offering of software or special services that can be offered on top of the product, thus giving you an opportunity to take advantage of the lure of free.

The Free-to-Scale Axiom	If you can use the lure of free to attract a large number of potential customers who *will* eventually become paying customers, a free offer may be a great tool for architecting profitable growth and scaling your innovation.

Step 2: Choose the Right Flavor of Free

As we've explained, there are three flavors of free: freemium, free trial, and fully free. If you determine that a free offer makes sense for your business, your next task is to decide which of these strategies is best for you.

When freemium makes sense: At its heart, a freemium offer splits off a portion in the offer as free with access to more or better features coming at a price or at a premium. Naturally, this approach allows for users to experience only a limited portion of the product, but they're able to experience that portion very deeply if they desire to.

This strategy fits well when you are offering goods whose full value becomes apparent only through in-depth use. It also fits well if you can afford to give away a forever-free product (freemium) in exchange for getting market share (i.e., by keeping customers in your ecosystem rather than letting them go to a competitor) and have sufficient product benefits reserved for a paid offering (for getting wallet share).

The Freemium Evaluation Checklist can make it easy for you to decide whether freemium is the right strategy for you.

Consider adopting a freemium strategy if:

☐ *Your product or service lends itself to viral adoption,* with existing users spreading the word to create more users. Example: PayPal, where account holders spread the use of the service because only other account holders are eligible to receive payments.

☐ *Serving free users can be done at low cost.* As a rule of thumb, you should be able to achieve a positive return on a free user investment in the first year, after factoring in all your variable costs—marketing, customer service, data storage, and so on.

☐ *There's a clear, compelling migration path from free to paid.* Example: A basic Dropbox account provides 2GB of storage at no cost to users. But users are driven to upgrade to paid as they accumulate and upload content over time, requiring increased storage capacity.

☐ *Your offering provides increased value over time (stickiness).* Example: The longer customers make use of note-taking tools, the more notes they amass—which makes it increasingly difficult for them to stop using the service or to switch to a rival app.

☐ *Your product or service benefits from network effects.* Network effects occur when a product's value increases as more people use it, making it more attractive to new users. Freemium makes sense when you can leverage network effects by allowing free access, driving rapid adoption and increasing product value as the user base grows. Example: Dating sites like Tinder benefit from a larger free user pool, which provides customers with more choices and a better chance of finding a match.

☐ *There's a potential for third-party monetization.* Example: LinkedIn benefits from a large freemium membership through increased ability to sell services to professional recruiters seeking talent.

☐ *It's relatively easy to prevent users from gaming the system.* Some users will try to bypass usage limitations—for example, by creating multiple user accounts. You may be able to prevent this or at least discourage it by using automatic bill-through on customer accounts or by requiring a combination of data points (address, email, credit card info) to identify each account.

☐ *There's a large potential paid market base among free users.* Use a 10% conversion rate—generally the "gold standard" in the freemium world for the percentage of free who convert to paid—to estimate whether the potential market is sufficient for you to pursue.

The last item on the checklist may be the most important factor of all. Deciding whether freemium will work for you is, in part, a numbers game. The larger the potential pool of customers, the more attractive the freemium model will be. As an article in *Harvard Business Review* puts it, "All other things being equal, you would do better to convert 5% of two million monthly visitors, for example, than 50% of 100,000 visitors."[1]

When free trial makes sense: The freemium experience can be limited, since by definition most customers will enjoy only a portion of the benefits that your product or service offers. By contrast, free trial provides a taste of the full range of premium features for a limited time. If your core value proposition is contained within the premium version, this enhanced experience will make it easier for customers to recognize what's most compelling about your offering and thereby increase the likelihood that they will make a commitment to pay.

The Free Trial Evaluation Checklist can help you determine whether free trial is the right strategy for you.

Consider adopting a free trial strategy if:

☐ *The key factor in customer acquisition is engagement with your offering.* If your ability to convert customers from free to paid depends on a deep engagement with all the benefits of your product or service, then a free trial period may be your most powerful acquisition tool. A limited time window incentivizes focus and effort from your customers to learn about your product via exploration and usage.

☐ *Your offering is relatively simple to use.* If a significant portion of the value of your offering can be realized in a relatively short period of time, the likelihood that free trial users will convert to paid will be relatively high.

☐ *The most compelling value features of your offering can be experienced only through the premium version.* Example: Amazon Prime offers a long list of customer benefits, of which the most attractive by far is the free delivery feature, which reduces the cost of every purchase from the Amazon site. Many customers who get a chance to experience this feature of Amazon Prime through their free trial are hooked for life.

☐ *Your primary goal is increasing the number of paid customers rather than creating network effects based on total customer numbers.* The free trial strategy forces users to choose whether to convert to paid when the trial period ends. Thus, if retaining unpaid customers has significant value for your business, the free trial strategy may not be your best choice.

The free trial strategy has one powerful psychological factor on its side—namely, the well-known universal psychological trait known as loss aversion. Loss aversion is the human tendency to feel more strongly the pain of losing something we've previously owned than for something we've never had. First identified by economists Daniel Kahneman and Amos Tversky, the theory of loss aversion explains why most people will turn down the opportunity to take a bet that offers an equal chance of winning $400 and of losing $200: Losses loom larger than gains.[2]

Because of the power of loss aversion, once consumers enjoy a taste of the value created by your product, they are loath to give it up. Hence the effectiveness of the free trial strategy.

There is an interesting variant of the free trial strategy—the *reverse trial*, which combines the best aspects of the freemium and free trial approaches. This trial starts every new sign-up on a free trial, usually without needing an opt-in or a credit card, and gives customers access to all paid features (i.e., the best possible products you can offer). This trial will be timed—limited, for example, to two weeks—after which customers can either buy or downgrade to a freemium tier. This trial gives your users time to explore the most advanced features your product has to offer and decide whether they should pay; in the worst case, by downgrading them to a free plan when their trial is up, it creates the opportunity to reengage with them and keep them in your ecosystem.

When fully free makes sense: The fully free model is viable only when there is an option for *third-party monetization* through selling advertisements or other services to businesses that want access to your customers. Use the Fully Free Evaluation Checklist to help you decide whether this strategy makes sense for you.

Consider adopting a fully free strategy if:

☐ *Your product or service benefits significantly from network effects.* Example: Instagram and other social media sites, which attract users largely because of the large numbers of other users already active on the site. The sense that "Everybody is on Instagram" is the single most powerful user benefit that the service can offer.

☐ *It's unlikely that free users of your offering can be converted to paying customers.* If your product or service is such that customers are unlikely to be willing to pay to enjoy it, you need to look for other ways to monetize your offering.

☐ *There's a strong potential for third-party monetization—including the potential to create a two-sided marketplace.* In a two-sided marketplace, one set of customers participate on a fully free basis while another set of customers pay for the benefits they receive.

Step 3: Decide What Should Be Free

Both freemium and free trial models require a *fencing strategy*—that is, a carefully designed limit on the value a customer can receive for free. The nature of the fence you build and the narrowness of the limits you set will depend on the kind of business you have and the level of value customers need to experience to feel motivated to spend more. For many businesses, deciding exactly what should be free is the most difficult of the three steps.

The Gate-to-Growth Axiom	Designing your fencing strategy is the most crucial step for creating a successful migration path to paid offers.

There are several common ways to fence your free offer. Let's examine each one.

Fence by Consumption Limit

In this strategy, you fence the freemium offering based on the user's level of consumption, establishing clear limits between what is free and what must be paid for. For example, Zoom permitted free users of their service to make calls of up to 40 minutes, which enabled them to realize most of the value of Zoom. However, serious users are likely to opt for the flexibility that the paid version provides (calls of any duration).

Fencing by consumption offers a number of benefits. It's generally perceived by users to be fair. It also allows users to experience the full value proposition of your offering, even as you create increasing switching costs as users build up their level of engagement with your product or service. Finally, it creates a clear conversion event, which kicks in whenever users bump up against the explicitly defined consumption limit.

Fence by Performance Limit

In this strategy, you fence the freemium offering based on performance differences with a view that paid users primarily will pay for better and faster performance. For example, ChatGPT's free users have limited availability during peak times, have access only to standard models (e.g., GPT-3.5 instead of GPT-4), and experience standard response times. These fences effectively encourage users to experience the value of ChatGPT for free while incentivizing power users to upgrade to the paid subscription for enhanced benefits. This balance maximizes market share while driving wallet share.

Fence by Time Limit

As we've seen, this is the fencing mechanism used in the free trial strategy. For example, Amazon Prime offers one-month free trial memberships, and in this case, it makes good sense for the business. This time-limited access showcases the enhanced capabilities of the premium service, making it more compelling for users to continue with a paid subscription after experiencing its advantages for free for a month.

The most crucial element, however, in designing a time-limit strategy is deciding the length of the term. It should be long enough to provide a full experience, so users appreciate the value of your offering, but not so long that they lose interest or find ways to game the system to milk it of all its value. You may need to experiment to determine the ideal time limit for your free trial offering.

Fence by Product Feature

In this strategy, you keep certain premium features behind a paywall, available only to paying customers. As mentioned earlier in the chapter, this is the fencing mechanism Spotify used. This kind of fencing has two major benefits: It provides users with a clear incentive to upgrade to paid, and it can help your company to control customer service costs in direct ways. For example, some software companies use a fencing strategy in which only paying customers have access to live customer support.

Landing but Also Expanding

Regardless of the type of fence you choose, you will need to give freemium or free trial users enough benefits so that they will recognize the value your product or services provide and want more—but not so much that they will be satisfied with the free version of your offering and fail to convert to the paid version. In other words, you need to focus on the long-term growth (i.e., expanding) that leads to scaling, not just short-term customer acquisition (i.e., landing).

The Land-and-Expand Axiom	To scale, you need to have a strategy not just for landing (acquiring customers) *but also* for expanding (monetizing and retaining these customers).

Unfortunately, most startup companies claiming to have a land-and-expand strategy for scaling innovation fall into the trap of landing without expanding. This happens, in part, because the customer psychology underlying your land-and-expand strategy can be tricky. Customers who enjoy the use of your product or service without paying for it may end up being trained, consciously or unconsciously, to feel that your offering has no monetary value. Because they don't take it seriously as a commercial offering, they may feel offended when you ask them to pay for it; after all, by providing it for free, you've suggested that it is a kind of public utility, an entitlement, rather than a product that must be purchased.

To avoid training customers to undervalue your product or service, the availability of *an attractive offering that customers must pay for* is an essential element of the freemium strategy. In other words, some truly great features *must be excluded* from the free package. This is one of the most important things to do. It's also one of the hardest for a customer-obsessed business leader, who wants to give and give and give to customers. But if you don't hold something back, then how can you expand?

Another dominant reason for landing without expanding stems from a fundamental imbalance in product development and monetization strategies. What we have seen often is that 20% of a product's benefits drive 80% of a customer's willingness to pay. Ironically, this critical 20% tends to be the easiest to build, as it delivers the most obvious and immediate value. In their eagerness to launch and acquire customers, founders frequently build just this 20% of the product and call it their minimum viable product (MVP). Many offer this MVP for free to attract a large user base, believing that expansion and monetization will follow naturally.

However, the reality is often less straightforward. Once the MVP is live, these companies find themselves scrambling to build the remaining 80% of the product, which, despite being complex and resource-intensive, drives only the remaining 20% of customer willingness to pay. These companies have already delivered the core value for free, leaving little incentive for customers to upgrade or expand. Your MVP could be your most valuable product (not just viable)!

Hence, to avoid the landing-without-expanding trap, it's critical for founders to deeply understand what drives willingness to pay and strategically structure their offerings. By thoughtfully fencing premium features and aligning them with what customers truly value, companies can land effectively while ensuring room to expand into sustainable revenue.

Ultimately, the companies that thrive are the ones that understand this balance requires deliberate planning and discipline.

The 20/80 Axiom	The 20% of a product that drives 80% of willingness to pay is often the easiest to build; if you give it away, you inadvertently lock yourself out of monetization from day one—a paradox where the pursuit of adoption undermines the path to revenue.

Beyond the Basics: Insights, Tips, and Tricks About the Lure of Free

To take full advantage of the lure of free, let's now consider some advanced insights, tips, and tricks you may find useful when crafting and implementing an effective free offer that can help you achieve scale.

- *Measure the activity rate of freemium customers.* The most important KPI to track for freemium users is their level of activity and engagement. Those with high engagement over a period of time—usually the top 10% to 20% of customers based on usage—are the ones you should prioritize and focus on converting.

- *When possible, default to the best free trial experience.* Perhaps, like many companies, you have two or more versions of your products—for example, good, better, and best. Which version should you use for a free trial offering? When possible, give your customers the best product for your trial experience. Loss aversion kicks in, encouraging more people to select the best version when the time comes to convert to paid.

- *Don't obsess over whether customers will game the system.* Some of your customers will find a way to squeeze unintended value out of free offers. Don't go crazy about trying to stop them. Instead, focus your energy on minimizing the cost of serving each customer and—even more important—converting free users to paid customers.

- *Gamify to increase engagement in free.* Dropbox provided additional "free storage" (the primary metric by which it fences free products) when customers engaged with the product in designated ways—for example, by filling out checklists, by referring others into the system, and by being active in their user community by posting comments. Incentivizing engagement by gamifying such activities will help turn casual users into committed customers.

- *Always remember that attaching a price to a product makes it more attractive in the eyes of customers.* The price often serves as a signal of value to customers, especially when the product or service in question is one that most customers lack the expertise to judge or evaluate themselves. An experiment by Stanford marketing professor Baba Shiv demonstrated this in dramatic fashion. Shiv had a group of subjects sample red wines from five different bottles, each of which was tagged with a price ranging from a low of $5 to a high of $90. The subjects believed they were tasting five different Cabernet Sauvignons, but in fact they were tasting just three. One wine was offered in two bottles, one bearing the real price of $5, the other bearing a fake price of $45; another wine was served in two bottles, one with the real price of $90, the other with a fake price of $10. (The third wine was served in a bottle showing its real price of $35.) The results: Not only did the experimental subjects claim that the wines labeled with more expensive prices taste better, but functional MRI scans showed that, when tasting the supposedly higher-priced wines, their brains exhibited higher levels of neural activity in the medial orbitofrontal cortex, the region where pleasure is experienced. In effect, raising the apparent price of the wine actually made the wine "better."[3] Remember this experiment when developing your fencing strategy, and make sure you are not inadvertently minimizing the value of your product or service in the eyes of your customers.

- *Don't overdo free.* There are many ways to boost customer acquisition, from cleverly designed pricing models to tailored promotional offers. We explore these in the chapters that follow. Don't become overly addicted to the lure of free, powerful as it can be. To scale innovation, you need a holistic acquisition strategy that is well balanced with acquisition, monetization, and retention.

Chapter Summary: How This Strategy Avoids the Single-Engine Trap

Free is powerful—but dangerous when used in isolation. The strategies described in this chapter help avoid the Disruptor trap of chasing customer acquisition without a path to monetization as well as the Community Builder trap of giving too much away to please early users. When designed with a clear migration path from free to paid, it fuels both market share (by lowering the barrier to try) and wallet share (by converting to meaningful revenue over time). That's what Profitable Growth Architects do—they use "free" not as a giveaway but as a gateway.

CEO Questions

- Has your company critically examined the potential for using the lure of free as a tool for customer acquisition?

- Have you studied the differences among the three flavors of free: freemium, free trial, and fully free? Which of the three is most appropriate for your company, and why?

- Have you optimized your fencing strategy to produce the highest possible conversion rate from free to paid?

- Are you landing and expanding? If not, why not?

Chapter 4

The Most Important Decision: Choosing Your Pricing Model

*H**ow you charge* trumps *what you charge*. It is the game changer that distinguishes a winning company from a losing one. Choosing the right pricing model, as early as possible, is one of the most critical decisions you will take during the startup phase for driving both market share and wallet share and for architecting for profitable growth.

The reason for this is simple yet compelling. A pricing model that makes intuitive sense makes it easy for customers to buy. The best models also let you share in both your customers' successes and their risks, and ensures you're capturing a fair share of their willingness to pay. Moreover, a pricing model that is perceived as sensible and fair will make it likely that customers will stay. In other words, developing and implementing a winning price model is crucial to gaining both market share and wallet share. Your customer's rationale is simple: "The pricing model makes sense, the value is great, and the cost is reasonable. Why would I ever cancel?"

The How-You-Charge Axiom	If customers don't like how they have to pay for your product offer, it doesn't matter what they have to pay—because they simply won't buy from you.

Which pricing models are best suited to your business? Most likely, you will be selecting between subscription (a fixed payment at regular increments), usage (payment based on consumption or use), and outcome (pay for a specific outcome or result.). But how do you decide which model is most appropriate for your business? Read on.

Subscription, Usage, or Outcomes? Three Companies, Three Paths to Success

Netflix, Amazon, and Bayer are innovative giants, each achieving remarkable success in its respective industry. They've achieved this by implementing (and experimenting with) very different pricing strategies. Netflix's subscription-based model was key to disrupting Blockbuster. Amazon Web Services (AWS) employs a (primarily) usage-based pricing model. Bayer's Crop Science division pioneered the outcome-based pricing revolution in the farming sector, sharing in both the risks and the rewards its products deliver to farmers. Let's look at these examples in detail.

In September 1999, Netflix revolutionized the video rental industry by introducing a subscription-based pricing model, allowing customers to rent an unlimited number of DVDs for a flat monthly fee. This innovative approach eliminated late fees and shipping costs, two major pain points for customers of traditional rental stores like Blockbuster, which relied on a pay-per-rental model. The subscription model's success was so transformative that Netflix retained it when launching its online streaming service in 2007.

As streaming became more popular, Netflix introduced its first tiered subscription plans in 2011 to cater to customers with different needs and preferences. These plans varied in terms of video quality, the number of simultaneous streams, and the ability to download content for offline viewing.

Over the years, Netflix has continued to adjust and optimize its subscription plans, introducing new tiers and features while raising prices to reflect the increasing value of its content library and services. For instance, Netflix launched the Premium plan in 2013, allowing customers to stream on up to four devices simultaneously while streaming in 4K Ultra HD. In 2022, to continue to accelerate the growth in its subscriber base, Netflix launched the Basic with Ads plan, offering a lower-cost option for price-conscious consumers. The result: Thanks to this flexible roster of subscription plans, Netflix has attracted hundreds of millions of subscribers worldwide, solidifying its position in the streaming industry.

Let's switch gears to Amazon. Most people know Amazon for its "everything store," offering fast, reliable home delivery of almost any product, from groceries to home furnishings. However, a significant part of Amazon's success lies in its B2B division, which is invisible to ordinary consumers. Amazon Web Services (AWS) is the leading provider of cloud computing services. Led by Andy Jassy, who became Amazon CEO in 2021, a year in which AWS accounted for more than 60% of Amazon's total operating profits. How did AWS achieved this impressive scale? By developing a highly effective usage-based pricing model that creates enormous value for both AWS and its customers.

AWS serves over a million customers, from startups to global enterprises, all of which need cloud computing services. To meet the diverse needs of customers, AWS offers a flexible pricing model. Customers can choose a usage-based pricing option or make purchase commitments for discounts. They can also modify their contract lengths and payment terms for further discounts. Usage is measured with various metrics based on specific services, giving customers control over what they buy and how much they pay based on what they use. For instance, cloud access is priced by the hour, with compute instances measured in increments as small as one second.

There are many other examples of companies that have propelled their growth with expertly crafted usage-based pricing models. Twilio, for example, developed a usage-based pricing model that accounts for more than 70% of its revenue. Snowflake, the cloud data warehousing giant, parlayed its usage-based pricing model into one of the most impressive tech IPOs in history. Utility companies like Pacific Gas & Electric Company charge customers based on the amount of electricity used (measured in kilowatt-hours). Coin-operated laundries charge per load.

Let's now turn to Bayer and, more specifically, Bayer's Crop Sciences division. Prior to 2019, Bayer used standard per-product pricing. That year, the company introduced an outcome-based pricing model, aiming to align the cost of agricultural products with their performance outcomes. In essence, Bayer's experts establish an expected yield outcome from a product or seed based on a farm's data regarding historical performance. If the actual yield falls below the expected value, Bayer rebates a portion of the product's price to the farmer. Conversely, if the yield surpasses the expected value, the farmer shares a preagreed portion of the additional income with Bayer.

The advantage of this outcome-based pricing model is the risk management it offers farmers. If Bayer's products perform as advertised, farmers see additional yield and share a portion of the gains with Bayer. If not, their downside risk is protected, with a portion of production losses reimbursed.

Bayer isn't the only company to experiment with outcome-based pricing models. Intercom introduced a pure outcome-based pricing model for its Fin AI Agent product, which is designed to resolve customer questions. If the AI makes a resolution by delivering a satisfactory answer to a customer's question, Intercom collects $0.99. If a resolution can't be made and human intervention is necessary, there's no payout. Similarly, Salesforce designed its Agentforce pricing to align directly with business outcomes, tying costs to the value delivered through customer interactions. By charging per conversation, the model ensured that companies pay Salesforce in proportion to their use of AI-driven customer support, directly linking pricing to improved efficiency and enhanced customer experiences. This approach incentivized businesses to scale their usage as the outcomes—such as faster resolutions and better engagement—drove measurable impact, making the pricing inherently outcome oriented.

Orica, one of the world's largest providers of commercial explosives, charges based on the volume of rock blasted away. ENERCON offers service contracts based on the energy yielded by its wind farms. Signify (formerly Philips Lighting) launched an outcome-based pricing model called Light as a Service, where no up-front investment is required, and a customer's payout is driven by performance commitments on light levels and energy savings.

Companies also have soared by shifting from ineffective pricing models to smart ones, effectively turning struggles into triumphs and achieving significant scale as a result.

Consider the example of Zocdoc, a digital platform for scheduling medical appointments. The service is free to patients, with revenue coming from participating physicians and healthcare companies. Zocdoc initially charged caregivers a flat annual subscription fee of $3,000, which by 2015 was generating annual revenues of $71 million. However, the company struggled as new sign-ups were nearly offset by customer churn.

In 2018, Zocdoc switched in selected states from a subscription model to a usage-based model, charging healthcare providers per patient booking. This pay-as-you-go (PAYG) model made it more affordable for new customers to try Zocdoc. The results were striking: Zocdoc's provider network grew by 50% in states that adopted the new model.[1]

LegalZoom improved its business performance by moving in the opposite direction. Initially it operated as a legal document website that monetized via individual transactions. In 2011, LegalZoom added subscription to most of its products. Instead of selling a single document for a will, it also offered a wills package with legal advice, including 30-minute phone consultations with independent attorneys and attorney reviews of completed documents. The shift from PAYG to a subscription model enhanced LegalZoom's ability to acquire and monetize customers, putting it on a strong growth trajectory for a multibillion-dollar IPO.

For each of these very diverse company examples, having the right pricing model has made a huge difference in its ability to gain market share and wallet share. But how can you decide which of these models is best for you? And having decided, what should you do to design the details of your pricing model for optimal value creation? That's what we explain in the next section of this chapter.

How to Design Your Pricing Model: What Best-in-Class Companies Do

Designing your ideal pricing model involves three steps: selecting the right model type for your business, choosing the best pricing metric(s), and crafting the pricing structure. Let's explore each step in order.

Step 1: Decide on the Type of Pricing Model

Your first task is to decide which model makes sense for your business, focusing particularly (as we've recommended) on the subscription, usage, and outcome-based pricing models. Each of these flavors fits certain types of businesses best. To make the right choice, consider the next sets of criteria and compare them with the characteristics of your company.

Consider adopting a subscription pricing model if:

☐ *Your customers demand predictable bills.* In some markets, customers consider predictable, consistent costs to be the most important factor in determining their level of satisfaction. If your conversations with customers have highlighted this need, then subscription pricing may be the way to go.

☐ *Customer usage tends to be stable from one month to the next.* One reason that direct-to-consumer razor company Harry's, now part of Mammoth Brands, made a sizable dent in the market dominance of incumbent companies like Gillette is that the subscription model was a natural one for the razor market. Most men shave almost exactly the same number of times every month, which makes the I-never-have-to-think-about-it convenience of a subscription purchase simple and attractive.

☐ *Customer usage is intermittent or episodic but the value delivered is ongoing.* Consider services that provide identity theft protection, such as LifeLock or Experian. Customers don't use the service continually, but they're happy to have it on the relatively rare occasions when their personal information has been compromised (which is also the last time people want to receive a sudden bill from their identity protection company). Subscription pricing offers the right solution.

☐ *Locking in customers is a critical competitive strategy.* In markets where customers have many alternative sources competing for their business, subscription pricing at favorable rates can be a great way of capturing their business long term. For example, in the fragmented food delivery business, DoorDash has built a loyal customer base by waiving delivery fees for DashPass subscribers, thus incentivizing them to use the Door-Dash app over others.

☐ *You and your customers will benefit from simplifying the pricing conversation.* In some businesses, it's tedious and alienating for customers to have to navigate a buying decision for every single transaction. That's what the online music business was like until subscription-based services like Spotify arrived, simplifying the process and winning millions of loyal customers in the process.

Consider adopting a usage-based model if:

☐ *A low commitment cost and minimal transactional friction are key to making it easy for customers to buy.* A great example of this is Twilio. Twilio provides application programming interfaces (APIs) for communication services like SMS, voice, and video, allowing businesses to integrate these features seamlessly into their applications. With Twilio's usage-based model, customers pay only for the messages, calls, or minutes they use, avoiding up-front costs or long-term commitments. This approach lowers the barrier to entry, making it easy for businesses to experiment with new features and scale their usage as needed, particularly in scenarios with unpredictable or variable demand.

☐ *Customers especially demand price transparency and fairness.* This is another trait that may be uncovered in your customer conversations. If transparency and fairness are especially prized, then a usage model may be perceived as better than a subscription model. Note that "fairness" typically is defined according to usage and value derived—for example, if a customer doesn't use a subscription-based service for a few months, it may feel "unfair" that they are being charged for those months.

☐ *Both customer usage and value delivered are intermittent or episodic rather than continual.* Cloudflare is a prime example of usage-based pricing working well for intermittent or episodic usage. The company provides web performance and security services, such as content delivery, distributed denial-of-service (DDoS) protection, and serverless computing, which are often needed during specific events like product launches, marketing campaigns, or cyberattacks. These short bursts of high usage deliver significant value but aren't consistent over time. By offering usage-based pricing for features like bandwidth or additional protection, Cloudflare allows customers to align costs with actual use, making the model both flexible and appealing for businesses with irregular demand patterns.

☐ *Your business carries underlying costs that scale with customer usage.* One reason that AWS uses the usage-based model with its cloud computing customers is that the infrastructure cost associated with the service increases as usage grows. A pure subscription model would mean that AWS customers with huge usage needs would get a great bargain while those with small needs would be grossly overpaying—and probably would drop the service.

☐ *The product or service is especially sticky.* When the perceived value enjoyed by using a product or service increases steadily with usage—and especially when it is increasingly difficult for customers to drop the offering after using it extensively—then the usage model offers significant benefits to the company. Once a company starts using the AWS cloud infrastructure to host its own services, for example, switching to a different service is inconvenient and painful.

Consider adopting an outcome-based pricing model if:

☐ *The value delivered by your product or service is easy to measure.* Attribution is the primary challenge that comes with outcome-based pricing models. The metric to determine attribution is of vital importance. In the example of Intercom, attribution is simpler because it is easier to measure the volume of customer questions answered by its AI agent. By contrast, Slack illustrates the challenges of implementing an outcome-based pricing model when the value delivered is obvious, but it is very difficult to measure and quantify that value. Although Slack undeniably enhances collaboration and productivity by streamlining communication, quantifying those benefits—and attributing them directly to Slack—is extremely difficult. An outcome-based model, charging based on productivity gains, would be complex and subjective, potentially leading to disputes over metrics and perceived value.

☐ *The upside is large enough to compensate for the risk you're undertaking.* Implementing an outcome-based pricing model comes with its own share of risk: If your product or service can't deliver upside, your payout will be significantly lower than it would have been if you had considered a subscription or usage model instead.

☐ *Your customers' revenue model can be closely aligned with your own.* When you share both risk and reward with your customers, both parties will work toward the same objectives. Think about it like this: If your customers know that you will win if they win, they're more likely to use your products optimally, exploring all the benefits that your products have to offer.

☐ *You are attempting to win over customers from competition.* Outcome-based pricing models can be a highly effective way to attract customers, especially those loyal to a competing product. A well-defined outcome-based model aligned with the value that your customers gain from your product can lower their barrier to switching by providing a clear mechanism to protect their downside.

Considering these three sets of characteristics should enable you to determine which model is more likely to be best for your business. Now you're ready to move on to step 2 in the process.

Exhibit 4.1 Monetizing AI—Getting the Model Right from Day One!

AI companies cannot afford to postpone pricing decisions. Monetization is not just a go-to-market detail; it's a core architectural choice that can make or break the business. Why? Because AI businesses live at the intersection of intense cost pressure and extraordinary value potential.

Unlike traditional software, many AI solutions can be expensive to operate from the outset. Inference and model tuning can incur real-time compute costs. At the same time, AI, particularly agentic AI, has the potential to tap into *labor budgets*, which are often 10x larger than IT or software budgets. That's a massive opportunity—but only if you have the right monetization model to capture it.

If you use the old SaaS playbook—anchoring your pricing on seats, bundling in unlimited usage, or failing to link pricing to impact—you risk systematically undermonetizing your innovation from day one. Worse, you train customers to expect more for less, a hard habit to undo.

To help founders and leaders navigate this high-stakes terrain, we've developed a 2x2 pricing framework for AI companies, based on two key dimensions:

- *Autonomy*. How independently does the AI operate? Does it augment a human or replace humans entirely?

- *Attribution*. How clearly can the AI's actions be linked to measurable outcomes?

This gives us four strategic pricing zones:

1. Copilot + Low Attribution → Seat-Based Pricing Model (Bottom Left)

    You're augmenting humans but can't clearly tie actions to outcomes. This is common for AI tools embedded in productivity apps (e.g., email summarizers, writing assistants). Your best bet is to price per seat, but beware: Doing so caps your upside and doesn't scale with value delivered. Make every effort to increase attribution and move to bottom-right quadrant.

2. Copilot + High Attribution → Hybrid Pricing Model (Bottom Right)

    You're still a helper, but now you can prove impact. In this quadrant, it's smart to layer usage on top of seats. That might mean credits, tiered packages, or consumption-based thresholds. Think: Copilots in finance or legal where you can show how time or cost was saved. Over time, push attribution deeper so you can move toward an outcome model.

3. Autonomous + Low Attribution → Usage-Based Pricing Model (Top Left)

    Here, the AI is operating independently, but you can't (yet) tie its work to business results. That's okay; you can still win with task-based or volume-based pricing. This is where AI platforms that automate back-end processes (e.g., document classification or coding assistants) live. Usage is your best proxy for value.

4. Autonomous + High Attribution → Outcome-Based Pricing Model (Top Right)

    This is the holy grail. You're not just replacing human effort; you're directly moving the needle on metrics that matter (e.g., increased sales, reduced costs, higher throughput). If you can prove attribution, you can ask for a slice of the upside. Examples include AI-driven autonomous agents or AI for cost optimization. The key is trust and data visibility, and you must constantly reinforce the value brought to the table in order to capture a portion of it.

Four Strategic Pricing Zones

Autonomy High	**Usage-Based Pricing Model** • Charge per task, job, API call, etc. • Use where usage = perceived value • Seats are irrelevant	**Outcome-Based Pricing Model** • Autonomous + High Impact • Monetize on outcomes • Take a percentage on incremental value
Low	**Seat-Based Pricing Model** • Anchor on per-seat model • Risk of undermonetizing • Make efforts to increase attribution	**Hybrid Pricing Model** • Combine Seats + Usage • Explicit: Meter and charge usage • Implicit: Tier packages by usage
	Low **Attribution** High	

Step 2: Choose the Price Metric

A *price metric* is the unit of measurement used to calculate the total price a customer pays for a product or service. It defines how value is quantified and priced, aligning what customers are charged with the value they receive. Selecting the right price metric is crucial, as it directly impacts how customers perceive the fairness and flexibility of your pricing and how well the model scales with their needs.

Price metrics are everywhere, tailored to reflect the specific value delivered by the product or service. For instance, cloud storage providers like AWS use metrics such as storage space (e.g., gigabytes used per month) or compute hours for virtual servers. Slack's pricing scales based on the number of active users, while HubSpot charges based on the number of marketing contacts managed within the platform. Twilio charges customers based on a per-transaction metric, such as the number of text messages sent or voice minutes used. Intercom charges businesses based on the number of AI-resolved customer conversations (resolutions). Financial services like Klarna and Affirm charge fees tied to the number of transactions or loans processed, making their revenue proportional to the volume of business their clients conduct.

Beyond tech, other industries also use creative pricing metrics that align with the value delivered. For example, transportation services charge based on distance traveled and time taken, reflecting the utility provided to the rider. In hospitality, hotels use room nights as a price metric, while in healthcare, companies may price based on the number of patients treated or procedures performed. In business services, it is common to charge by the hour. Even in utilities, providers charge for water, gas, or electricity based on units consumed, ensuring costs align with actual usage.

The concept of price metrics is more common than you might think. Consider your local pizza place: It uses two price metrics—"by the slice" and "by the pie." This approach aligns pricing with customer preferences, whether someone wants a quick bite or a meal for the whole family. Similarly, in tech or any other industry, a well-chosen price metric ensures customers pay in proportion to the value they derive, making pricing intuitive, fair, and scalable.

For a whole host of reasons, it is critical to get your price metrics right. The price metrics you choose can serve all of these purposes:

- *Extracting a fair portion of the value delivered to customers.* Good metrics are directly tied to the value your product delivers. Michelin introduced a pay-per-mile pricing model for truckers, where costs were tied to the miles driven rather than purchasing tires outright. Because the main value proposition for Michelin's innovative tires was durability, the choice of a per-mile metric made clear sense and enabled the company to be rewarded for the value it was providing.

- *Addressing distinct customer segments.* Different metrics can allow you to appeal to different segments with varying needs. For example, when you travel on the Deutsche Bahn railway, you can pay per ride or subscribe to a BahnCard with a duration of between three and 12 months. These two metrics make it easy for Deutsche Bahn to serve both occasional travelers and dedicated commuters.

- *Synchronizing payment with consumption.* The right metric can allow you to schedule payments to coincide with the use of your product or service. This approach leads to a better customer experience while also improving your company's cash flow.

- *Overcoming customer buying constraints and psychological thresholds.* Michelin's per-mile usage pricing allowed trucking company purchasers to buy the new tires without having to worry about larger-than-expected capital expenses.

- *Controlling the level of transparency.* Mailchimp displays detailed pricing on its website, with calculators to estimate costs based on their customers' audience size. Similarly, Stripe's pricing is openly displayed and straightforward with no hidden fees or complicated add-ons. Customers can easily calculate costs based on their usage. Your choice of pricing metric is an opportunity to choose the level of transparency you consider most advantageous.

- *Differentiating your company from the competition.* Using different metrics from your competitors can effectively differentiate your business, especially if your chosen metric is hard to imitate.

How do you decide which price metrics make sense for your business? Start by brainstorming a list of potential metrics—the more, the better. Think

Table 4.1   Possible Metrics for a Software Offering

Pricing by User	Pricing by Customer Characteristic
User	Number of business processes
Active user	Number of networks connected
Server	Number of employees
Pricing by Usage	**Pricing by Return on Investment**
Number of AI-generated reports	Increased service level
Number of AI resolutions	Gains in productivity
Number of transactions	Cost reductions

outside the box and strive to understand your customers: how they define value, how they use your offerings, how often, and so on. For example, Table 4.1 shows a list of possible metrics created by a software company during the process of defining its pricing model.

Once you've created a list of possible metrics, you need to evaluate the options according to the benefits they bring to you and the benefits they bring to your customers. The next frameworks will guide you through this two-part evaluation process.

A. *Benefits to You.* Rank each metric you are considering on a scale of 1 (low) to 5 (high) on each of the listed criteria. Then calculate an average score.

- *Strategic objectives.* To what extent is this metric likely to drive customer adoption and maximize customer lifetime value?

- *Value extraction.* To what extent will this metric help you capture a fair portion of the value you deliver to your customers?

- *Competition.* To what extent will this metric help differentiate your company from its competitors?

- *Future growth.* To what extent will this metric enable you to grow with the customer's growth and/or make it easier to upsell future products?

The Most Important Decision: Choosing Your Pricing Model

- *Implementation.* To what extent will this metric make it easy for you to administer, monitor, control, and enforce prices?

B. *Benefits to Customers.* Rank each metric on a scale of 1 (low) to 5 (high) on each of the next criteria. Then calculate an average score.

- *Perceived fairness.* To what extent will this metric make it easy for customers to accept the pricing as fair and reasonable?
- *Budgets and thresholds.* To what extent will this metric help customers overcome buying constraints and any psychological price thresholds that may make them reluctant to pay?
- *Value alignment.* To what extent will this metric generate payments that scale with value received?
- *Predictable.* To what extent does this metric provide predictable costs for customers or allow them to calculate total cost of ownership?
- *Flexibility.* To what extent does this metric enable customers to choose and pay for the exact scope of services desired?

Your goal is to identify a metric—or a combination of metrics—that score high on both the A scale and the B scale. The ideal pricing metric will provide benefits both to your company and to the customers you serve, thereby creating a strong basis for long-term, mutually beneficial growth. In other words, you should aim to select a metric within the green zone shown in Figure 4.1, avoid the red zone, and, if necessary, settle for the gray zone as a last resort.

Now you're ready to tackle the third and final step in the process.

Step 3: Design the Price Structure

The *price structure* is the way the price of a product or service is charged to the customer. Price structures range from those that involve the least variability (fixed) to those with the greatest variability. In selecting the best price structure for your offering, you need to consider to what extent, and in what way, you want your price structure to account for differing levels of customer usage.

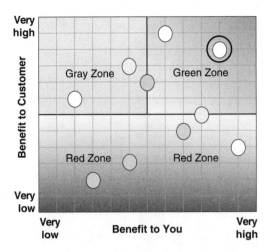

Figure 4.1 Price Metric Choice: Aim for the Green Zone

To begin addressing this challenge, look at Figure 4.2, which illustrates in simple graphical form eight common pricing structures that companies have used successfully.

Let's review these eight structures, from the least variable to the most, and consider some of the key criteria that determine which structures work for which companies.

1. *Flat.* This is the simplest structure: The price charged remains the same, no matter how the usage may vary. Think of your Netflix subscription—the monthly price is the same regardless of how many movies you watch. This structure has a number of advantages for your company: It's easy to communicate; it generates stable, recurring revenues; and it promotes retention. It also offers some clear advantages for your customer: It's super-easy to understand and provides predictable pricing that people find easy to commit to. The classic marketing/sales pitch for this structure is "all you can eat."

2. *Adaptive flat.* This structure modifies the flat structure by adjusting the fixed price according to customer usage in the previous period. For

The Most Important Decision: Choosing Your Pricing Model

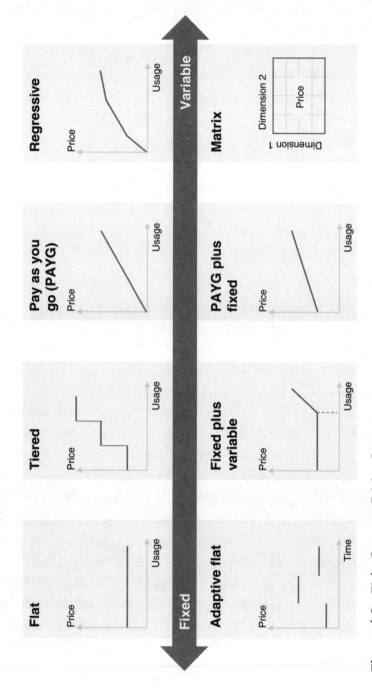

Figure 4.2 Eight Common Pricing Structures

Scaling Innovation

example, in Year 1, the price remains fixed and unchanging; but in Year 2, the price might go up or down, depending on the level of usage during Year 1. Within the year, however, the fee is fixed. This structure has most of the same advantages as the flat structure, provided there is alignment between you and your customers regarding the relationship between usage and value. The marketing/sales pitch for this structure is "Your fixed fee adapts based on how much you use the product."

3. *Tiered.* This structure is common in B2B software, where the price is flat but tiered. The price charged remains the same, no matter how the usage varies within the tier—for example, a customer might pay $100K for the first tier of usage, then pay $200K for the next tier of usage, and so on. The marketing/sales pitch for this structure is "All you can eat, within a tier." The disadvantage of the tiered structure is that it is based purely on volume tiers rather than on true usage, which could result in you leaving money on the table (compared to a more usage-based structure like pay as you go, structure 5).

4. *Fixed plus variable.* In this structure, the price is fixed until a specified usage level is reached, after which an overage charge kicks in. This structure is familiar from cell phone plans, which typically include a certain number of minutes for a fixed fee, with an additional charge based on the number of incremental minutes you use. The advantage of this structure is that, when it's designed properly, it guarantees a minimum recurring revenue while keeping most customers on the fixed fee alone. Since most customers think long and hard about exceeding the fixed-rate level, you can promote this structure as one that provides customers with both simplicity and peace of mind. At the same time, however, the ability to charge an overage fee allows your company to capture a fair share of value from customers who use your product a lot. The marketing/sales

pitch for this structure is "You can get started for a fixed initial invest-ment that should allow you ample usage."

5. *Pay as you go (PAYG).* As we've already discussed, this structure allows customers the flexibility to pay only for what they use. The advantage of this structure for your company is that it is easy to pitch to new customers, it is guaranteed to cover any variable costs you incur, and—most important—it automatically scales with value delivered. The big advantage for customers is that they don't have to commit to an up-front cost and can avoid a capital expense they might find onerous or daunting. The marketing/sales pitch for this structure is "Only pay for what you use."

6. *Pay as you go (PAYG) plus fixed.* This structure modifies the PAYG structure by introducing a basic fixed payment—what you might call a pay-to-play charge. The advantage of this structure for your com-pany is that it lets you recover a minimum amount of revenue on every deal, which could be crucial if you have a significant fixed cost (e.g., integration services and other setup costs to get started) that make a pure PAYG structure risky. As for customers, they do have the disadvantage of having to pay a minimum fee, but otherwise this structure has the major benefits of the PAYG structure. The marketing/sales pitch for this structure is "You pay a minimum fee to get started, then only pay for what you use."

7. *Regressive.* This structure is a more advanced version of the PAYG with incentives for customers to use more. In other words, the rate which you pay as you go decreases as your usage increases. Think of this as a volume discount on the PAYG rate. For example, Twilio charges a PAYG rate that varies by usage—$0.0079/message for the first 150K messages, $0.0077/message for the next 150K messages, $0.0075 for the next 200K messages, and so on. The main advantage for you is that this structure builds on top of the advantages of the PAYG struc-ture, further incentivizes usage by providing a volume discount, and,

most important, allows you to message on fairness (since the rate comes down with high usage). The advantage for the customer is both low commitment and a guarantee that the price goes down with usage. The marketing/sales pitch for this model is "Only pay for what you use. The more you use, the cheaper your price."

8. *Matrix.* This pricing structure is built around two key dimensions: one typically reflecting a volume metric and the other representing an action that drives value for your business. For example, as shown in Figure 4.3, the pricing (in this case price per document) is determined by the number of documents produced by an AI agent (the volume metric) and the number of departments deploying the AI agent (the measurement that benefits your business). The price per document is highest in the upper-left corner and lowest in the bottom-right corner. In other words, customers are incentivized to scale usage across more departments as well as to use the AI agent

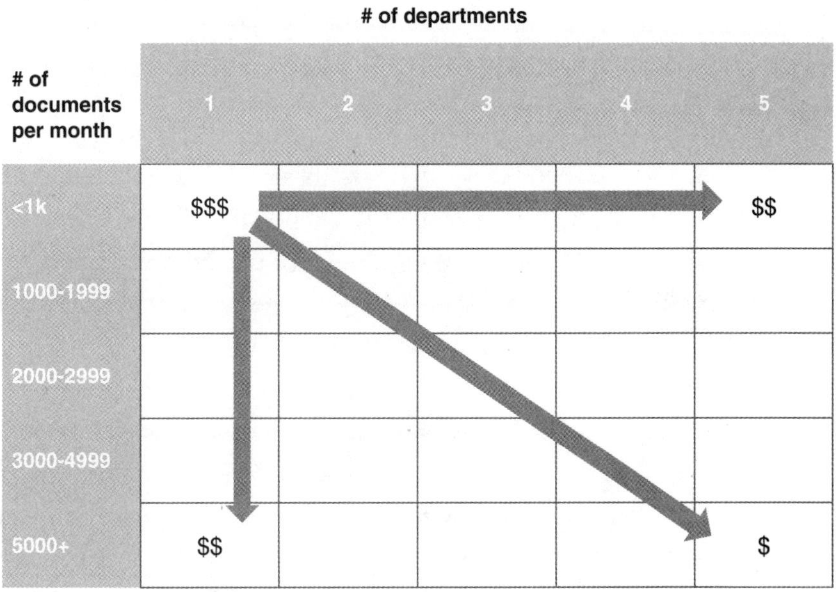

Figure 4.3 Sample Matrix Structure

The Most Important Decision: Choosing Your Pricing Model

freely within each department. For your company, this approach creates value by driving broader adoption (more departments) and higher engagement (more documents generated), leading to a stickier, enterprise-wide implementation and larger overall deals.

The advantage of the matrix structure for your business is that it lets you incentivize fast, broad usage of your offering, rewarding customers when they use it a lot and when they realize a large amount of value. All of this can help to make your offering really sticky. The marketing/sales pitch for this structure is "We empower you to pick the price you want. The more you use and the more value you receive, the better your pricing."

Having chosen the type of model that's right for your business (i.e., subscription, usage, or outcome based), the best pricing metrics, and the most appropriate pricing structure, you have now assembled all the elements for a pricing model that should work for you. But how can you be sure you've made the right choice?

The Breakeven Exercise: A Neat Trick to Test for the Best Pricing Model

Over the years, we've found that customers always have an inherent preference for a particular pricing model. It's important to align with that inherent preference. Doing so is one of the most powerful ways you can make it easy for customers to buy—but it's not always easy to figure out which model your customers intuitively prefer.

One of the most effective ways we've found to test for price model preference is to put customers through what we call the "breakeven exercise." Here's how it works.

The exercise starts by pitching the product or service to customers, so they understand the value it offers. In other words, first have the classic sales and marketing conversation. Then put them into one or more hypothetical usage situations and provide them with breakeven options. The way they react will tell you all you need to know about whether your pricing model is the right one.

Let's take an example from a marketplace company that we worked with. The common practice is to charge a commission for every item sold in the marketplace. However, our client was not sure about the best way to price that commission. To find out, we put the client's customers through the next hypothetical exercise:

Imagine that you are selling a $200 item in the marketplace. You know that you will have to pay a commission on the sale. But there are three pricing models that could be used to determine the amount of that commission. Model A is a flat fee of $10.00. Model B is a flat fee of $3.00 plus 3.5% of the total sale price. And Model C is a charge of 5% of the total sale price. Which of these three models do you prefer? Or are you indifferent as to which model is used?

In the actual experiment, the names of the three models and the order in which they were presented were both randomized to avoid any bias. Imagine you were the one selling the item and take a moment to decide which of the three models you would prefer. Then read on to find out what our study revealed.

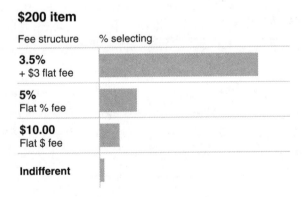

Figure 4.4   Results of a Sample Breakeven Exercise

The Most Important Decision: Choosing Your Pricing Model

As Figure 4.4 reveals, one of the three models was overwhelmingly preferred—*despite the fact that, if you do the math, all three models would generate the same $10 commission.* And almost no one declared themselves indifferent about the choice of model, even though there was literally no difference among them.

One of the basic assumptions of classical economics is that human beings make economic choices for reasons that are fundamentally rational. If this were true, then everyone in this experiment would choose the "indifferent" option. Yet we have applied this technique across thousands of companies and have never observed the "indifferent" option prevail.

Thus, even when it may seem illogical, customers *do* care about how you charge them—which means you must make the effort to determine which pricing model will make it easy for them to buy.

The Mental Model Axiom	Customers instinctively gravitate toward a pricing model that feels right to them, and are rarely indifferent.

Beyond the Basics: Insights, Tips, and Tricks About Choosing the Best Pricing Model

You now understand the basic process for designing the best pricing model for your business. Now let's consider some advanced insights, tips, and tricks you may find useful as you work your way through the process.

- *Monetizing metrics versus fencing metrics.* One of the finer points to consider when choosing a metric is the distinction between *explicit* and *implicit* metrics. When you explicitly charge your customers based on units consumed, you are using a *monetizing metric.* (The per-mile charge for Michelin's long-lasting tires is an example of a monetizing metric.) In other cases, however, you may choose to implicitly charge your customers by limiting or fencing the availability of product or service functionality. The result is what we call a "fencing metric." Here's an example: Netflix uses a subscription model where the number of screens you can watch on simultaneously depends on the plan you choose. The standard plan allows streaming on two screens at a time, and the premium plan allows up to four. In this case, the per-month price is the monetizing metric, and the number of screens is the fencing metric.

- *Primary and secondary metrics.* Don't feel you must limit yourself to a single metric. Companies often employ a combination of metrics to cover broader usage segments across their customers. The primary metric typically scales with value, while the secondary metric typically scales with costs. For example, a lab management software company that we worked with charges customers based on the number of lab test results generated per day. This primary metric is aligned with the value that customers receive. The company also charges fixed fees based on the number of lab instruments used. This secondary metric tracks the need to cover the costs and risks associated with the third-party software installed for each lab instrument.

- *Hybrid models.* For some companies, a hybrid pricing model that combines features of the subscription, usage, and outcome-based pricing models makes sense. Consider HubSpot, which markets software products for marketing and sales management. HubSpot's three plans—Starter, Professional, and Enterprise—are sold on a monthly basis, and each covers a specified number of marketing contacts. If you want to exceed that number, you can purchase packs of contacts for an additional fee. For example, the Professional plan ($800 per month) includes 2,000 contacts; a pack of 5,000 additional contacts is available for $250. Thus, HubSpot's pricing model is a subscription/usage hybrid. Similarly, you could

83

design a subscription/outcome-based hybrid where customers pay a lower annual subscription fee, but, in return, they share in the upside/downside that your solution generates for them.

- *Offering a choice of models.* Don't feel constrained to offer only one pricing model. In many cases, offering a choice of pricing models is a great way to appeal to different customer segments. To help remember this, think of the pizza example mentioned earlier in the chapter: It can be purchased by the pie or by the slice—two different models catering to two different needs. If pizza can be sold with two different models, your product can, too.

- *Using outcome-based pricing as a negotiation tool.* Even if your customer does not want to go down the route of being charged based on an outcome, bringing it up as one of the options can serve as a powerful negotiation tool, particularly in B2B settings. For instance, by presenting an outcome-based option alongside a fixed-fee alternative, you not only provide flexibility to your customer but also demonstrate confidence in your product and a willingness to share the risk—putting your own skin in the game. Even if the customer ultimately chooses the fixed-fee option, offering an outcome-based deal can enhance the perceived value of the fixed-fee model. This approach can also enable you to justify charging a higher fixed fee than you might otherwise, as the outcome-based pricing acts as a natural anchor. Additionally, it provides a strategic defense during price negotiations. If a customer pushes back on price, you can point to the outcome-based option as a low-risk alternative, reinforcing the fairness of the fixed fee while maintaining your pricing integrity. This dual-option approach not only positions you as a partner invested in your customer's success but also creates leverage to optimize pricing outcomes.

- *Special tactics when you use a usage model.* If you adopt a usage-based pricing model, it's important to proactively address potential pitfalls. The following tactics can help you minimize downside and maximize both customer trust and revenue performance.

o *Rethink sales incentives.* Traditional sales comp plans reward teams based on up-front contract value. But in a usage model, much of the revenue unfolds over time. Snowflake, for example, redesigned its sales compensation to reward both committed bookings *and* recognized consumption—with the latter paid out as usage is realized. This approach incentivizes salespeople to sell usage models.

o *Offer customers peace of mind on overall pricing and predictability.* Usage-based models can create anxiety for customers worried about unpredictable bills or runaway costs. Ease these concerns by offering a transparent discount schedule that improves per-unit pricing with increased usage. If predictability is critical, agree on a budget and implement a drawdown model against that budget— charging based on actual usage. When the budget is exhausted, you can renegotiate the next tranche. These tactics typically go a long way in managing customer anxiety around pricing volatility. As a last resort, think about caps (see next entry).

o *Keep caps in the back pocket.* Usage caps can be a powerful negotia- tion tool to reassure hesitant customers, but use them sparingly and strategically. Once introduced, caps are nearly impossible to remove, as customers tend to react emotionally to changes in perceived pro- tections. If you must offer a cap, always try to time-bound it. For example: *"Let's set a capped contract for the first year so we can both get comfortable with your usage patterns. After that, we'll transition to a true usage-based model, using the data we've gathered to establish fair pricing that reflects your actual needs."* This method positions the cap as a bridge, not a permanent fixture.

• *First establish the right pricing model; then optimize price levels.* It is far easier to change price levels after getting a new pricing model in place than to start with high price levels and face resistance. Take inspiration from Ryanair, the first airline to introduce a new pricing model that included a fee for a specific weight of luggage (20 kilograms). When Ryanair launched the model in 2006, the charge was €3.50, a level specifically chosen to minimize the uproar caused by the new fee. By 2016, the level had risen to €35.00.

- *Consider future trends when designing your pricing model.* It is important to take future trends into account when coming up with pricing models, especially if those trends include increased costs. In 2008, a leading logistics company created a pricing model that based flat-screen TV deliveries on a per-screen price. It even signed multi-year fixed-price contracts locking in this model in order to retain customers. These decisions backfired on the company in subsequent years as TVs became much larger, causing delivery costs to skyrocket while revenues stayed flat.

Chapter Summary: How This Strategy Avoids the Single-Engine Trap

A well-chosen pricing model prevents the Money Maker trap of optimizing for revenue at the expense of reach and the Disruptor trap of choosing a model that scales monetization poorly. The strategies described in this chapter fuel market share by making your offering accessible to more segments, and they build wallet share by aligning price with value delivered. Profitable Growth Architects choose pricing models that grow with their customers—and with their business.

CEO Questions

- Do you have the right pricing model that enables you to best capture market share and wallet share? How do you know?

- Have you examined the advantages and disadvantages of the subscription, usage, and outcome-based models to determine which model is most appropriate for your business?

- Have you examined a wide range of possible metrics to use before arriving at your current choice? Have you spent time developing your ideal price structure?

- Have you done tests to determine which pricing model your customers intuitively prefer?

- Have you explored the possibility of using multiple metrics and/ or providing a choice of pricing models to appeal to a range of customer segments with varying usage patterns, needs, and preferences?

Chapter 5

Making It Easy to Buy: Beautifully Simple Pricing

In the early days of a startup, countless decisions vie for a founder's attention. Amid this whirlwind, pricing often takes a backseat, treated as a quick decision rather than the strategic cornerstone it is. Yet pricing is not just about numbers; it's about the story you tell customers, the way you signal value, and how you set the stage for profitable growth.

Beautifully simple pricing is not just a nice-to-have, it's essential. Pricing that is clear, intuitive, and aligned with value reduces friction in decision making. When customers understand and trust the price, they are more likely to take the plunge, especially in markets saturated with alternative options. On the flip-side, pricing that's confusing, misaligned, or overly complicated can drive customers away before they even get started.

Moreover, simple pricing is not just a mechanism for customer acquisition; it's a tool for signaling brand intent. Pricing high—premium pricing—can signal that a product is the market leader, while low, competitive pricing can position it as an accessible option. By architecting pricing that balances market share with wallet share, startups can lay the foundation for sustainable growth and profitability.

This chapter is a deep dive into what creates beautifully simple pricing and how that simplicity can help startups scale effectively. Before we delve into a detailed 10-point checklist that you can use to assess your own pricing to make it beautifully simple, we start with two case studies that exemplify these principles in action: Superhuman and Subway.

The Price-Value Axiom	Pricing is never just a number—it's a measure and signal of value and a core part of your narrative. If you're not intentional about it, you're letting your pricing tell the wrong story.

The Power of Simple: How Beautiful Pricing Fueled Superhuman and Subway

Superhuman, the lightning-fast email client, did not stumble on its pricing strategy by chance. From the outset, founder Rahul Vohra understood that the product wasn't just an email service: It was a productivity tool for high-achieving professionals who value their time as much as their money. The challenge for Superhuman was to craft a pricing strategy that reflected its premium positioning while remaining accessible and easy to grasp. As Rahul puts it, "It is truly impossible to separate pricing from positioning. And when founders ask me, 'How do I figure out what my pricing should be?,' my answer is always 'You should first figure out your positioning.'"

The journey began with understanding customers. The Superhuman team conducted extensive customer interviews, diving deep into understanding what its users truly valued. The insights revealed that users saw Superhuman as more than an email client; it was a time-saving powerhouse. Professionals estimated they saved hours each week using the tool. Quantifying this benefit allowed Superhuman to frame its pricing in terms of value delivered. Team members realized they weren't just selling software; they were selling reclaimed time, improved focus, and a stress-free inbox.

The second critical question: How much should customers pay for these benefits? To answer this, Rahul and his team engaged their first 100 users with a series of well-crafted questions (which careful readers may recognize as techniques we introduced in our book *Monetizing Innovation*):[1]

- At what price would you consider Superhuman to be so expensive that you wouldn't buy it?

- At what price would you consider Superhuman to be so inexpensive that it might compromise perceived quality and cause concern?

- At what price would you consider Superhuman to be starting to get expensive—not out of reach, but requiring some consideration before buying?

- At what price would you consider Superhuman to be a bargain—a great buy for the money?

Using the responses, the team identified a price point that aligned most closely with the third question: When would Superhuman feel expensive, but you'd still buy it anyway? The median answer was $30 per month. Superhuman had its new price point.

Reflecting on this decision, Rahul explains, "This wasn't an arbitrary choice but a carefully considered figure. The pricing decision wasn't just about numbers; it was about psychology. The price had to signal premium quality without alienating potential customers."

The $30 price point resonated with the psychological threshold of Superhuman's target audience, busy professionals who were accustomed to investing in productivity-enhancing tools because they valued their time. Even better, it allowed the company to craft a straightforward, compelling narrative connecting the price with value: "It's just $1 a day to save up to four hours a week." Phrasing it this way put the cost in simple, relatable terms, making it easier for customers to justify the expense.

Further, by choosing a round number, Superhuman avoided making its price feel overly calculated or arbitrary—it was $30, not, say, $29.49. This approach aligned with the company's overall philosophy and positioning.

Making It Easy to Buy: Beautifully Simple Pricing

Packaging was also simple. Superhuman had just one offer, without complex add-ons or hidden fees. Customers knew exactly what they were paying for and what they would get: a faster, cleaner, and more efficient inbox that saved them valuable time. The combination of a beautifully simple price point, a clear connection to value, and a seamless user experience made the $30 per month feel less like an expense and more like a worthwhile investment.

Superhuman's pricing became a core part of its branding. By charging more than other email applications, the company positioned itself as a premium product, which suggested both quality and exclusivity. This latter characteristic was amplified by their invite-only initial launch.

The result of this well-thought-out strategy was a beautifully simple pricing model that not only attracted loyal customers but also made them evangelists for the brand. Superhuman's pricing wasn't just about revenue; it was about signaling value, building trust, and creating a product that people believed was worth every penny.

Now let's turn our attention to Subway, the well-known sandwich shop chain. In the mid-2000s, Subway was grappling with fierce competition in the fast-food industry. Sales were stagnant, and the brand was losing market share to rivals offering compelling promotions. Subway needed something bold to capture attention and drive foot traffic. Enter the $5 footlong, a pricing strategy so simple and memorable that it not only revived Subway's fortunes but also became a cultural phenomenon.

The idea came from a franchisee in Florida, where the $5 footlong started as a limited promotion. The straightforward premise stood out from the complex meal deals and combo offers promoted by other restaurant chains: Any 12-inch sandwich for just five bucks. The simplicity of the premise was carried through in its execution. There were no asterisks, no fine print, and no tricky upsells. The clarity and simplicity of the offer resonated with customers who knew they could walk into Subway, hand over a $5 bill, and leave with a satisfying meal. Soon they were doing just that, in the millions.

As with Superhuman, the connection between price and value was simple enough to be captured in a single, memorable phrase. Subway rolled out the promotion with a catchy jingle—"Five Dollar Footlong!"—which became an earworm for millions of customers. The pricing, paired with clever marketing, hit the sweet spot of affordability and value. In a postrecession era when customers were watching their wallets, the $5 price point felt accessible without cheapening the brand. It wasn't just a deal, it was a promise.

Perhaps the most clever aspect of the $5 footlong was how it incorporated consumer psychology. A "foot-long" sandwich sounded substantial to customers, a full meal that could satisfy their hunger. For many, $5 was a key psychological threshold—it didn't feel like a splurge, nor did it require much deliberation. The simplicity of the pricing also made it easy for restaurant workers to communicate with customers: There was no confusion at the counter, just a straightforward offer.

The results were astounding. Sales surged, with Subway reporting an increase in revenue of over $3.8 billion within the first year of the promotion. Franchise owners embraced the offer, as it drove higher traffic and upselling opportunities. Customers who came in for the $5 footlong often paired it with drinks or chips, boosting the average order value while maintaining the simplicity of the core offering.

Inevitably, rising food costs and overall inflation made Subway phase out the deal. But the initiative had done its job, improving both Subway's financial position and its brand power. The $5 footlong lives on as a demonstration of the power of beautifully simple pricing: It captured attention, drove sales, and created billions in company value. Not bad for something based on a five-dollar bill.

These stories highlight the transformative power of beautifully simple pricing. Whether it's an exclusive tech tool aimed at professionals or a universally appealing fast-food offer, simplicity in pricing can reduce friction, build trust, and create a memorable value proposition that accelerates profitable growth.

The Beautifully Simple Axiom	When pricing is beautifully simple and aligned with brand value, it becomes a catalyst for explosive growth.

Making It Easy to Buy: Beautifully Simple Pricing

The 10-Point Checklist for Beautifully Simple Pricing

Beautifully simple pricing doesn't happen by accident. It requires deliberate design, clear principles, and a deep understanding of both your product and your customers. In this section, we present a 10-point checklist to help you craft pricing that fits all these criteria. Each principle in this list is drawn from real-world success stories and proven strategies. Collectively, they can turn pricing from a challenge into a competitive advantage.

1. Clarity

When customers encounter your pricing model, it should be immediately clear what they are paying for and what they are receiving in return. This clarity is the cornerstone of beautifully simple pricing. It eliminates confusion and reduces hesitation in decision making. Clarity also builds trust, a key advantage since customers have grown increasingly wary of fine print and alert to unexpected fees. Clarity in pricing shows customers that your company operates with integrity. An example is the personal-use pricing plan DropBox created early in its history: $9.99 per month for 2TB of storage. The clarity of both price and value left no room for ambiguity about limitations or additional costs.

Moreover, clarity streamlines the decision-making process for potential buyers. In a crowded market where customers often compare multiple options, easily understood pricing becomes a competitive advantage.

2. Avoid Price Points That Seem Calculated

When customers encounter an oddly specific price, like $36.47, they are likely to pause and question the reasoning behind the number. This situation creates unnecessary cognitive load, forcing buyers to think harder about the price. The resulting moment of hesitation can interrupt the purchasing flow, leading to lost sales.

By contrast, round numbers, or price points with common ends like .99 or .95, resonate better with customers. A price like $30 or $39.99 is easier to process and feels better aligned with what buyers expect. A .99 or .95 ending suggests a deal, which can accelerate adoption. Alternatively, a round number creates a sense of trust and authenticity, signaling that the company values straightforwardness. Slack successfully leveraged this principle with its per-user pricing of $8 or $15, avoiding overcomplication while still feeling competitive and fair.

Calculated-looking pricing can unintentionally come across as manipulative. Customers may perceive the company as trying to extract every penny from them, eroding trust in the brand. Beautifully simple pricing avoids this pitfall by embracing figures that make it easier for customers to rationalize spending.

3. Align with Value

A beautifully simple pricing model must be anchored in the value delivered to the customer. This alignment ensures that customers feel they are receiving enough benefit for the price they are paying, creating a perception of fairness and reinforcing their purchasing decision. Value alignment is particularly important for startups, where pricing often serves as the first tangible indicator of the product's worth.

Starbucks is a prime example of how pricing can align with the value customers perceive. The company goes beyond simply selling coffee; it delivers a distinctive experience that combines high-quality beverages, comfortable seating, complimentary Wi-Fi, and the ability to customize an order to the customer's taste. Many people who go to Starbucks aren't just there for what they buy at the counter; they pay for the opportunity to relax, work, or socialize in an inviting environment. The abundance of value on offer allows Starbucks to charge premium prices. In tying its pricing to the overall experience, Starbucks reinforces its position as a premium coffeehouse and creates lasting loyalty among its customers.

Making It Easy to Buy: Beautifully Simple Pricing

4. Ability to Scale/Grow with Customers

Startups, in particular, thrive when their pricing models scale along with their customers. A rigid pricing structure that doesn't allow changes risks alienating users who outgrow the product or feel constrained by its limitations.

As an example, AWS, mentioned in Chapter 4, allows startups to start small and scale usage as their needs grow. This strategy allows AWS to connect with a wide range of customers, from individual developers to large enterprises. By aligning pricing with usage, AWS creates a seamless growth journey for its customers while capturing increased revenue as they scale.

This approach could also benefit customers with seasonal or fluctuating needs. For instance, a company that offers dynamic pricing based on consumption can cater to customers who might otherwise hesitate to commit to fixed monthly plans.

5. At First, Offer Fewer Choices

In pricing for the startup phase, less is more. Offering fewer options simplifies the decision-making process for customers, reducing the friction created by comparing multiple options. When faced with too many choices, customers can experience decision paralysis, where the abundance of options overwhelms them and leads to inaction.

A critical step for any startup, as outlined in *Monetizing Innovation*, is to conduct a segmentation exercise to identify the core customer groups based on what they value and their willingness to pay. However, this recommendation doesn't mean rushing to create products and pricing for every potential buying group. Instead, prioritize clusters of buyers for whom your product delivers the most value and among whom it's easiest to achieve traction. Even there, offer only a limited number of pricing options.

By offering a deliberately restricted set of alternatives—or even a single option—you will simplify decision making for customers. (Doing so has the additional benefit of allowing you to streamline operations.) Recall that Superhuman initially offered only one price—$30 per month—targeting busy professionals who valued time saving and productivity. This clarity allowed the company to focus on delivering exceptional value to its core audience while building a strong brand.

Over time, as your market presence expands and your company attracts new sets of buyers, you can develop additional offers to address other segments. For example, during the scale-up phase of its trajectory, Superhuman added new plans—Teams and Enterprise—to capture the growing diversity of its buying base. This staged approach ensures that your startup remains focused and simple during its early days while laying the groundwork for future scalability. Starting simple isn't a limitation; it's the first step in a strategy for success.

6. Signal Your Intention

Pricing is more than just a number—it's a powerful signal of a company's brand positioning and market intentions. Startups must carefully consider how their pricing reflects their brand narrative and growth aspirations.

Apple has long leveraged the brand communicative aspect of pricing, setting premium price points for its products. This intentional strategy reinforces Apple's position as a leader in innovation and design, appealing to customers who value quality and are willing to pay for it. Conversely, Zoom adopted competitive pricing during its startup phase to capture market share rapidly. This tactic signaled the company's intention to be a mass market product, which played well with its value proposition: If everyone was going to be on Zoom, shouldn't you be on Zoom, too?

The intention behind pricing also influences customer perception. A deliberately chosen price point can evoke excitement, urgency, or exclusivity, shaping how customers view the product and its value.

7. Be Predictable

Beautifully simple pricing means pricing that is stable and predictable. Consumers demand consistent pricing because they generally operate within a set budget, and the most successful startups respect that fact. For example, when Spotify launched, it offered straightforward monthly fees—$9.99 for individual users and $15.99 for a family plan. Customers knew exactly what they would pay each month, which removed uncertainty and lowered the barrier to adoption. For consumers, who often manage multiple subscriptions, this predictability is not just a convenience but a necessity.

In the B2B space, the dynamics are different but the result is the same. Companies don't demand fixed monthly fees. However, they do require a means of forecasting their approximate spend, such as pricing calculators that allow them to estimate future costs based on usage. Another approach in B2B is the use of caps or ceilings in contracts. For example, an AI analytics provider might offer a contract based on usage but limiting monthly costs to a predefined cap. Restrictions like these give businesses confidence that costs won't spiral out of control, addressing their desire for predictability while maintaining the flexibility of a PAYG model. Moreover, these caps can be revisited and adjusted during renewals, allowing companies to scale revenue as client needs grow.

Although the paths to predictability differ, the underlying goal is the same: to foster trust and remove friction in decision making. In B2C, it's about simplicity and consistency, while in B2B, it's about providing tools and structures flexible enough to fit the needs of a dynamic business environment while still offering clarity and control. By tailoring approaches to the audience, businesses can ensure their pricing remains beautifully simple and effective.

8. Be Transparent

Few things can erode trust faster than an unexpected charge on a bill. Some customers react almost as if they were the victim of a crime. Hidden fees can damage a company's reputation. Companies with beautifully simple pricing, like Slack, go out of their way to avoid even unintentional mistakes of this nature. The company's Fair Billing Policy ensures that customers are only charged for active users, a practice that has earned widespread praise. There are no hidden costs in Slack's easy-to-understand per-user-per-month pricing. This level of openness not only builds trust but also aligns the company's interests with those of its customers.

Furthermore, transparent pricing reduces friction in the sales process. When customers understand the full cost up front, they are less likely to hesitate or ask for clarifications, resulting in faster decision making. For startups, this transparency can significantly improve conversion rates and reduce the length of the sales cycle.

9. Be Easy to Contextualize

Framing your price in terms of everyday costs or clear, intuitive returns on investment—contextualizing it, in other words—makes your fees relatable and easier for customers to justify. This technique is particularly effective for startups looking to make their offerings accessible and memorable.

Recall how Superhuman framed its pricing as a comparison between the value delivered, "four hours saved per month," and the price, "$1 per day." This evaluation resonated with its productivity-focused customer base, which often calculated that those four hours were worth hundreds of dollars. Furthermore, it allowed customers to view the price in terms of a small daily investment rather than a larger monthly expense, making it easier to rationalize.

Contextualization can also apply to the price model, meaning the way the customer will be charged. AWS presents its pay-as-you-go, usage-based pricing as, "similar to how you pay for utilities like water and electricity. You only pay for the services you consume, and once you stop using them, there are no additional costs or termination fees." This framing is a masterclass in clear and simple contextualization.

This technique can also be used to clearly communicate outcomes. For instance, a software company might frame its pricing as delivering a

Making It Easy to Buy: Beautifully Simple Pricing

"5x return on investment within the first month," helping potential buyers connect the cost to a tangible benefit. Framing pricing in terms of outcomes not only justifies the price but also reinforces the product's relevance, making it easier for customers to see the connection between what they pay and what they gain. By making the pricing relatable and results oriented, companies can significantly increase perceived value and willingness to pay.

10. Make Communicating Easy

The ultimate test of whether a pricing model is beautifully simple is how easily it can be understood, both internally and externally. If sales teams struggle to explain the pricing structure, or if customers need extensive guidance to understand how they will be charged, the model is too complex. By contrast, Netflix's early pricing is a textbook example of clear communication: "$8.99/month for unlimited streaming." This succinct and memorable messaging enabled customers to understand the offer effortlessly, leading to widespread adoption. Beautifully simple pricing should empower anyone—whether a sales representative, marketer, or satisfied customer—to explain it in just a few sentences.

Clear communication of pricing also facilitates referrals. When customers can easily explain why they're paying for a product and what they're receiving, they are more likely to recommend it to others. For startups, this organic word-of-mouth marketing can be a critical driver of growth, especially in the early stages.

In conclusion, beautifully simple pricing is more than a strategy. It's a philosophy that aligns a company's goals with its customers' needs. By prioritizing clarity, transparency, and value, startups can create pricing that not only attracts customers but also fosters loyalty and drives sustainable growth. Companies that embrace simplicity in pricing in their startup phase will remain agile, competitive, and well positioned for long-term success.

Chapter Summary: How This Strategy Avoids the Single-Engine Trap

Simplicity in pricing removes friction—not just for you, but for your customer. It helps avoid the Community Builder trap of undercharging loyal users out of fear and the Money Maker trap of overcomplicating pricing in a way that overwhelms or freezes buying decisions. When pricing is easy to understand and act on, it expands your reach (market share) while giving customers clear, confident paths to pay for value (wallet share). Profitable Growth Architects simplify with purpose—removing barriers to adoption while making it easy for customers to say "yes" to more.

CEO Questions

- Does our pricing clearly communicate value to our target audience? If customers don't immediately see the connection between price and value, they may hesitate to buy.

- Is our pricing model simple enough for anyone on the team to explain? Complexity can confuse both customers and employees, hindering adoption and sales efforts.

- Does our pricing align with our brand's market positioning? Pricing sends a strong signal about quality, exclusivity, and accessibility. Ensure it reflects your brand identity and your positioning.

- Are we flexible enough to adapt to customer growth and market changes? Rigid pricing models can limit scalability and alienate customers whose needs evolve.

- Are we monitoring pricing performance and iterating based on feedback? Continuous improvement is critical to ensure your pricing remains relevant and competitive.

Chapter 6

Mastering Value Messaging: Speak Benefits and Not Features

Let's consider a typical product launch scenario. You are confident you have built a fantastic product, and you believe strongly that you should be able to achieve an amazing product-market fit. You've developed a packaging structure and a price model that you feel good about. Your website has been updated to reflect your new offer, and if you're selling to other businesses, you have your sales team ready to go.

But fast-forward six months and the results aren't what you expected. Conversion rates are lower than anticipated. Your sales team is struggling to sell, often asking for even bigger concessions to close deals. Customers are gravitating toward competitors, and your efforts to upsell or cross-sell to existing buyers are falling flat. You're left wondering, "I built a great product—what went wrong?"

It's likely time—if not past time—to ask another crucial question: *Are you effectively communicating the value that you're providing?*

Value messaging and its communication are critical to realizing the full economic potential of your product. Without a clear articulation of your product's benefits, customers may fail to understand its worth, resulting in missed opportunities for sales, upsells, and long-term loyalty. Building a fantastic product simply isn't enough. If you aren't able to communicate the value of your product in a way that resonates with your customers, you're doomed from the start.

Simply put, **if you don't speak the value, no one will get it.**

The Say-It-to-Sell-It Axiom	If you don't speak the value, no one will get it.

Effective value messaging is the key to achieving both market share and wallet share. How do you craft a strategy that effectively communicates value during your next product launch? Let's begin by examining cases where ineffective value messaging led to notable failures and then contrast them with a success story of getting it right.

Misstep in Messaging: What We Can Learn from Quibi and the Tata Nano

In 2020, Quibi launched as a short-form streaming platform with big promises and even bigger names. Backed by nearly $2 billion in funding and led by media and tech heavyweights Jeffrey Katzenberg and Meg Whitman, Quibi aimed to revolutionize the way people consumed video content. The platform offered "quick bites" of premium content, designed to be viewed in under 10 minutes, catering to the fast-paced lives of modern consumers.

However, despite its ambitious vision, Quibi shut down just six months after its launch, becoming one of the most high-profile failures of the streaming era. Quibi's core issue wasn't its technology or content; it was its inability to communicate a clear and compelling value proposition to its target audience. The platform marketed itself as a mobile-first streaming service but failed to explain why users should choose it over competitors like YouTube, TikTok, or Netflix, all of which offered either free or more versatile content. Additionally, Quibi limited viewing to mobile devices, excluding users who wanted to watch on larger screens, which further restricted its appeal.

The messaging also didn't address a specific audience or its pain points. Unlike Netflix, which emphasizes binge-worthy content, or TikTok, which thrives on user-generated creativity, Quibi's value proposition was vague. It promoted itself as premium content for on-the-go viewing, but this messaging clashed with the reality of a global pandemic, where people were largely at home. Without a clear articulation of what made its offering unique or essential, potential subscribers couldn't see the value in paying for yet another service. Despite a star-studded lineup of original shows, Quibi struggled to capture market share and wallet share. By the time it shut down, it had burned through most of its $1.75 billion funding and failed to gain a foothold in the crowded streaming market.

Another example of poor value messaging comes from Tata Motors' ambitious launch of the Tata Nano in 2008. Marketed as the world's most affordable car, the Nano was envisioned as a transformative solution to meet the transportation needs of India's aspiring middle class. It was marketed as the "one Lakh rupees car" (approximately $1,200), emphasizing its affordability as a replacement for scooters and motorbikes. While the Nano was innovative in concept, the execution of its value messaging proved disastrous. The Nano's low price became its defining feature, but instead of being seen as a triumph of engineering and affordability, it was branded as "the world's cheapest car." This label created a perception problem, associating the car with low quality and a lack of prestige. In a market like India, where car ownership is often a status symbol, this branding alienated the very audience Tata Motors sought to attract. Compounding the issue were reports of quality problems, including several incidents of Nanos catching fire, which further damaged the car's reputation.

The result? What could have been a revolutionary product was seen as undesirable and low value, leading to lackluster sales and significant losses for Tata Motors. Tata could have reframed the Nano as "India's smartest car for city living," emphasizing its innovative design, fuel efficiency, and practicality for navigating congested urban streets. By highlighting its long-term cost savings and safety advantages over two-wheelers, Tata could have appealed to first-time car buyers upgrading from scooters, focusing on the Nano as a stepping stone toward upward mobility. A narrative centered on being a "smart choice" rather than a "cheap car" might have helped transform the Nano into a symbol of innovation and progress.

Mastering Value Messaging: Speak Benefits and Not Features

Value Messaging Done Right: Square

In stark contrast to Quibi and Nano, Square, the payment processing company, launched with a product that was equally groundbreaking in its category but succeeded by nailing its value messaging. Square introduced a small, portable card reader that plugged into smartphones, allowing small businesses to accept credit card payments on the go.

Square's leadership team understood that its target audience—the small business owner—wanted simplicity, transparency, and empowerment. Square aligned its value messaging with its customers' aspirations and pain points. Instead of focusing solely on the technology, Square emphasized the freedom and flexibility its product offered, turning a simple payment solution into a symbol of empowerment for small business owners to compete with the larger players.

The messaging emphasized Square's straightforward approach to payment processing. Unlike traditional providers, which often required complicated hardware, long-term contracts, and opaque pricing structures, Square communicated a single, clear value proposition: Plug in the Square Reader, swipe a card, and start accepting payments. Square's messaging also emphasized transparency by promising a flat, easy-to-understand pricing model: 2.75% per swipe, with no hidden fees or commitments. Last, Square's messaging reinforced the ease of adoption by highlighting that its solution was portable, affordable, and didn't require any specialized knowledge. It appealed to business owners who wanted a quick, frictionless way to start accepting card payments.

The result? Square didn't just capture market share and wallet share; it built trust and loyalty with an underserved audience.

The stories of Quibi, the Tata Nano, and Square highlight the critical importance of getting value messaging right for scaling innovation. A great product alone isn't enough to succeed; how you communicate its value can make or break your efforts to attract customers, drive engagement, and build loyalty. To learn how to master value communication in practice, read on.

The Value Blueprint: What Best-in-Class Companies Do

The three key steps that best-in-class companies take to mastering value communication and messaging are:

1. *Understand your customers.* Build a deep understanding of their needs, pain points, and what they truly value.

2. *Tailor your value messages.* Create differentiated messages that align with the unique priorities of each customer segment.

3. *Highlight competitive advantages.* Showcase how your offering stands out, emphasizing benefits in a way that resonates and compels action.

Let's look at each of these steps in detail.

Step 1: Understand Your Customers' Needs and Pain Points

There is a subtle but significant difference between your customers' needs and the pain points they experience. For instance, a busy professional may *need* a convenient and reliable way to get meals delivered to the workplace because they have limited time to cook due to their hectic schedule. The same professional's *pain points* may include long delivery times, high delivery fees, inconsistent food quality, and similar problems. When building a product and articulating its value to your customers, ask yourself: "What need is my product addressing?" and "What pain points am I reducing or eliminating?" The answers to both questions should be front and center in your value messaging.

Customer research often is needed to uncover answers to these questions. To illustrate, let's examine Figure 6.1, which exhibits the research outcomes from work we did with a large restaurant chain.

Mastering Value Messaging: Speak Benefits and Not Features

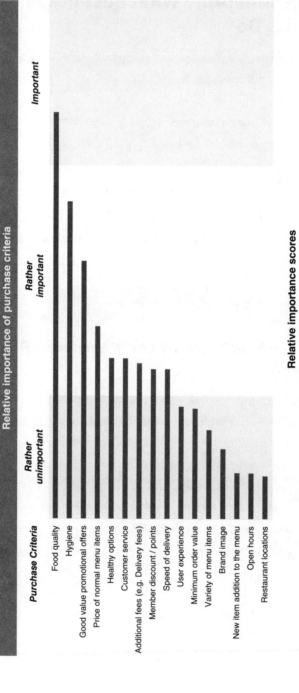

Figure 6.1 Example Relative Importance Scores

Scaling Innovation

As part of our work, we sought to understand the needs and purchase criteria that drive customers' choice of restaurants. The results were surprising. For starters, our client believed that "brand image" would be a significant purchase criterion, and it believed that its reputation and legacy in the market would hold a lot of weight. Unfortunately, this client was wrong. Brand image was a much lower purchase criterion for its customers, who indexed heavily on food quality and hygiene. Interestingly, this was a new trend; traditional purchase criteria such as menu variety had taken a backseat.

The implication of these results was simple: Our client had to *change its value messaging*. It decided to document the stringent hygiene standards that employees were subject to in company kitchens and make this completely transparent. It also made efforts to communicate about the quality of the ingredients, their freshness, and where they were sourced from.

As this example illustrates, tying your value messages to the purchase criteria that drive consumer decision making is of the utmost importance. What's more, your customers' needs probably *differ significantly* from what you might otherwise believe internally.

To conduct a similar study for your product or service, start with a list of possible needs and purchase criteria and run studies with your customers that let them rate the criteria from unimportant to very important. One way to force trade-offs is to have your customers allocate 100 points across the criteria. Remember to always leave a few "other" spaces that customers can use to name and rate their own criteria. Doing this helps to ensure you eliminate bias and uncover additional criteria that you might not have considered. You should also include questions to rate and rank pain points.

The Echo Chamber Axiom	More often than not, your customers' needs and pain points will be significantly different from what you believe them to be.

Step 2: Tailor Your Value Messages

Effective value communication begins with a robust segmentation strategy. Many companies believe they have this area covered but often rely on customer personas based solely on demographics like age, income, or location. Although useful for general insights, demographic-based personas can be misleading; customers who share similar demographics often have vastly different needs, motivations, and pain points.

True customer segments go beyond demographics and focus on specific needs that tie directly to the value your product or service delivers. By identifying these needs and linking them to the benefits you provide, you can create targeted, impactful value communication that resonates with each segment. Without such communication, your messaging risks being too generic, failing to address the real reasons customers choose your offering.

We worked with a global SaaS player specializing in customer engagement. In essence, it was in the business of helping businesses engage and retain customers across digital channels. One of our primary objectives was to build our client's value story, making sure it aligned best with different customer segments and how they derive value from their platform (which was often very different). We launched a large-scale study in which we spoke to customer teams from hundreds of our client's existing and prospective customers. Soon their segmentation became very clear: Customers derived value differently from the product based on their own business models. For example, a subscription business using our client's platform to engage with customers was looking to optimize for customer lifetime value.

By contrast, an e-commerce business working on a transaction basis was using our client's platform to nudge customers toward conversion events or to bring them back after a period of dormancy.

Based on this insight, we aligned our client's value story with the different business models it served, even though the platform remained the same across the board. We enabled our client to speak the same language of the customers it was targeting by aligning its value messaging to the KPIs customers were hoping to solve for.

In short, align your value communication to reflect what truly matters to each segment—not just who they are, but what they need and how your solution delivers that value.

The One-Size-Fits-None Axiom	Tailoring value messages to segments is not optional. If your value message doesn't match how each segment thinks, feels, and buys, it will be ignored, no matter how true it is.

Step 3: Highlight Competitive Advantages

The next step in defining an optimal value messaging and communication strategy is to identify your competitive strengths and use those strengths to define your value proposition. To do this, let's introduce Figure 6.2, which showcases what we call the "Matrix of Competitive Advantage."

The y-axis in the matrix ranks the relative importance of different purchase criteria or needs from a customer's perspective. This is a direct input from the kind of information shown in Figure 6.1. The x-axis ranks how your company performs relative to competition across each purchase criterion. Any position to the right of the center of the x-axis indicates you are overperforming; any position to the left of the center indicates you are underperforming relative to competition.

111

Strategic Competitive Advantages

5 Quality of information/analysis

4 Comprehensiveness of information/analysis

3 Availability of information/analysis based on needs

2 Ease of use/navigation of website/search

1 Authority and brand recognition

Outperform

7 Ability to obtain all this information from a single source

6 Cross-country comparability/consistency

8 Customer service/option of speaking to consultants/analysts

Consistent

9 Price perception

External view

Internal view

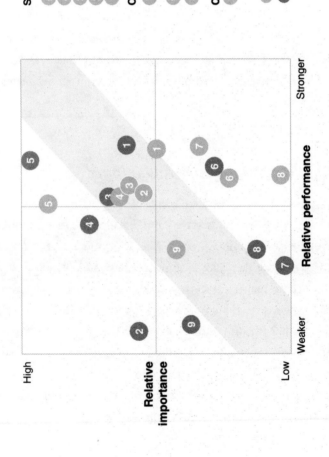

Figure 6.2 Sample Matrix of Competitive Advantage

Let's break down how the four quadrants in the matrix should be interpreted and how they can be used to define your value proposition:

- *Top-right quadrant* depicts your competitive advantages—criteria that are important to your customers on which you outperform your competitors. These advantages should anchor your value proposition and messaging.

- *Top-left quadrant* shows your competitive disadvantages—criteria that are important to your customers on which you perform worse than your competitors. For these criteria, you need to develop value defense arguments and know what to say when asked.

- *Bottom-right quadrant* depicts criteria on which you perform better than your competitors, although these criteria are relatively unimportant to your customers. There are two ways to use these in your value messaging: You can either choose to reduce your focus on them, since they're unimportant, or you can try to elevate their importance for your customers through messaging. For example, a company that took a largely overlooked purchase criterion and managed to thrust it onto the main stage was Apple with the iPhone's touchscreen. In Steve Jobs's iconic 2007 presentation, he showcased the iPhone's intuitive touchscreen, followed by the "Touching is believing" ad campaign. At the time, touchscreens weren't a top purchase criterion for most customers, but Apple's compelling value message and demonstrations transformed perceptions.

- *Bottom-left quadrant* shows criteria that aren't important to your customers on which you underperform relative to the competition. Your customers won't be anchoring their purchase decisions to these criteria; hence you can avoid them in your value communication.

Following these three key steps that best-in-class companies take will ensure you are well on the way to creating compelling value communication and messages that resonate with your target audience(s), drive initial sales, and foster long-term loyalty.

Four Fatal Flaws: Avoiding Common Missteps in Value Messaging

When you are determining your value messaging, you should avoid the next four critical flaws.

Flaw #1: Talking Features and Not Benefits

Your customers aren't buying features; they're buying the benefits those features deliver. While it's natural for product teams to talk about features, as that's what they've built, what truly matters to customers is the value they gain. Instead of using technical jargon that is feature centered, make sure that your marketing and sales team use language that resonates intuitively with how your customers perceive the benefits.

Flaw #2: Overlooking the Emotional Drivers of Buying Decisions

Logical, fact-based arguments that spell out consumer benefits are important elements of the value conversation, but neglecting the emotional aspects of value can be a fatal error. Consumers often make decisions based on how a product makes them feel or the aspirational identity it offers. And the same considerations apply in B2B settings as well—after all, business decision makers are human beings, too. Make sure you integrate emotional appeals and tap into the psychological factors that drive decision making when building your value messaging strategy.

Flaw #3: Overcomplicating Your Value Messages

Overcomplication is one of the most treacherous pitfalls when it comes to value communication. It can come in several forms: the use of jargon; being overly technical, especially when trying to speak to nontechnical audiences; trying to focus on too many kinds of benefits; or simply making ambiguous statements that don't clearly communicate the value you offer. The results can include confusion among customers, a severely diluted brand message, and ultimately commercial failure.

Flaw #4: Ignoring the Importance of Competitive Differentiation

Whether you like it or not, customers make comparisons among products and services. They compare prices, features, benefits, promotions, and a whole lot more. All you can do is create the most compelling reason possible for them to choose your product while creating a strong and memorable brand identity. This type of competitive differentiation is based on communicating the benefits that your product brings to customers and how those benefits outshine those offered by competitors.

Beyond the Basics: Insights, Tips, and Tricks to Optimize Your Value Messaging Strategy

Let's conclude with some additional suggestions you may be able to use to make your value messaging strategy even more powerful.

- *Have your customers describe your product to you.* Some companies find it hard to fully grasp the customer perspective on their brands and their products. A helpful exercise we recommend is to ask customers to describe your product and its benefits, without any help from you. For example, you can put customers in a scenario where they're actually pitching your product on your behalf. The benefits they emphasize may surprise you—and they can help you improve your value communication strategy.

- *Make sure you refresh your understanding of customer needs periodically.* Refresh your understanding of customer needs either every 18 months or whenever there is a significant shift in market trends. For instance, we spoke earlier about the project we conducted with the large restaurant chain. The pandemic had changed customers' purchase criteria significantly, leading them to focus more on ingredient quality and hygiene than ever before. If the restaurant chain had not refreshed its understanding of customer needs, it would have failed to update its value messaging strategy accordingly.

- *Value messaging doesn't stop at the sale; it's a continuous process that builds long-lasting customer relationships.* From effective onboarding to sustained education, regular value reinforcement, and incorporating customer feedback, every stage of the after-sales journey is an opportunity to communicate and amplify the benefits your product delivers. Businesses that prioritize ongoing value communication not only enhance customer satisfaction but also drive upselling, loyalty, and advocacy.

- *When addressing competition, stick to facts, not rumors.* We once advised a global SaaS platform whose competitor had resorted to using social media to spread false rumors about our client's platform. Our client was understandably concerned about the negative impact this might have on sales. But when we talked to customers and prospects, we realized that the company's fears were groundless. In fact, some customers explicitly stated that they did not want to do business with a company that badmouthed its competition in public. When building your own competitive messaging strategy, stick to facts and let your product speak for itself. And if customers bring up a competing product on their own, don't shy away from setting the story straight with facts, not rumors.

Chapter Summary: How This Strategy Avoids the Single-Engine Trap

Value messaging is the connective tissue between your product and your price. When done poorly, it fuels the Disruptor trap of overpromising during acquisition and the Community Builder trap of being too modest to charge appropriately. The strategies described in this chapter help your prospects see why your product is worth paying for, which makes it easier to attract new customers (market share) and justify meaningful spend (wallet share). Profitable Growth Architects don't just build value; they communicate it proudly with precision.

CEO Questions

- Before developing your value communication strategy, do you have a strong sense for the needs, purchase criteria, and pain points of your customers? Have you validated your beliefs through objective external research with customers and prospects?

- Is your segmentation strategy based on demonstrable customer needs or on pure demographics? Has your company developed a targeted value messaging strategy to address differences in customer segments?

- Do you have a clear definition of your value proposition and how it stands out compared to the competition's? Have you validated your competitive differentiation with your customers and prospects?

- Do you continue to emphasize your value messages in all the after-sales stages of the customer journey?

Mastering Value Messaging: Speak Benefits and Not Features

Scale-up Strategies

Chapter 7

When You Give, Get Something Back: Discounting and Promotions

When it comes to attracting customers during the scale-up phase of your business, promotions and discounting are frequently used strategies. They are widely recognized for their potential to drive sales, convert new customers, and clear out inventory. The underlying logic in both these concepts is similar and straightforward: Offer customers a lot of value at a reduced price to incentivize purchases.

However, despite the apparent simplicity of this underlying concept, most companies falter in executing these strategies effectively. The missteps routinely stem from a failure to grasp the essential principle of smart promoting or discounting: *You always need to get something back in return for what you give.*

Those who fail to follow this essential principle often fall into the trap of using promotions and discounts excessively. Although promotions and discounts can generate short-term sales spikes, they can also erode profit margins and diminish the perceived value of a product. Customers may come to expect promotions as the norm, waiting for sales before making purchases, which can disrupt cash flow and create inconsistent sales patterns. Frequent discounting can harm brand equity and potentially alienate customers who purchased at full price. Moreover, customers who were acquired through deep promotions or discounts are frequently the most likely to churn.

The Give-and-Get Axiom	Arbitrary or excessive discounts train customers to expect more for less; always give with intention—and get something in return.

To avoid this pitfall, whenever you give something to customers in the form of a discount or promotion, always think about what to get back. For example, if you are in a B2B negotiation, you could provide a discount in exchange for a longer-term contract (the "get"). In B2C, this approach could take the form of earning a promotion through actions your customers are willing to take. When customers need to invest effort to earn a promotional reward, they value it even more. For example, *tiered promotions*, like a coffee shop offering a free drink after a fixed number of regular purchases, encourage repeat business and a sense of achievement or completing a challenge. *Educational promotions*, such as software discounts as a reward for completing tutorials, not only add value but also increase user engagement.

Leveraging a give-and-get mechanism not only sets you up for longer-term success but creates a sense of balance and reciprocity. It makes such conversations feel like fair exchanges rather than one-sided concessions. Without this balance, customers may question the value of the offer, often thinking they could have received even more, which can undermine the perceived authenticity and fairness of the deal.

The Earned Reward Axiom	If customers invest effort to earn a promotion or discount, they value it even more.

Now let's look at some examples of companies that have demonstrated how to give smartly and get something back—the key to attaining market share and wallet share.

Good Rates for Good Driving: How Progressive Transformed the Insurance Industry

In the crowded field of insurance companies, standing out requires more than just catchy commercials or clever slogans. It demands innovative thinking that addresses the needs and concerns of customers.

Progressive Insurance, founded in 1937, has consistently demonstrated such ingenuity. The company has a history of being at the forefront of insurance innovation, whether through offering the first drive-in claims service or providing comparative insurance rate information online. One of its most notable contributions to the industry is the introduction of safe-driving discounts, rewarding policyholders who exhibit responsible driving habits. This concept not only transformed the way car insurance premiums are calculated but also helped cultivate safer driving behaviors across the country.

Progressive's journey toward pioneering safe-driving discounts is rooted in its commitment to leveraging technology for better service—specifically the development of usage-based insurance (UBI) models. These models assess premiums based on individual driving behaviors rather than simply on traditional factors like age, gender, or location. Progressive's version of UBI, branded as Snapshot, was among the first of its kind when it launched in 2008.

The Snapshot program revolutionized the car insurance landscape. It used telematics technology—a combination of telecommunications and informatics—to monitor and record driving patterns. Snapshot tracks metrics such as mileage (how far the driver travels), braking (the frequency and intensity of hard braking events), and time of day (since nighttime driving is typically riskier). By analyzing these data, Progressive could offer discounts to drivers who demonstrated safe behaviors, such as avoiding late-night driving or refraining from sudden stops.

This approach offered two key advantages:

1. *Fair and meaningful incentives.* In give-and-get terms, to get the discount, drivers needed to give back safe driving. Putting in the effort made the discounts more meaningful.

2. *Data-driven insights.* Progressive gained a wealth of data, helping refine its risk assessment models and improve customer offerings.

Customers quickly embraced Snapshot, appreciating the opportunity to lower their premiums by proving their safe driving. Progressive's leadership in safe-driving discounts not only set a new industry standard but also serves as a masterclass in giving smartly and getting something back.[1]

The same basic give-and-get principle can be applied to promotions and discounting in many industries beyond insurance.

A classic example of a promotion that made the customer earn the reward is a 1960s case study from Renault. Back then, Renault was struggling to clear out an inventory of old Dauphine models to make space for newer vehicles. Even offering hefty discounts on the cars didn't move them off the lots. George Lois, a New York ad man, intervened with a clever twist. He created small, hidden nicks in the cars' paint and covered them with Band-Aids. A newspaper ad then promised $500 off to anyone who could spot the flaw. The result? The cars sold out by lunchtime on the day the ad appeared. Turning the discount price into a challenging activity that customers could "win" through their own efforts created engagement and created a new cohort of Renault drivers.

A more complex story unfolded at a well-known B2B Silicon Valley unicorn that was suffering from a poor bottom line. The sales team had adopted a Wild West approach to discounting, offering hefty price cuts left and right to close deals. Although this approach kept sales high, profits were dwindling. The random discounts were also eroding the company's value and confusing customers about the real worth of its products.

A newly appointed VP of Sales recognized that the chaos in the discounting strategy was her first major challenge. She decided to implement a structured discounting program to address the issue and started by analyzing past sales data to identify patterns in discounting practices. She then realized that while some deals required discounts to close, many customers were getting price cuts unnecessarily; targeted and segmented discounting could preserve profit margins without losing sales.

Next she divided the customers into segments based on factors like deal size, industry, and purchasing history and established guidelines to ensure that discounts were offered only when essential to close a deal. More important, discounts now were granted based on a give-and-get principle. To ensure adherence to the new strategy, sales reps were required to submit discount requests describing what they would get back in exchange for the discount—longer-term renewals, better payment terms, a multiple-department sell, or a valuable testimonial. Each request was reviewed based on its strategic fit within the segmented discounting plan.

Initial resistance from the sales teams quickly gave way to acceptance as they saw the results. The structured discounting program not only maintained deal flow but enhanced the company's image by emphasizing the true value of its products. Within a quarter, the company's profit margins improved significantly, and the sales team found that customers respected the consistency and rationale behind the new pricing structure. Structured discounting turned the company's financial health around.

As these examples show, well-designed promotions and discounts have two things in common: They are thoughtfully targeted, and they employ the give-and-get principle.

In the pages that follow, we look first at how to design compelling promotions and then at how to design an effective B2B discounting strategy.

How to Design Compelling Promotions

A significant challenge for many businesses today is overcoming a reliance on constant promotions. When customers come to expect discounts every time they shop, it diminishes the perceived value of the product and creates a dependency on deals to drive sales.

To ensure promotions benefit you and your customers, you should adopt what we call the "SPAM framework": *Strategize, Plan, Apply, Monitor.* Here's how it works.

Step 1: Strategize

This step involves doing three things: (a) defining the goal of the promotions, (b) selecting promotions that align with your brand personality, and then (c) tailoring promotions by customer segments to unlock the give and get.

Defining the Goal

Start by asking a few critical questions: Why do you want to run the promotions? What are the goals? How does the goal change by segment?

To make it easier for you to get started, we've outlined some of the most common goals companies pursue through promotions:

- Attracting new customers
- Driving incremental purchases from existing customers
- Clearing inventory
- Driving cross-sell/upsell
- Increasing engagement
- Increasing enrollment in membership programs

Decide which of these goals you want to pursue for each customer segment. Once that's clear, you'll know exactly what you want to get out of the promotion.

Selecting the Type of Promotion Based on Brand Personality

Of course, the promotions you choose need to reinforce the goal you picked in the previous section. Less obviously, the promotions you pick also need to be aligned with your brand's personality. Take the case of one well-established retailer. In an effort to appeal to price-conscious customers, it started running constant promotions for all—with devastating effects. Establishing everyday value became very hard because the company trained customers to purchase only on promotion. This approach led to long-term dilution of its margins while leaving money on the table for brand loyalists. Worst of all, it destroyed the company's brand identity.

Once you map your brand to a personality (e.g., using the framework provided in Jennifer Aaker's groundbreaking paper),[2] you can pick promotions that reinforce your positioning.

Figure 7.1 shows the four most common brand personalities along with promotional strategies that can serve to reinforce each one.

- *Sincerity*. If your brand is based mainly on sincerity, your promotions should be simple, straightforward, and transparent. Consistent with Warby Parker's sincerity, the company offers straightforward promotions like "Add a pair and save 15%" and even message "No promo code required"!

- *Excitement*. If your brand personality is centered on a constant buzz of news and emotion that helps you to acquire or retain customers, you have to come up with new and different ways to use promotions to engage your base. To get customers through its doors, Starbucks uses myriad themed promotions, perks, and offers like the Happy Hour offer to generate curiosity and attention.

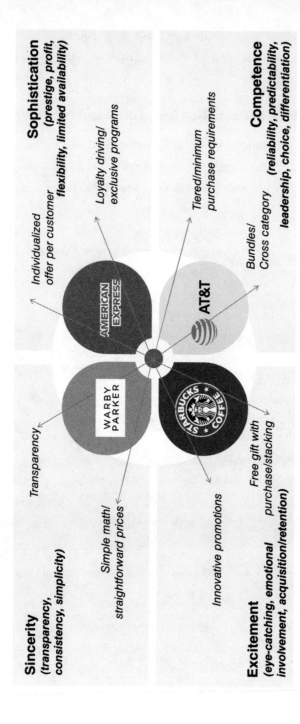

Figure 7.1 Four Common Brand Personalities and Appropriate Promotional Types for Each

- *Sophistication.* If you have a brand that exudes sophistication, your promotions have to mirror that image. That's why you see American Express offering exclusive promotions that no other credit card has. Amex cardholders receive offers based on their shopping habits and other criteria such as location. Big meat eaters might find they are mostly targeted with special offers at steakhouses, while fashionistas receive discounts on apparel shopping for their favorite brands.

- *Competence.* If your brand personality is built on values like choice and differentiation, your goal is to use promotions to increase customer spend through buying bundles and similar offers. Think of AT&T's family plan or promotional add-ons.

Tailoring Promotions by Customer Segment to Unlock Give and Get

Without a clear tie back to customer segments, promotions and discounts can become spray-and-pray exercises that fail to deliver meaningful results. Think of it this way: Not everyone might need a promotion to entice them into using a ride-hailing company. If a ride-hailing company gives everyone the same deep discount or promotional offer for booking a ride, it simply is giving money away for no good reason. A smarter approach would be to tailor promotions to key segments and unlock specific gets. For example, the company could offer a promotion on basic rides to attract the price-sensitive segment and get incremental transactions while providing a promotion on high-end black-car service to target quality-focused customers and get a minimum spend.

In other words, for each customer segment, you need to employ promotions that are aligned with the segment needs, values, and willingness to pay so that you can drive specific and targeted behavior and get something meaningful back. The list of most common gets is detailed in the "Beyond the Basics: Insights, Tips, and Tricks on Giving Smartly and Getting Back" section later in the chapter.

The Purpose-Driven Promo Axiom	Effective promotions have a clear goal, align with your brand identity, and are tailored by customer segments to unlock both the give and the get.

Step 2: Plan

Even well-run companies can flop if they fail to plan their promotions properly. In 2018, the popular toy chain Build-A-Bear announced a one-day "Pay Your Age" event that would allow a child to take home a stuffed animal—normally priced anywhere from $14 to $60 or more—for the price of their age. The plan generated enormous excitement—so much so that on July 12, 2018, lines of hundreds of families appeared at Build-A-Bear locations around the United States and abroad. The numbers were so large that many stores had to close the lines by 10 am, leaving huge numbers of kids disappointed and their parents angry. Making matters worse, the families who were turned away were handed vouchers for use at a later time with a value far short of the special discount they'd been promised by the company. It was an interesting idea, but the execution was a disaster, causing enormous damage to the company's reputation and its connection with customers.[3]

To ensure your promotions go off without a hitch, meticulous planning of each element is crucial. Figure 7.2 shows six essential questions you should answer to help you plan a solid campaign.

- Why *are you running a promotion?* Promotion incentives should align with your goals and brand identity. Are you aiming to attract new customers or reengage those you haven't heard from in a while? Big gestures like creative promotions or heavy discounts can draw people in while personalized promotions can recapture the attention of existing customers. Price discounts drive traffic while value-added promotions increase basket size.

Scaling Innovation

Anatomy of a Promotion

Why Promotion objectives	**How much** Depth
Who Target segments	**When** Frequency/Calendar
Which Product role	**Where** Channel

Figure 7.2   Elements of a Promotional Campaign

- Who *are you targeting with your promotion?* Ensure your promotion appeals to the right audience. Different messages and deals resonate with different segments. Successful promotions tailor offers to a segment's preferences, budget, shopping habits, price sensitivity, and purchase history. Poorly targeted promotions can alienate your target customers and waste your budget. Do you know which segments you want to acquire and where you want to increase your share of wallet?

- Which *products are you promoting?* A common mistake is focusing on signature products only. Instead, choose products for promotion based on their role in your portfolio, aligning with your objectives and target segments. Explore cross-selling and bundling opportunities, like pairing everyday items with specialty items or traffic drivers with basket fillers.

- How much *will you give away?* When offering percentage discounts, consider the depth needed to trigger a purchase without cutting too deeply into your margins.

- When *will you run your promotion?* Tie promotions to dates and milestones relevant to your target segment or create urgency with short deadlines.

When You Give, Get Something Back: Discounting and Promotions

- Where *will you run your promotion?* Choosing the right promotional channel depends on the type of promotion and your target audience. In-store displays might increase basket size with a mix of items while social media channels are ideal for reaching your existing customer base.

Step 3: Apply

After the strategy and plan phases, it is time to apply your insights and ideas to the successful launch of your promotion. Here are few best practices to ensure that everyone sees the benefits offered by your promotion:

- *Highlight your deal prominently.* Ensure your promotion grabs attention. Avoid hiding key details in fine print; use large, clear fonts and contrasting colors. If a significant discount is your main draw, make it the focal point. Use icons like "Top Seller" or "Selling Out" to guide customers. Always emphasize the key benefits and what customers stand to gain.

- *Leverage psychological tactics.* Use behavioral psychology to enhance your promotions. Highlight the affordability of your products with phrases like "As low as" or "Up to X% off." Tiered promotions, such as saving 10% on $100+, 20% on $200+, and 30% on $300+, encourage customers to spend more to save more. These strategies can improve value perception and motivate higher spending.

- *Craft a clear call to action.* Create a call to action (CTA) that emphasizes urgency, scarcity, and exclusivity with messages like "Limited quantities available," "While supplies last," "Hurry, offer ends soon," or "For you." A study in three Sioux City supermarkets tested the impact of a clear CTA and scarcity effect on Campbell's Soup sales. Signs alternated between "Offer limited to 12 cans per person" and "No limit per person." The 12-can limit CTA increased average sales per buyer from 3.3 to 7.0 cans.[4]

- *Time and place your promotions wisely.* To maintain their effectiveness and perceived value, avoid overusing promotions. Running promotions too frequently or on the same items can teach customers to wait for discounts. Instead, vary the type of promotion and the products featured.

Table 7.1 summarizes some very specific dos and don'ts that can help you apply your promotional campaigns effectively.

Table 7.1   Top 5 Dos and Don'ts for Running Effective Promotions

Do	Don't
Generate interest by emphasizing key benefits.	Overuse promotions to the point that customers rely on them and will buy only when there are promotions.
Design marketing materials using large text in clear fonts and colors; include visuals and icons.	Bury key details in fine print and annoying pop-up windows.
Increase perceived affordability to encourage customers to spend more.	Mislead customers with vague or unfulfilled promises.
Use customers' fear of missing out by applying time pressure.	Continuously run predictable promotions for the same items.
Train your ecosystem partners (such as retailers) to run promotions aligned with your brand strategy.	Allow for confusing inconsistencies between retailers and channels.

When You Give, Get Something Back: Discounting and Promotions

Step 4: Monitor

When we ask companies about the effectiveness of their promotions, we repeatedly find that most cannot explain with confidence whether their promotions have worked or not. The key to being able to monitor effectiveness of promotions is to correctly define the list of KPIs that will enable you to measure progress toward the goals you selected for the promotion. Your full list of KPIs should answer such questions as: How many additional customers did the promotion attract? How does this impact vary by segment? Did existing customers increase frequency of purchase? How much did we increase cross-sell/upsell? What was the total revenue impact? How has the basket size changed after promotions? Did we increase membership sign-ups? Did we increase product usage and engagement, and if so, by how much?

Depending on the design of your promotions, multiple KPIs may be needed to ensure promotion success. An approach for measuring effectiveness in such cases assigns different weights to different KPIs. The results are combined into composite scores that can be used to interpret the overall result.

Now that we have looked at how to design the best promotions using the SPAM approach, let's switch gears to discounting.

How to Design an Effective B2B Discounting Strategy

Promotions can apply to both B2B and B2C, but discounting is more prevalent in the B2B sales context. Accordingly, let's look at how to develop an effective discounting strategy for B2B negotiations.

In the typical B2B situation, you can set pricing guidelines for your product or service, but the actual pricing generally comes down to sales teams having a conversation and arriving at a price for a deal. Hence it becomes critical that your sales teams are trained well on when to offer discounts, how to offer them, and what to get back in exchange. If your sales team is unprepared in the moment, the most natural thing is for them to provide a deep price discount just to close the deal. In the process, however, they may have left a lot of value on the table and trained customers to expect even lower prices in the future. Chapter 10 in this book is devoted to acing negotiations. Here we limit the discussion to the gives and gets as they pertain to discounts.

Effective discounting begins with recognizing that price reductions are just one form of concession; anything you're willing to give in a negotiation can be considered a discount. Start by creating a comprehensive list of potential concessions your team can offer. Ideally these concessions will be valuable to customers but don't cost you much. Table 7.2 lists common "gives" to jump-start that creation process.

Next, develop a clear plan for how and when to offer these concessions during negotiations. A powerful tool for this purpose is what we call a "concession matrix," which provides a structured approach to guide your sales team in offering concessions strategically while preserving the overall value of the deal.

The Price-Last Axiom	Think of three non-pricing concessions that you can offer before using a pricing concession.

The concession matrix itself has two axes, one reflecting what the discounts cost to the seller (your company) and the other reflecting how valuable or important the discounts are to the buyer (your customer). (See Figure 7.3.) The result is four quadrants, known as the opening quadrant, the defense quadrant, the battleground quadrant, and the closing quadrant. Place each of the discount levers you came up with in one of the four quadrants, based on how costly it is to provide and the value you believe it delivers to your clients. Finally, plan a list of gets, or counterconcessions, that you can ask for in exchange. See the list of the most common gets in the "Beyond the Basics" section later in the chapter.

When You Give, Get Something Back: Discounting and Promotions

Table 7.2 Top 10 Gives

The Give	Description of the Give
Invitation	Free pass or invitation to the next user conference or company event
Early access	Early access to product roadmap
Training sessions	Provide free training sessions for onboarding users
Payment terms	Provide extended payment terms (e.g., offer 30 days instead of typical 15)
Event sponsorship or cobranding opportunities	Waive sponsorship fee for next company user event
Dedicated account manager or priority support	Provide direct access to a named person to provide the first line of response to manage all inbound requests
Discount on future purchases	Discount provided as credit for future purchases
Additional products or licenses or usage allowances	Provide additional products (e.g., add-ons) or licenses or usage allowances for free (instead of price discounting)
One-time fee	Waive setup or integration fees (rather than discounting price on primary product)
% discount	Price discount that you are willing to concede

Once you have mapped out all the concessions in the matrix, you need to pick a few for use in specific negotiations. Prepare what to concede when, what value arguments to use, and which "gives" to pair with which "gets." Not all concessions need to be used for every negotiation, and certain

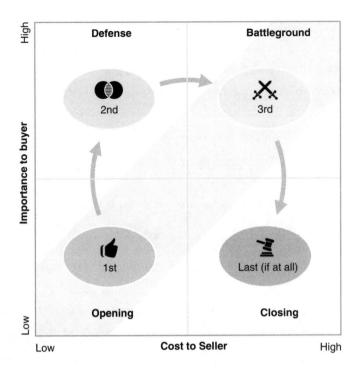

Figure 7.3 Concession Matrix

concessions may make more sense with certain customer segments; this is why advance preparation before the negotiations is key. We talk further about this topic in Chapter 10.

The typical discounting process will proceed in this way:

- *Start from the opening quadrant.* If needed, concede discounts in this quadrant first. Begin with aspects that are insignificant to both you and the customer. Emphasize their importance, telling buyers "This is a tremendous concession!" to start the negotiation on a positive note and build goodwill. For example, offer passes to your next user event, which normally cost money.

When You Give, Get Something Back: Discounting and Promotions

- *Move to the defense quadrant.* Next, focus on aspects that are important to customers but less crucial for you. Examples of typical concessions in this quadrant include training sessions, a dedicated account manager, and the like. Avoid giving these away for free; instead, ask for a counterconcession before tackling the more challenging issues that you will face in the next quadrant. The counterconcessions are the "gets" for the "gives" that you plan through your concession.

- *Move to the battleground quadrant.* Prepare value arguments for any concessions you plan to make. Don't concede anything in this quadrant for free; always *demand* something in return. Fight hard for a fair exchange and educate customers that the concessions cost you. The classic example for a concession in this quadrant is the price discount.

- *Finally, move to the closing quadrant.* Ideally the negotiation is already over by now. If necessary, use the concessions in this quadrant last. Concede only if you really are forced to do so. There is no reason to concede here, as these concessions are not as much value for the client but do cost you to provide. Be prepared to say "no." Examples of concessions for this quadrant include waiving event sponsorship fees or waiving one-time setup fees.

Beyond the Basics: Insights, Tips, and Tricks on Giving Smartly and Getting Back

Having covered the basics to promote and discount smartly, let's now consider some advanced insights, tips, and tricks you may find useful when crafting and implementing promotions and discounts.

- *Add more value before promoting or discounting.* It is common for the sales team to get into a discount mode or for the marketing team to get into a promotion mode to drive acquisition. However, before jumping into discounts or promotions, focus on enhancing the value of your product or service, and try to give value before you try to discount or promote. This approach is more effective in the long run, as it emphasizes quality and customer satisfaction rather than just lowering prices. Here are some tried-and-tested strategies to add value before promoting:

  o *Services.* Provide services that are of value to customers for "free" rather than discounting the primary product; in other words, preserve the price by adding value. Example of services could be training services, customer support services, and so on.

  o *Product.* Rather than discounting, give customers an add-on or upgrade them to a better tier (give them the "better" package instead of the "good" package) to preserve the price.

  o *Alternative currency.* Rather than promote, provide value in an alternative currency, such as loyalty points or credits that customers can redeem for valuable benefits.

- *Learn the full roster of possible gets.* As we've emphasized throughout this chapter, promotions and discounts are worthwhile only if you gain something in return. But what exactly should you aim to get back? Identifying all the potential gets to ask for requires creativity and experience. Don't worry; we've done the heavy lifting for you. Drawing from our extensive review of thousands of companies, we present Table 7.3: Top 10 Gets in B2B and Table 7.4: Top 10 Gets in B2C.

Table 7.3 Top 10 Gets in B2B

The Get for the Concession	Description of the Get
Logo	Use of client logo in your marketing and sales material. If not logo, at least try for permission to use client name.
Case study	Ask client to present case study at user conference or as a whitepaper.
Reference	Ask for taking up to five reference calls. Key is to use a specific number to prove that the ask is concrete and genuine.
Payment terms	Ask for favorable payment terms—net 14 days, annual payment instead of monthly, etc.
First look or exclusivity	Start by asking for exclusivity—e.g., you will provide discount if client will give you 100% of the contract (and stop multisourcing) and keep you as exclusive; or you retain the exclusive rights to serve any future needs (and competition is called only if you cannot deliver). Worst case: Concede for a first look (the right to bid on any work before it can be made into a request for proposal) if client is hesitant for exclusivity for future contracts.
Broader adoption	Provide concession if product is adopted more widely (e.g., if used across at least three company departments). This is a very powerful get for companies trying to achieve a wall-to-wall adoption.

(continued)

Table 7.3 *(continued)*

The Get for the Concession	Description of the Get
Minimum commit	Discount provided only if minimum purchase is met (e.g., software purchased at least for minimum of "x" usage).
End user access	Provide access to product end users (i.e., getting to know end users likely will come handy in renewals and upsells as they can vouch for the value). You can also go beyond access and ask that up to five end users will beta test any new innovations.
Value audits	Provide concession if client agrees to do periodic value audits. Such audits can cut both ways and are useful only if you truly bring a lot of value to the table and are confident to measure it and use it in renewals and upsells to command a better price.
Bundled product discount	Provide discount only if multiple products are purchased.

Table 7.4 Top 10 Gets in B2C

The Get for the Concession	Description of the Get
Membership	Users must join a club membership to unlock promotions. This method enables you to collect data and provide better customer service and create a switching cost to lock in the customer (e.g., the grocery chain Safeway offers promotions only to Safeway members).

(continued)

When You Give, Get Something Back: Discounting and Promotions

Table 7.4 *(continued)*

The Get for the Concession	Description of the Get
Subscribe	Provide promotions or special deals only to subscribers (e.g., delivery fees are waived only if you are a subscriber).
Referral	Provide referral bonus when people bring people. Uber used this strategy in the early days to build a lot of users quickly.
Payment terms	Ask for favorable payment terms (e.g., annual payment instead of monthly unlocks a discount).
Future credit	Provide promotions that can be redeemed in the next purchase. This method brings users back for more (e.g., offering a promotion for the next food delivery purchase that is unlocked right after users order food now).
Outcome	Provide promotions that are unlocked on demonstrating good outcome (finishing course, safe driving, achieving weight loss goal, etc.). Remember, if people have to earn the promotion, they value it more.
Minimum spend	Provide promotion only if minimum spend is met.
Social media	Offer discounts if users engage with social media to help promote the brand or to provide reviews.
Alternative currency	Provide loyalty points or credits that can be redeemed.
Bundled product promotion	Provide discount only if multiple products are purchased.

Chapter Summary: How This Strategy Avoids the Single-Engine Trap

Unstructured discounts and promotions often fall into the Disruptor trap—giving away too much in pursuit of acquisition without asking for anything in return. The strategies described in this chapter reframe promotions and discounts as strategic tools where every give has a corresponding get. Done right, promotions can expand reach without eroding value. They unlock growth by driving trials and urgency (market share) while setting the stage for meaningful monetization and future expansion (wallet share). Profitable Growth Architects use discounts not as bribes but as levers.

CEO Questions

- Do you have a clear strategy for giving promotions and discounts smartly? Do you practice the rule of give and get when planning promotions and discounts?

- Have you thought about adding value before you consider promotions or discounts?

- What are your goals from promotions, and how do they vary by segment? Is your promotion aligned with the brand identity you are trying to build?

- Have you developed a concession matrix for use by your sales team?

Chapter 8

Blow Up Your Packaging: Time to Redefine Your Offer Structure

When your business enters the scale-up phase, it's critical to revisit your product packaging and bundling. By now, your customer base, market, and offerings likely have evolved, making it essential to create a structure that reflects this new reality. Without adapting, you risk losing potential buyers and alienating existing customers who may feel they've outgrown you. Packaging designed for your early buyers must now be reimagined to appeal to the segments you can reach today.

Many companies overlook this step because their original packaging worked well enough to get them from startup to scale-up. But with growth comes new challenges. Early on, you likely identified customer segments based on needs, perceived value, and willingness to pay, but resource constraints meant focusing on just a few. Now, with greater resources and a broader product lineup, you can expand your reach and addressable market. This is the moment to inspect and refine—or completely redesign—your packaging strategy.

The key is to structure your products in ways that cater to multiple segments simultaneously. A one-size-fits-all approach won't work. Nor will trying to position the same product for different segments. Instead, you need to productize your offerings to fit the needs, perceived value, and willingness to pay of the segments you're now targeting.

If you didn't conduct a proper segmentation exercise during the startup phase, now is the time. The methods we outlined in our book *Monetizing Innovation* for segmenting customers remain just as relevant during scale-up.

The Build, Don't Spin Axiom	You need to productize your offerings to the various segments you serve rather than positioning the same product to various segments.

Let's look at some examples of companies that went through the journey of blowing up their packaging—then redefining it—when they hit the scale-up phase.

Scaling at Asana: How Strategic Packaging Unlocked Growth

Asana was founded in 2008 by Dustin Moskovitz, a cofounder of Facebook, and Justin Rosenstein, a former Facebook engineer. While at Facebook, they developed an internal tool called "Tasks" to address inefficiencies in team collaboration and task management. The tool significantly improved operational efficiency at Facebook, inspiring Moskovitz and Rosenstein to realize its broader potential. Believing they could help organizations worldwide streamline workflows, they left Facebook in 2008 to build Asana as a stand-alone product. Launched commercially in 2012, Asana grew over the next decade, serving millions of users worldwide and becoming a leading tool for productivity and collaboration.

In its early startup days, Asana focused on small teams, offering a Free plan that supported up to 15 team members. Asana also offered a Premium plan, allowing unlimited members and providing additional features, such as the ability to collaborate on private projects and receive priority support. The Premium plan was designed to cater to more substantial and demanding teams. (See Figure 8.1.)

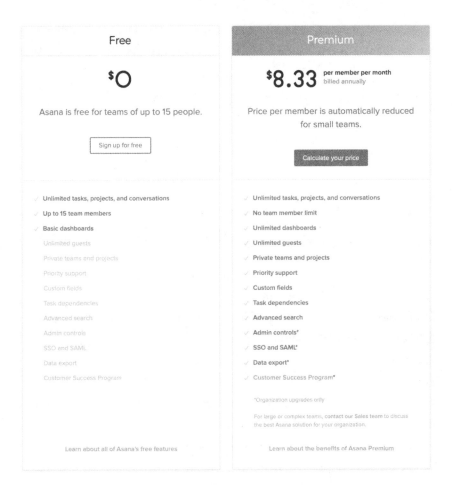

Figure 8.1 Asana Packaging During the Startup Phase

As Asana's features grew more sophisticated, it became evident that potential enhancements would continue to emerge for years to come. The challenge, however, lay in organizing this expanding functionality into a clear and intuitive set of offerings that could appeal to a diverse user base. By 2015, the company faced a pivotal moment in its evolution, and with the arrival of Chris Farinacci as chief operating officer, a new chapter began.

A seasoned executive with deep expertise in business strategy, Farinacci quickly recognized that the existing approach of continuously adding features to both the free and premium plans was unsustainable in

Blow Up Your Packaging: Time to Redefine Your Offer Structure

the scale-up phase. This approach risked overwhelming users and hindered the company's ability to fully monetize its advanced capabilities. Additionally, the free product had essentially become the primary competitor to the paid offering.

The critical questions to address were:

- What is the optimal boundary between free and paid offerings?
- How many packaging tiers should we offer?
- What pricing metrics and price points are appropriate for these packages?

To tackle these challenges, Farinacci assembled and led a comprehensive cross-functional team comprising a monetization lead and the heads of Customer Operations, Sales, Data Science, Product, and Marketing. Their first step was commissioning a customer study to gain deeper insights into the diverse needs and value perceptions across Asana's customers and prospects.

The findings were transformative. For instance, the study revealed four distinct customer segments, each with unique requirements and willingness to pay. Armed with these insights, Farinacci and the team implemented a strategic pivot to the packaging and pricing that fundamentally reshaped Asana's business. The key outcomes are listed next.

- In 2016, Asana introduced the Enterprise plan, designed to cater to large organizations. This allowed Asana to attract new buyer segments and expand the packaging portfolio. Soon after, the company launched the Business plan, which bridged the gap between Premium and Enterprise. This new tier targeted midsize teams seeking advanced features beyond task management but without the full range of capabilities required by enterprise-level customers. (See Figure 8.2.)

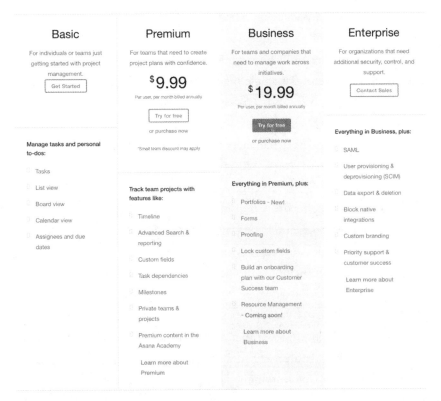

Figure 8.2 Packaging at the Scale-up Phase

- Asana enhanced its Premium package by introducing power features along with a corresponding price adjustment. This upgrade significantly increased conversions from the free tier, as customers clearly recognized the added value and responded with their purchases. In effect, the distinction between free and paid became much clearer to customers.

- Lastly, Asana launched a 30-day free trial experience for the paid products on top of the existing Free package. This trial allowed customers to explore the new features in the paid plans and experience their value before committing to a purchase. The free trial introduction significantly boosted conversion rates and revenue.

Blow Up Your Packaging: Time to Redefine Your Offer Structure

This reimagined packaging strategy marked a turning point for Asana. By aligning its product offerings with the distinct needs of its customer segments, the company unlocked significant growth. As Farinacci reflected, "Packaging was one of the single biggest pivots to grow Asana in the scale-up phase and helped set us up nicely for the IPO in the coming years."

What began as a simple task management tool created by a team of Facebook alumni evolved into a powerhouse in enterprise software. The journey from startup to scale-up illustrates the transformative power of reimagining packaging. By leveraging segmentation and introducing tailored product tiers, Asana effectively transitioned from a niche solution to a global leader in project management, proving that strategic pivots during the scale-up phase can unlock extraordinary opportunities.

A similar transformation unfolded at LifeLock, a leading provider of identity theft prevention services, which ultimately sold to Symantec for $2.3 billion. In its early startup phase, LifeLock offered a straightforward, single-plan subscription model that catered to all customers equally. However, as the market matured, subscriber demands and expectations evolved, prompting the company to rethink its approach. LifeLock introduced multiple packages tailored to diverse customer needs and willingness to pay—a strategic shift that wasn't without internal debate.

As then-CEO Hilary Schneider explained in an interview, "There was a constant debate about whether to keep our offerings simple with one plan or to diversify into multiple packages." Advocates for simplicity argued that a single plan would make customer decisions easier and improve acquisition rates. Proponents of segmentation believed that offering tailored packages at varied price points would appeal to a broader audience, improve retention by aligning products more closely with customer needs, and ultimately drive greater growth.

Schneider's decision to launch segmented packages marked a pivotal moment in LifeLock's evolution. "Blowing up and redefining our packaging was *the* pivotal move," Schneider emphasized. The results spoke for themselves: a revenue surge of over 40%, proving that addressing distinct market segments wasn't just a theoretical exercise but a powerful strategy for driving growth. This bold move redefined LifeLock's trajectory, solidifying its position in the market and paving the way for its successful acquisition.

We hope these examples have convinced you that you need to rethink your packaging and bundling strategy when you hit the scale-up phase. Oh, by the way, even Superhuman, the example we discussed in Chapter 5, evolved its packaging to a three-tier structure in the scale-up phase to better serve its growing customer base.

But how should you go about it? The next section gives you a step-by-step framework to blow up and redefine your offer to different segments that you want to service in the scale-up phase.

Redefining Your Packaging: What Best-in-Class Companies Do

What follows is a five-step process you can use to redefine your packaging and bundling strategies to closely tie with your target segments, ensuring that you tailor your products specifically to each segment.

Step 1: Redefine Your Customer Segments at the Scale-up Phase

As we've noted, *Monetizing Innovation* explains how to do a segmentation exercise. If you did such an exercise in the startup phase, you should consider rerunning it when you reach the scale-up phase. In the intervening time, you have probably learned a lot more about your segments and how customers use your product. You may have a better idea for buyer personas for each segment. You may even have a hunch that there are untapped segments that your earlier segmentation study did not reveal. Rerunning the segmentation study can tell you whether the market has evolved and whether you need a refined view on size and potential of each segment.

If you've never conducted a segmentation exercise, your understanding of whether your product truly serves different customer segments may be little more than guesswork. You might also have settled on a single product that you believe—or hope—represents product-market fit. If that's the case, now is the time to undertake a segmentation study to define and measure each customer segment based on its needs and willingness to pay.

The key to customer segmentation is defining how you should treat the various segments differently. Doing this involves dividing your market into distinct groups based on shared characteristics, with a particular focus on their specific needs, what they value, and their willingness to pay. (Note: Other segmentation methods—such as those based on behavior, demographics, or personas—are often nonactionable and less useful for driving profitable growth.) To define your customer segments at this stage in your company's life cycle, you need to run a *willingness-to-pay study* with both your current customers and your prospects. The latter group includes customers who are new to the category as well those that have chosen a competitor (yet could be prospective customers of yours in the future). The primary goal of the study will be answering two questions: What features and services matter most to your future buyers? And are they willing to pay for them?

Chapter 4 of *Monetizing Innovation* explains how to run a detailed willingness-to-pay study. If you don't have the bandwidth to take on a full project of this type, here are two quick and easy ways to achieve the majority of insights:

1. *Ask your customers and prospects a series of needs-based questions.*
   List no more than 10 to 15 features that your product currently offers or that you are building. In each case, describe the benefits the feature offers rather than its technical specifications. Then ask respondents to indicate whether the feature is a *must have* or a *nice to have* or if it is *not needed.*

2. *Follow up with basic willingness-to-pay questions.* For each feature, ask respondents to indicate whether they *will definitely pay for it, would consider paying for it, would most likely not pay for it,* or *will definitely not pay for it.*

The insights from this straightforward research will enable you to prioritize product features based on their value to buyers and buyers' willingness to pay. In addition, you can conduct a *clustering analysis* on these responses that will help you define your segments by identifying groups of customers who share the same sets of feature preferences and willingness to pay.

You will also need to ask questions in the study that elicit criteria that will help you *identify* buyers from these segments, such as firmographic or demographic information, as well as questions that will help you understand your buyers' personas.

Step 2: Determine Your Packaging/Bundling Structure

Next you need to determine the correct packaging/bundling structure based on the results from Step 1. In general, there are five packaging/bundling structures to choose from, as illustrated in Figure 8.3.

The most relevant packaging structures for the scale-up phase are 2, 3, and 4. Structure 1 is applicable in the startup phase, and Structure 5 makes sense when you are way past the scale-up phase and thinking of "debundling" to provide further revenue optimization.

Don't rush the process of selecting the best packaging structure for your scale-up phase; take the time to choose wisely based on your segmentation analysis. In particular, don't be unduly influenced by the packaging structure you see competitors using. Remember, there is a good chance these rivals also need to redefine their packages, so you might be following an outdated example. Alternatively, they might be throwing stuff against the wall to see what sticks. In that case, copying them could be a classic case of the helpless being led by the clueless.

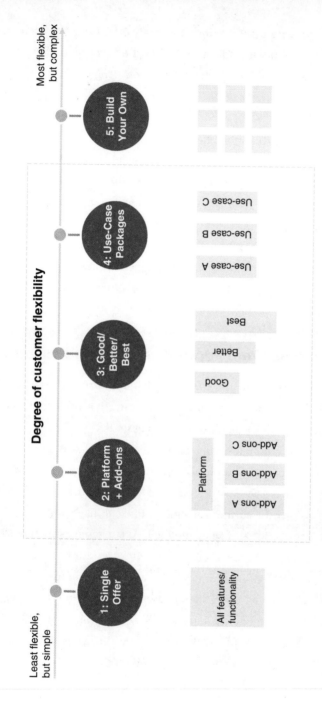

Figure 8.3 Packaging/Bundling Structures

The Build, Don't Borrow Axiom	Looking to competitors for packaging ideas may feel safe, but companies that win are the ones that design packaging grounded in customer insight, not competitive benchmarks.

To help you decide which of the five structures shown in Figure 8.3 is best for your company, use the next description of each structure, its benefits, and when it is most appropriate.

- *Structure 1: Single Offer.* In this model, all the product features and benefits that you have developed are crammed together into one offer. This is the simplest offer structure but also the least flexible: You only have one thing to sell to all your customers, regardless of their needs, providing the least opportunity to differentiate. The benefit of this packaging is its simplicity, which allows you to focus on acquisition and engagement. A single-offer structure can make sense in the startup phase, especially if you are working with tight resource constraints and have a high need to focus. If this is the case, hopefully you did your segmentation homework prior to launch and picked the single best segment to productize to. Once you reach the scale-up phase, it's usually time to move on to a structure that allows for somewhat higher complexity, enabling you to serve a range of customer segments directly.

- *Structure 2: Platform + Add-ons.* This structure consists of a core platform—a required base offering that all customers must purchase—combined with optional modules or add-ons that provide additional functionality. It allows buyers to tailor the offering to their specific needs. For this structure to be effective, the core platform must include features that are essential for all customer segments, ensuring universal appeal. The platform + add-ons approach works particularly well when certain features are highly valued by specific segments but

Blow Up Your Packaging: Time to Redefine Your Offer Structure

not by others. Some customers may consider these features must-haves or nice-to-haves and be willing to pay for them, while others may see them as unnecessary or not worth the additional cost. By isolating these features as add-ons, companies ensure they are available to those who want them without burdening others who do not.

This structure is highly effective for companies developing multiple products, as it enables them to present their vision as a cohesive, integrated platform—a true one-stop shop for customers. It reassures buyers that future purchases will integrate seamlessly with the existing platform, offering peace of mind and simplifying vendor relationships. However, there is a limit to how many add-ons this structure can support before it becomes overly complex. If more than five optional modules are needed, a different approach—such as Structures 3, 4, or 5—may be more suitable to maintain clarity and ease of use.

- *Structure 3: Good-Better-Best (GBB).* This classic structure consists of a series of packages, each offering progressively more products, functionality, and features at higher prices. The entry package serves as the basic offering, the mid-tier package incorporates the entry package but adds more enhancements, and the top-tier package encompasses still further features. Note that despite the name "Good-Better-Best," there is no reason that this structure has to have three tiers, so long as the fundamental principle that each tier builds on the one before it is observed; as we saw, Asana began with a two-tier structure, then added Business and Enterprise to go to four tiers, and ultimately added a fifth tier, Enterprise+.

This tiered structure enables businesses to cater to various customer segments by providing options that align with different levels of needs and willingness to pay. Over time, this approach can lead to better customer retention, as the act of empowering customers to select a specific package based on their needs and willingness to pay fosters a stronger connection and commitment to the product or service and builds brand loyalty. The GBB structure can also boost customer acquisition. Price-sensitive customers can opt for the Good package, while those who prioritize quality will tend to choose the Best package. Many customers will gravitate toward a middle package, the Better package, perceiving it as a balanced option that avoids the extremes. In other words, this tiered approach helps mitigate indecision, which otherwise could result in lost sales. You might ask, "If the GBB structure comes with so many advantages, why not use it all the time?" In reality, using the GBB structure blindly is the most frequent packaging/bundling mistake companies make. For this structure to work well, you need distinct clusters of customers with escalating needs and willingness to pay. Use the GBB structure only when the segmentation analysis from Step 1 shows that the customer segments differ by key product features in such a way that a tiered structure makes sense. If needs of your segments differ but not in a way that progresses steadily upward, you may be better served by a platform-plus-add-ons model or a use-case approach.

- *Structure 4: Use-Case Packages.* The essence of use-case packaging lies in serving distinct buying groups with minimal overlap in their needs. A classic example is the distinction between "teacher" and "student" editions of a textbook—each group has specific requirements, and a teacher would rarely purchase a student edition (or vice versa). This structure involves creating packages tailored to specific use cases or customer types and works particularly well under two scenarios.

The first scenario arises when certain features or benefits are highly relevant to specific segments but irrelevant to others. For example, DocuSign offers a package specifically tailored to the real estate industry, which includes access to standard real estate forms that simplify transactions—an essential benefit for that segment but

Blow Up Your Packaging: Time to Redefine Your Offer Structure

unnecessary for others. The second scenario involves products that serve diverse verticals or functions with varying levels of willingness to pay. LinkedIn provides an excellent illustration with its distinct solutions for hiring managers and sales professionals. For hiring managers, LinkedIn offers Talent Solutions, designed to help them connect with "candidates" and manage hiring workflows. For sales professionals, the platform offers Sales Navigator, which focuses on identifying "leads" and includes features like dashboards for tracking outbound sales messages. These aren't merely repurposed versions of the same product but are fully productized solutions with unique features that resonate deeply with each group.

Use-case packaging can be one of the most effective ways to align your offerings with customer needs, allowing potential buyers to find precisely the right solution while enabling you to tailor your product with remarkable precision. However, implementing this structure can be challenging. Catering to a large number of customer segments may create unwanted complexity, and sometimes the lines between segments are blurry rather than clear-cut.

If your segmentation analysis reveals a manageable set of distinct buying groups or verticals with clearly defined needs and personas, use-case packaging can be a highly effective strategy to consider. It empowers you to deliver tailored solutions that enhance customer satisfaction and maximize willingness to pay, driving both adoption and long-term loyalty.

- *Structure 5:* Build-Your-Own (BYO). The BYO structure is centered on a configuration process that lets customers choose exactly what they want. It can be a good fit when customers with diverse needs value maximum customization, such that they can be accommodated only by a highly flexible offer. It is also suitable when a product has an extensive array of options that are hard to fit into standard packages. However, the BYO structure carries a high degree of overhead and complexity, making it a very unusual choice for the scale-up phase. It generally is not a reasonable option until a company is operating on a truly massive scale. In such cases, the product offering may have evolved to the point that a simpler packaging model is no longer effective, and a BYO structure may be needed.

Step 3: Create Packages/Bundles

In this step, you need to create packages or bundles based on the segment needs identified in Step 1 and the structure selected in Step 2. You need to determine the composition of each package or bundle, specifically which features to include and which to exclude. A framework we refer to as "Leader, Filler, Killer" is particularly useful for this process. The basic idea is to organize the features based on expected adoption and perceived value (Figure 8.4). Let's analyze the elements of this framework.

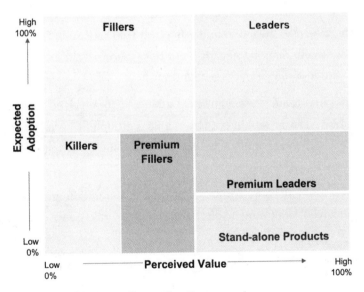

Figure 8.4 The Leader, Filler, Killer Framework

159

Blow Up Your Packaging: Time to Redefine Your Offer Structure

- *Leaders* are the essential features or benefits that serve as the primary drivers of a package's appeal for a specific segment. They represent the key reasons why customers choose to buy and often are what initially captures their interest. Leader features typically have high expected adoption rates and significant perceived value.

- *Fillers* are supporting features that enhance the overall value of the package/bundle but are not the primary reasons for its purchase. Ideally fillers make the package/bundle more attractive with no more than a proportional price increase, such that the trade-off makes sense to potential buyers. For fillers, the expected adoption level is high, but the perceived value is low to medium. For this reason, be careful to limit the set of filler features for each package/bundle. Adding too many fillers can lead to the phenomenon we called "Feature Shock" in *Monetizing Innovation*—a situation in which customers are so overwhelmed by the profusion of benefits that the basic value of the product gets lost.

- *Killers* are features that potential buyers do not want to pay for. In the eyes of customers, they add little or no value, and their inclusion likely will detract from the package's appeal and lead to lost sales. The expected adoption and perceived value for such features is not just low but literally negative. For this reason, avoid including killers when designing a package/bundle.

- *Premium Leaders* are features that have high perceived value but are expected to be sought only by a limited group of buyers. Hence, they are good candidates for inclusion in premium packages rather than all packages/bundles.

- *Premium Fillers* are features that rank in the middle ground of both perceived value and likely adoption. They are good candidates to pad out premium packages.

- *Stand-Alone Products* are features that possess high perceived value but are essential only to a small portion of customers who are willing to pay for them. (Twenty percent of customers or fewer is a good guideline to define the size of such a group.) These features should be offered as add-ons or stand-alone products.

Step 4: Cross-Check Your Packages/Bundles for Effectiveness

Now that you have created packages/bundles for your different customer segments, it is time to cross-check them to make sure they will help you unlock market share and wallet share. A package/bundle should be considered effective if it:

- *Encourages initial adoption.* Your packages/bundles should be designed to lower barriers to entry and encourage new customers to try your products. They should make it easy and attractive for customers to start using your product, and the value should be clear early on. Packages/bundles that offer enough functionality to solve immediate needs help build trust and encourage future purchases.

- *Aligns with the customer life cycle.* Your packaging/bundling strategy should allow the buyer to see how it fits their needs today—and how it will continue to be the right choice for them in the future. Highlighting the ability to grow with the customer's needs reinforces the long-term value of your proposition.

- *Facilitates upsell.* Your packages/bundles should be structured to encourage expansion of the relationship between you and your customer, offering clear upgrade paths that highlight the added value and benefits of higher-tier packages or add-ons.

- *Enables easy product explanations to customers.* Finally, your packages/bundles should be easy to communicate and understand. Use simple language and clear visuals that emphasize benefits—especially from leader features—as well as the differences among packages. Simplicity and clarity make packages/bundles easier for you to pitch and for customers to choose. By ensuring that the structure of your offerings is easy to explain, you will avoid complexity that could otherwise deter potential customers.

Step 5: Test and Refine Your Packaging/Bundling

The last step to perfecting your packaging/bundling strategy is to do a final test with customers and prospects and refine the offerings before a full-scale launch. It is crucial that these tests include pricing to ensure realism and to measure customers' level of willingness to pay. One simple approach that can generate highly useful insights is a form of simulation we call a "shopping-cart exercise."

The Beyond A/B Axiom	To tap into the mental models and rules people use to make buying decisions, you need to run simulations, such as shopping-cart exercises, with customers and prospects. Given the complexity and number of possible variations, traditional A/B testing is not a viable approach.

A shopping-cart exercise involves putting customers or prospects through a series of simulated scenarios that reflect possible real-world outcomes and observing how they choose among various options. This method provides valuable data on customer preferences and price sensitivity. To perform a shopping-cart exercise, follow these five steps:

1. *Develop the set of alternatives to be tested.* Create a handful of versions of your packaging for testing, based on the steps outlined earlier in this chapter. These should reflect your best guesses at the optimal solution. They may vary in feature placement, number of packages, pricing, and value messaging. Focus on the most critical variables to

test and avoid unnecessary details. Clearly highlight the different features in each scenario to enable respondents to make informed choices. Make the simulated buying process as realistic as possible. For example, if you are an online business, create a landing page for each scenario; for a sales-led business, present the scenarios as a sales team would pitch them to customers or prospects.

2. *Attach a price to each package/bundle.* Incorporate realistic pricing into the scenario. Doing this will force customers or prospects to make trade-offs so that they select the option that fits their actual purchase criteria. Later you may wish to follow up the shopping-cart exercises with additional tests to optimize pricing.

3. *Include your current package/bundle as a baseline.* One of the scenarios presented to respondents should reflect your current offer and pricing as a control. Doing this will allow you to evaluate the increase in revenue or adoption over status quo and give you a baseline against which to calibrate all the other scenarios you may consider.

4. *Simulate the real-world customer experience.* In each scenario, ask customers to perform actions they would take in real life. For example, ask, "Given this lineup of options, which one would you choose?" Always provide alternatives, such as "will not choose any of these options" or "will opt for the free plan" to make the scenarios as realistic as possible. Avoid the temptation to include elements that would not be present in the standard purchase path. For example, don't ask respondents to watch a video explaining the benefits of your product prior to making their selection, unless customers would also review the same video in real life before purchasing.

5. *Ask follow-up questions.* After respondents have made their choices, ask them why they made those decisions. Also follow up with: "If you had the opportunity to adjust your favorite scenario, what changes would you make?"

Based on how customers and prospects choose among scenarios, you can gain insights into the mental models and (often unconscious) rules they use to make buying decisions. This deeper understanding of the customer experience will prepare you to blow up your existing packaging strategy and redefine it to accelerate toward profitable growth.

Beyond the Basics: Insights, Tips, and Tricks on Redefining Your Offer Structure

Having covered the basic steps that will enable you to refine your packaging and bundling, let's now consider some advanced insights, tips, and tricks you may find useful.

- *Productize to willingness to pay as opposed to pricing your product.* When there is a significant difference in willingness to pay across the industry sectors you serve, or between distinct functional roles like Sales and HR, or between very different customer types such as professionals and amateurs, use-case-based packaging can be a powerful solution. For example, a leading provider of AI solutions for automating workflows offers different packaging and pricing for the legal and healthcare industries, as the willingness to pay varies dramatically between these industries. Said differently, the company has ensured that it productizes to the different willingness to pay of verticals (as opposed to pricing a product for different verticals), resulting in high rates of acquisition, customer satisfaction, and retention.

- *At its heart, packaging should be about doing right by the customer.* A core principle of thoughtful packaging is aligning pricing with customer value, not using it as a lever for coercion. A common misstep is gating essential features, like Single Sign-On

(SSO) in B2B SaaS, behind the most expensive plans, effectively forcing customers to pay a premium for a single critical capability they need, regardless of whether they use the rest of the bundle. A better, customer-first approach is either to include such foundational features across all relevant tiers or to offer them as reasonably priced add-ons. This approach empowers customers to pay for what they truly need, fosters trust, reduces friction in the buying process, and demonstrates long-term alignment with their success.

- *As your business grows and your product evolves, a combination of packaging structures may be optimal.* For instance, you could implement a GBB model *within* a specific use case. As an example, LinkedIn at the highest level has use-case packages for recruiters, Sales, and so on. However, Talent Solutions (the product for recruiters) has three tiers (a GBB), reflecting the fact that the needs and willingness to pay of solo recruiters are different from those of professionals working for large enterprises.

- *Initiate upsell conversations gradually rather than waiting until contract renewal.* A best practice is to allow customers to learn about or "experience" a better package a few months before their current package renewal. This approach facilitates smoother upsell conversations at the time of renewal.

- *Maintain an unpublished, defeatured package with only the core leader features to prevent customer churn.* For customers on the verge of leaving, consider providing a back-pocket option, called a "less expensive alternative," that offers only the essential features but at a lower price. This strategy can help retain customers who might leave due to perceived high costs, thereby reducing churn and maintaining customer relationships.

Chapter Summary: How This Strategy Avoids the Single-Engine Trap

Overly simplistic or overly generous offer structures ("all you can eat") often fall into the Disruptor trap of chasing customer acquisition without a plan to expand and often oversell features that customers don't need or value. The strategies described in this chapter help leaders structure packages that align with real customer needs and willingness to pay while preserving room for upsell. When customers see a package that fits their needs, they not only convert more easily but they stay longer, because they feel they made the right choice. This expands reach with tailored entry points (market share) and improves both retention and upsell over time (wallet share). Profitable Growth Architects know that great packaging doesn't just land deals; it builds trust that lasts.

CEO Questions

- If your company has recently reached the scale-up phase, have you considered redefining your packaging/bundling strategies?

- Have you conducted a segmentation study to identify your customer segments based on needs, value, and willingness to pay? Are you productizing for different segments, or are you trying to position the same product to different segments?

- Have you considered the five alternative packaging structures? Which of the five is most appropriate for your business given the needs, value perceptions, and willingness to pay of your key customer segments?

- Have you developed a clear understanding of which product features should be classified as leaders, fillers, and killers in relation to each customer segment?

- Have you used the criteria provided in Step 4 in this chapter to ensure the packages/bundles you've designed are effective?

Chapter 9

Price Increases: Ask Properly, and You Shall Receive

During a period of inflation, consumers are often frustrated to see their bills climbing higher and higher. Pundits then blame corporations for price gouging and demand relief. Politicians, seeing an opportunity to capitalize on this thread of public grievance, promise that they will return prices to the low levels of years gone by.

However, when prices actually start going down, there is often a disaster in the making. For example, Japan's long period of deflation, known in that country as the Lost Decades, saw the country's stock market crash 60% and unemployment double. Fortunately, deflation is rare. In 2024, 163 of the 172 countries tracked by economists experienced inflation. In nearly every place, and in nearly every period, prices went up.

But do yours?

Raising prices can be an emotional question for business leaders. There's often guilt: Is this any way to repay my loyal customers? After raising prices for the second time in the company's history, the chairman of popular dessert company Akagi Nyugyo apologized to customers by video, noting that the painful move came only after "we held on for 25 years"—a nod to the quarter century where their price had not budged.

Others feel they do not deserve to raise prices: There is still tech debt to be paid, there is some key improvement that hasn't been made or some killer feature that hasn't launched. Such leaders tend to forget that they (generally) *have* added value to their offering and that they do so in ways large and small all the time. They also overlook the fact that milk, bread, and butter do not get better, but their prices go up every year.

No wonder the famed venture capitalist Marc Andreessen said he was considering hiring a skywriter to write "RAISE PRICES" in the sky over San Francisco, where many of his investments have their headquarters. It's good advice, but not everyone follows it.

The Pricing-Paralysis Axiom	The reality is that most market rates—including goods and services—tend to rise annually, yet many executives hesitate to adjust their own pricing, often driven more by emotion than logic.

The biggest thing stopping leaders from raising prices is the fear that if they do so, they will lose buyers. To be sure, there is a risk that customers will walk away in response to a fee increase. But compare this with the bedrock certainty that if you do not raise prices, you will eventually get eaten alive by inflation. In fact, even if you do increase fees but fail to keep pace with inflation, your purchasing power will erode, and you might create a downward spiral. The dollars you bring in will cover fewer of your expenses. You will be left with less to fuel your product improvements, research and development, and any expansion you may have planned. You may not be able to hire the caliber of employee you had hoped for. The reward for keeping prices low is often death by a thousand cuts.

You may be thinking: Can't I make up for this with volume? To understand why you likely cannot, ask yourself which of the next two options you would prefer, all things equal:

A. 10% additional units sold but no change to price

B. 10% additional price realization but no change to sales volume

Some will go for option A, pointing out that increased volume implies more customers who could grow over time and that grabbing terrain that otherwise might have gone to other players in the market helps to defend against competition. Others will say there really is no difference between the two options.

Yet there is a clear advantage to option B. If you made $100 by pushing through a fee increase, every dollar drops to the bottom line—you keep all of it. If you followed option A and make $100 through sales, you keep only the profit, which would be $37 on average in the United States. In other words, to match the profits of option B, you would need to increase sales by a staggering $270.

The Price-Over-Sales Axiom	A 1% increase in price generates much more profit than a 1% increase in sales, all else being equal, because the additional revenue flows directly to the bottom line. In fact, most businesses would need a 2% to 3% increase in sales to achieve the same profit impact as a 1% price increase.

You may be thinking: Sure, but this assumes the price increase does not create lost sales. In practice, concerns about attrition far exceed actual churn. These worries are driven by the inevitable complaints when prices go up. However, if an increase passes without a whisper of response, it is possible you did not raise prices enough.

It takes nerve and resolve to do the right thing for your business. Price increases are unpopular and do carry risk, but they are 100% necessary. As Warren Buffett once said, "If you've got the power to raise prices without losing business to a competitor, you've got a very good business. If you have to have a prayer session before raising the price by 10%, then you've got a terrible business."[1]

The Courage to Raise Prices: How Arun Gupta Transformed Grailed

One leader who showed true courage in raising prices is Arun Gupta, the founder of online menswear marketplace Grailed, a company is in the secondhand resale market sector, which is growing at 15 times the rate of the traditional retail clothing. Arun built the company with his own hands, coding the website himself, hiring his first employee after the site had already been up for more than six months. Despite this growth, the Yale graduate initially took no fees from the transactions facilitated on his platform; he introduced a 6% sales charge only in 2016, two years after founding the company.

Meanwhile, Arun saw signs all around him that the little marketplace he'd launched was turning into a true rocket ship. The volume of sales transacted on his site was doubling every year or more. His users were starting to make serious money: In 2015, Arun told *Complex* magazine that the most expensive item ever sold in his marketplace went for $2,500, a Carol Christian Poell leather jacket; by 2018, that number had climbed to $47,000 (for a piece by designer Raf Simons). Within a few years, a single user reported selling more than $1 million of merchandise through Grailed.

Arun was rolling out major improvements to his marketplace, including "Binding Offers," which would stop buyers from endlessly haggling with sellers, and "Digital Verification," which gave buyers greater confidence in their purchases, increasing the speed and size of transactions. More were in the works.

It was time, Arun decided, to raise rates.

Under the heading "Platform Improvements and Seller Fee Update," he shed light on the massive efforts that had been undertaken to provide value to buyers and sellers in Grailed's marketplace. "Our team of expert moderators have digitally authenticated nearly 1 million items (and counting) this year alone," he pointed out, adding "digitally authenticated are more likely to sell, and sell faster." He also discussed exciting improvements in the works: improved listing and upload functionality, price intelligence tools, shipping and tracking features, and more. He then stated, in bold font, that the new fee would be 9%, "still making us one of the most affordable marketplaces. . .to reach nearly 1 million buyers worldwide."[2]

For Grailed, the increase would be transformative, since going from 6% to 9% meant an increase of 50% in terms of fees. Yet for sellers, it would only be three more pennies out of every dollar. Still, Arun knew he was in for a bumpy ride before he sent the announcement. His customers had grown accustomed to getting a lot for only 6% and would not appreciate the change.

The backlash was swift, loud, and public. A post with more than 100 upvotes claimed that users were no longer selling due to the increase; another read: "Sad, quickly losing [*sic*] respect for Grailed." A petition was launched on Change.org, begging the company to take its rates down to 7.5%. An article in the Australian edition of *GQ* talked of a "boycott," stating that "[a] surprise fee hike has users shunning the world's most popular menswear resale marketplace" and claiming that "the fee increase makes selling on Grailed almost untenable."

Arun struggled with the question of whether to respond, ultimately deciding to let his site's quality speak for itself. "When you increase prices, you also increase your ability to invest in a better experience for your customers," he noted. Sales held steady, then continued to climb—spectacularly. "Pricing is an important competitive advantage," Arun said. When his company was acquired by Goat Group two years later, the combined entity had 50 million users worldwide, and Grailed saw nearly half a billion dollars of goods sold.

Price Increases: Asking Properly

What sets leaders like Arun apart is their ability to deeply understand the context, craft a well-thought-out plan, and execute it with precision. Raising prices is a delicate process that requires careful consideration. Without a thoughtful approach, a price increase can lead to significant backlash and missed objectives. However, a well-planned strategy ensures that your price adjustments are aligned with customer expectations, minimizing friction and maximizing success.

To achieve a successful price increase, let's explore the three key pillars: understanding the context, creating a strategic price increase plan, and executing it effectively.

Understanding the Context

Before setting out to raise prices, it's critical to understand the relationship you have with your customers. Executives often follow generic advice on increasing prices, without realizing how sharply their business may differ from others. Fundamentally, there are three factors to consider.

1. *Do your customers expect prices to change or stay the same?* In some cases, customers may have entered into a written contract which limits the amount fees may be increased. At the other extreme, particularly when single-shot transactional purchases are involved, there is no expectation on either side that prices will stay the same. You do not expect to pay the same amount for your New Year's champagne this year as you did in years past.

   However, the question of price stability becomes fuzzier when there is an expectation of consistency but no contractual obligation exists. You may have such a pay-as-you-go relationship with a day-care facility or gym, where you're billed for each hour of care or every yoga class you attend. If the rate changes from one month to the next, you may be unhappy or even feel you've been treated unfairly. This issue can become compounded if you don't change price for a long time and train customers to expect more for less. Of course, your context becomes much simpler if your customers do expect a price increase.

2. *Are prices published?* Listing prices may attract buyers, but doing so robs you of flexibility. Consumer prices are communicated broadly, generally speaking; B2B organizations, particularly those that are sales-led, usually reveal much less price information to the public. If prices are listed, your competitors will immediately learn of any increase and may respond by attacking—or they may seize the opportunity to raise their own prices. Where prices aren't published, a competitive response will tend to be slower and is often less aggressive.

3. *What is your recent track record?* Have you raised prices recently? Increasing rates for the first time in a long time requires a very different approach than if you increase your rates frequently. Customers tend to show less gratitude for your track record of forgoing rate increases than you might anticipate. In fact, you may have set an expectation that prices will continue to stay where they are. In contrast, if you have already increased prices this year, it may be challenging to raise rates again, even if you have good reason. In general, setting customers' expectations that there will be higher rates in the future will play in your favor and make it easier to achieve full price.

Now that you understand the terrain, it's time to take action. First, carefully plan what you aspire to achieve and how you will get there. Then roll up your sleeves and execute against your strategy, bringing your organization together to win the fight. Ensure that you are monitoring results with the right metrics and that you have contingency plans ready should reality start to deviate from your forecast.

Creating a Strategic Price Increase Plan

A strategy for lifting fees goes well beyond the amount of the increase. Do you know what success will look like if the campaign goes as planned?

As part of your strategy, consider what parts of your offer are best suited to support the fee increase and assess what the resulting impact will be on different groups within your customer base. Calibrate your plan by thinking through competitive response. There will always be a "day after", so ensure you have planned for what comes next.

Creating a strategic price increase plan consists of five key steps, which are described below.

Planning Step 1: Set Your Goals—What Does Success Look Like?

As you start to plan out your fee increase program, you may realize that there are multiple objectives to be considered. Identifying and prioritizing these goals is a critical first step. Not only will doing so ensure you achieve your desired outcome, but without this step, you won't be able to communicate expectations to the people performing the hands-on work. If your teams do not know which objectives are more important than others, they may make moves you later will wish they hadn't. Worse, indecision may result in inaction.

Consider the trade-off between price achievement and customer satisfaction. A fee increase can create friction with parts of your base. Your position on the trade-off must be carefully chosen. Some business leaders want to ensure that they achieve the full price increase they have planned, no matter what blowback they receive. (And within this group, some actually hope to *create* churn by raising rates, as a way of firing their worst customers.) Others prioritize customer satisfaction, raising prices only if they are sure that doing so won't create too much attrition. Most are somewhere in between. For example, many feel that some churn is acceptable—but not for the most loyal customers or key accounts. And there's not just churn to consider, but customer sentiment as well.

Furthermore, given the effort involved in a fee increase, many companies hope to get more out of the effort than just a higher price. Here are just a few examples of the additional goals that are often considered:

- *Repapering.* For companies with explicit user agreements, getting all customers to sign on to the same contract, terms of service, or other legal language can be important to the enterprise value of the business and may support other goals, such as implementing an annual fee increase.

- *Discount normalization.* Many companies go through periods where they charge far below the optimal rate, especially during the early, formative years when they are particularly hungry for new sales. Others may have erratic streaks of high discounting due to a particularly aggressive salesperson or set of salespeople or as the result of an exceptionally generous promotional campaign. This lack of price integrity can create serious issues for the business, making discount standardization/normalization an attractive proposition.

- *Upsell/cross-sell.* During a fee-increase campaign, customers can be offered an opportunity to trial a higher-tier package or additional functionality for a limited time as a way to maintain customer goodwill while using the price increase conversation as an opportunity to have a up-sell conversation.

Before you advance to the next step, ensure that your goals are clear, prioritized, and well communicated so that expectations can be set for the project team. Note that your goals might be different for different customer groups.

The Prioritize-or-Pay Axiom	Fee increases can create value—or chaos. When multiple objectives are at play, failing to clearly prioritize and communicate them before the rollout invites confusion, resistance, and unintended consequences.

Planning Step 2: Determine What Fees Will Be Raised

When fee hikes are discussed in the news, they're usually blended together into homogenous statements like, "Airlines increased prices by 18% last year." However, it's generally a mistake to impose a blanket price increase.

The reason is because some of your products and services are likely in a better position to support a greater fee change than others. For example, if you have recently introduced a product, you may have done so at below the market-optimal price to gain early traction. If the new product now has a loyal base of customers, this is exactly the right time to bring it up to the fee level it deserves. If there's a product that you launched a long time ago and feel is growing stale, you may be inclined to discount—but if there are few good competitive alternatives and customers have unusually high lock-in, due to a high degree of training or integration, hold that price where it is or consider a boost. For customers of such a product, the cost of finding an alternative and retraining users might outweigh the impact of a price increase. Furthermore, products that are the dominant brand in their sector are generally more able to raise prices than those that have a small share.

Resetting customer discounts is another area of opportunity for generating higher fees. Many companies award steep price breaks early in their life cycle and never increase these long-tenured customers up to list price. This approach can create a sharp imbalance between what different customers pay for the same thing. Nudging older customers closer to what new buyers pay by pushing on their discount level is often a way to increase fees. You can still leave loyal customers with *some* discount, to thank them for standing by you—but charge a fair rate.

Not all fees can be raised. For example, a contract may cap the amount that fees can go up. As a practical matter, there may be groups of buyers whose fees you are unwilling to touch: influential customers and those who, if they left, would motivate others to leave as well.

Finally, you may be giving away products or services that customers would actually be willing to pay for. In such cases, consider whether you can begin charging for them going forward, keeping in mind that this shift may be perceived as a price increase.

Planning Step 3: Size the Increase

How high can your increase be? To answer this, you must consider both the achievable list price and the street price for the products you have targeted after any discount, promotions, or concessions. You should also check for price points that trigger the perception that a product or service is too expensive. For example, Grailed discovered that customers would experience great sticker shock should their fee cross 10%, information that helped CEO Arun Gupta choose 9% as the right fee level. To make this determination, he needed to find out what price customers might pay for the ongoing value that he added over the years. He followed the techniques for quantifying the willingness to pay as described in our book *Monetizing Innovation*.

Finally, recognize that there is a maximum fee increase that can be imposed in a given period. This ceiling differs according to industry and the prevailing economic environment. It also should reflect your strategic goals, as defined earlier. We find that, as a rule of thumb, a threshold of 15% to 20% for a single period is achievable. (There are exceptions to this, such as a low-dollar increase that creates a higher percentage change, such as the $1 example mentioned earlier.) Even if a customer would, in theory, accept a 50% increase, you may need to break that increase into smaller steps over a longer period of time. However, this is a question of strategy rather than a hard-and-fast rule; many successful fee increases have been conducted with much higher lifts; they just require more care.

Planning Step 4: Analyze the Impact on Your Customers

Next, consider carefully how your proposed prices will affect your buyers. Buyers include customers of today, represented by your current base, and customers of tomorrow, those whom you hope to attract in the future.

Price Increases: Ask Properly, and You Shall Receive

Start by forecasting how the new fees will impact the different customers that make up your base of buyers or subscribers.

- Start by playing out the new prices and structure against your base, generating an approximation of the fees they will pay after the change.

- If you have created a customer segmentation, assess how the fees will hit each group. If you have not, break your buyers into a set of bands based on the amount of sales they generate per customer (even a "low/middle/high" grouping will work).

- Within each group, assess the difference between what these customers pay today and what they will pay after the new pricing takes effect.

The resulting distribution should give you a first look at how the proposed price increase will affect different groups within your buying base. This information will be critical to creating an effective action plan. Look for these specific situations:

- Is the impact carried disproportionately by your largest or best customers? This is not necessarily a bad thing. However, such a situation may require a greater investment of time and effort and might need top people in your organization to participate.

- If it affects those with less ability to absorb a fee increase, plan to invest in concessions and messaging. A price hike that affects a large number of budget-constrained buyers, such as small businesses or lower-income consumers, risks a negative response in social media and the press, so you will want to prepare your response strategy in advance. Buyers with rigid budget cycles, such as those in education or government, may lack the ability to absorb a higher price unless you offer concessions that give them greater flexibility in terms of timing.

- Will pockets of customers be hit disproportionately or erratically by the price increase?

As much as possible, put yourself in the shoes of your customers and prospects, trying to anticipate how they will view the fee increase. Many cases of catastrophic fee increases could have been avoided had the proper analysis been performed up front. Unity, the popular mobile game development platform, introduced a charge for every time a game built on its platform was downloaded. While the per-download fee was small, the company overlooked the fact that some of its developers had signed fixed agreements with massive platforms like Xbox—meaning they could be hit for tens of millions of downloads without receiving a penny more in revenue. Since no exception was made for piracy, game developers would have to pay the download fee for illegal copies of their games. The community was furious. Unity lost a fifth of its value in little more than a week.[3] The company announced one month to the day after the fee increase was implemented that the changes would be rolled back completely.

Finally, many businesses make the mistake of executing fee increases as a "peanut butter spread": an even lift hitting all buyers equally. Instead, incorporate your customers' individual risk profiles into your plan. Assigning a somewhat smaller increase to the high-risk side of your population and a commensurately larger increase to the low-risk side will allow you to achieve the same overall price target with a lower level of attrition.

This approach can be visualized as a "lift" (raise list prices), "shift" (reduce discounting), and "differentiate" (adjust according to risk) method, as shown in Figure 9.1.

The Blind-Raise Axiom	Avoid the peanut butter spread of increasing price by the same amount for all customers. Matching the fee increase to your customers' churn propensity will allow you to reach the same overall lift with a lower level of attrition.

Lift

List Price Increase

- Standard annual escalators
- Additional price increases confirmed via willingness-to-pay studies

Shift

Peer Set Increase

- Customers are grouped by customer segment and product ownership.
- Customers with products priced below the median of their peer set will have those products increased toward the median.
- A minimum spend per product can also be applied.

Differentiate

Behavioral Adjustments

- Customers may receive a lean-forward or lean-backward price adjustment based on their perceived price sensitivity.
- A number of behavioral indicators can be used to measure perceived price sensitivity (such as correlation with churn).

Figure 9.1 Price Increases Using Lift, Shift, and Differentiate

Planning Step 5: Control the Message

Timing is everything, particularly when raising prices. There are two kinds of timing to consider. The first concerns the notice given to an individual account before a fee increase, which we sometimes refer to as the "inner loop." In some cases, a business does not let customers know about a price change until it is directly upon them. If you have ever signed into software and been greeted with a screen you must click through letting you know that "our terms have changed," including the price, or if you have ever received a bill that lets you know that prices have increased and the new rate will apply to your next invoice, you have encountered a very short inner loop. Since tight inner loops do not give customers time to react, they tend to promote high retention. However, tight inner loops can generate resentment, as buyers may feel they are not being given a choice. Other businesses signal a price increase far in advance, giving their customers a year or more of notice. This approach may be a more respectful way to treat their bases, but it also gives buyers enough time to seriously consider alternatives, creating higher attrition. Unfortunately, customers often grumble just as loudly about a future price increase as they do about one that is imminent—and while a fee hike sometimes is accepted once it is water under the bridge, one that is in the far future can prolong the period of resentment. Therefore, many companies try to find a middle ground, where the inner loop is neither so long as to encourage buyers to shop for alternatives nor so short as to make them feel like prisoners.

The second time span, what we call the "outer loop," is the period from the start of the overall price migration to its end. Sometimes this period exactly overlaps with the inner loop, as when a streaming service raises prices; geographic differences aside, everyone's fee increase takes place simultaneously. In other contexts, a fee increase may necessarily be longer. If a company intends the fee increase to take place at renewal, and some customers are on multiyear agreements, the outer loop will be quite long. The length of the outer loop is dependent on strategy and often informed by a company's own resource limitations. If a business has a large number of customers to be migrated but chooses to devote a limited set of personnel to handle the communication, the outer loop can be pushed out significantly.

Note the interaction between the inner and outer loops. If you have a particularly chatty customer base, meaning that they tend to discuss your prices among themselves and have ways of comparing rates, you may need a shorter outer loop, because customers will learn of the planned price increase long before you communicate it to them directly. Rather than risking buyers getting the wrong idea, it's generally better to increase resourcing so that you can carry the news yourself. Now that you have taken the first two steps for a successful price increase (understanding context and creating a strategic price increase plan), it is time to move on the third and final step—executing it to perfection.

The Controlled-Narrative Axiom	In price increases, timing is everything. Communicate too late—or inconsistently—and the narrative will take on a life of its own, especially if your customers talk to each other. Control the message before it controls you.

Executing Your Price Increase Plan

With your five-step preparation complete, there's nothing to it, but to do it, right? Not so fast. Now that it's time to take the field, you have to know what you're going to say about the new pricing. Additionally, you must prepare to address customer objections and motivate your team for success.

Execution Step 1: Draft the Communication

Depending on the size of your customer base, you'll need to determine whether the fee increase can be communicated through one-on-one human interaction or must be handled via broader channels such as email, in-app messaging, or physical mail. While direct, personal communication offers warmth and a more empathetic touch, it is resource-intensive and presents logistical challenges at scale.

To strike the right balance, develop a clear communication plan that preserves scarce human resources by prioritizing where personal outreach is most impactful. Use two key factors to triage your approach: the strategic importance of the customer and the relative size of the price increase they will experience.

Next, keep in mind that price is always the counterpart of perceived value, meaning that all things equal, people care a lot about getting a benefit in exchange for the money they hand over. Therefore, take time and care to explain the value you are delivering to the customer. Address any fee increase only after you have clearly articulated the benefits. Some guidelines:

- *Making the customer aware of the value does not always mean an exhaustive discussion of everything you do for them.* If you go on and on about benefits that are not relevant to buyers or are not of interest to them, you may invoke "snow blindness"—a blizzard of words that obscures the point you are making. Limit the message to what you believe the customer will truly be impressed by. Look for factors that will surprise and delight.

- *Don't constrain yourself to the current set of features, if you have good ones planned for the near future.* Unless you've burned customers with promises that did not come true, they will generally give you credit for your near-term roadmap. Remember, when communicating roadmap, focus on benefits to the customer as opposed to specific features you are building.

- *Avoid the temptation to apologize for the fee increase.* You offer something of value to the buyer, and you are asking for a fair exchange.

- *Similarly, blaming the fee increase on poor business conditions may backfire.* You are expected to run your organization well. Cries of hardship generally win little sympathy. Instead, focus on the value you're delivering.

- *Don't think that you must call the new price a price increase.* The important point, after all, is not the change in the fee. What you are

185

trying to communicate is that the price and the value delivered are in good balance. Therefore, instead of saying "Your price will increase by 10% to $500," consider simply stating "Your new price will be $500."

Execution Step 2: Handle Objections

List the points of pushback you expect to receive from buyers. Be expansive, since the worst place for salespeople to encounter a novel objection is when they are actually in the room with a customer. If you can fully armor up your contact team before they actually speak with buyers, they will perform better and will be more likely to maintain their morale. For each objection, identify questions the salesperson can ask that will allow them either to expose the root cause of the customer's concern—which can then be directly addressed—or, as often happens, to reveal that there is no real substance to their issue (apart from annoyance that the price is going up).

The Value-Led Increase Axiom	If you must raise prices, anchor your pricing message in the value you deliver, not the increase itself. Then speak with conviction, not apology.

Execution Step 3: Coordinate the Working Team

If your specific business context allows, create a small team of trusted individuals to run a proof of concept. This pilot will help you to flesh out your set of customer objections and, by gauging the response, allow you to adjust your plan to ensure you will hit your goals. A side benefit of running a pilot is that it will increase the confidence of the working team. Sometimes individuals within your organization may be skeptical about a change, perhaps believing that the proposed price increase isn't achievable. That attitude can be changed if those people see a few wins roll in, particularly if each victory is recognized and celebrated. The wins can help cement a positive attitude among the team members, which drives its own upward momentum. Soon everyone wants to be on the tiger team, sharing in the glory.

When preparing for a full launch, start by mapping out the key tasks that need to be completed and identifying the resources required to execute each one effectively. Success isn't just about having the right individuals involved; it's about ensuring alignment and coordination across all relevant parts of the organization. A well-executed fee increase program touches multiple teams, and cross-functional collaboration is essential. For instance, if the price increase is being supported by messaging around upcoming product improvements, it's important to engage leaders from Product early so they fully understand the expectations being set. Similarly, while Marketing may not be directly responsible for executing the fee change, it plays a critical supporting role: reinforcing product value, framing messaging, and helping to justify the price increase through broader brand narratives.

Beyond the Basics: Insights, Tips, and Tricks to Optimize Your Price Increase Campaign

And finally, here are some advanced tips to ensure you get your full money's worth from the effort you put into raising your prices.

- *If customers keep their discounts, remind them of that fact.* In addition to the value you provide your customers through your product or service, they may be benefiting from a discount you've given them against your list price. Ensuring that they are reminded of that during the fee increase communication can go a long way, particularly when you explicitly state that the discounts reflect your appreciation for their loyalty.

- *Put your best salespeople on the tiger team.* Running a pilot before going wide with a fee increase requires a good sample of diverse customers, to ensure you're getting an unbiased read on how your overall buying population will react to the new price. It may seem logical to use a mix of salespeople as well, with the idea of determining how to make different skill levels successful in handling the price increase conversation. However, it's a much better idea to staff the tiger team with your very best salespeople. Doing this will ensure that you have your top talent solving any issues that may arise in terms of customer objections or value communication. Furthermore, salespeople who are seen as leaders will inspire those who are farther down the scale. Finally, this approach gives you the best chance of achieving early wins, which will help cement the perception that the fee increase is a successful one—and, as explained earlier, perception in this matter often turns into reality.

- *Consider setting upper limits on the fee increase.* Customers may agree to a fee increase in the short term, knowing that they have little ability to find a new option without more time. But that does not mean that they won't begin looking for an alternative if the price hike is sufficiently jarring. Latent customer attrition can be like an avalanche waiting to happen. For this reason, it may be beneficial to set an overall cap on the amount of fee increase you permit salespeople to seek on a given customer over a two- to three-year period.

Chapter Summary: How This Strategy Avoids the Single-Engine Trap

The Community Builder trap of giving more for less leads many leaders to avoid price increases out of fear—worrying that even small changes will damage loyalty. The strategies described in this chapter show how to raise prices the right way: with empathy, evidence, and a clear value story. Done well, pricing changes reinforce the strength of your offering and signal continued investment and quality. They deepen revenue from existing customers (wallet share) without losing the trust that drives retention and advocacy (market share). Profitable Growth Architects don't avoid asking for more; they ask the right way.

CEO Questions

- Have you raised fees in recent years? If not, why not?

- Do you have a clear plan for a successful price increase? Do you plan to raise price for existing and new customers?

- Have you thought through all the objectives you have for your price increase, and are you able to put them in priority order?

- Are you clear on the set of customers for whom you cannot raise prices (e.g., due to legal obligations or long-standing relationships), and have you taken steps to make this "no-fly" population as small as possible?

- Are you clear on the KPIs to be tracked? What is your level of confidence in the contingencies to be adopted should the fee increase track lower than—or higher than—its original goals?

- Have you gotten your organization comfortable with the idea that there may be some attrition from a fee increase and that this is an acceptable trade-off?

Chapter 10

Acing Big Deals: Mastering Negotiations and Handling Objections

Picture yourself in the midst of a high-stakes negotiation with a prospective client. After weeks—or even months—of discussions, the moment of truth has arrived. You've put in the work: Your product or service appears to align seamlessly with the client's needs, and you've crafted a proposal you believe is compelling. The room is charged with anticipation, and the outcome of a pivotal deal hangs in the balance.

But as the conversation unfolds, obstacles emerge. The client raises objections: They challenge your pricing, question the implementation timeline, and bring up comparisons to competitor offerings. What started as a promising discussion now feels uncertain. Your confidence begins to waver as the client grows increasingly insistent, pushing for a lower price and pressing you to match or beat competitors' rates. The client tests the limits of your strategy, potentially undermining the value you've worked so hard to convey. Meanwhile, the weight of internal expectations looms large—closing this deal feels more critical than ever. The concept of value-based pricing, once your guiding principle, now seems fragile and elusive.

In moments like these, the stakes are high. How do you preserve your pricing integrity while addressing objections effectively? How do you strike a balance between offering competitive terms and maintaining profitability?

Success in this area requires more than a deep understanding of your product or service; it demands the ability to confidently communicate its value, justify the price, handle objections with composure, and guide the conversation toward a mutually beneficial outcome.

This chapter explores the nuances of negotiation, offering insights and strategies to enhance pricing performance along with behavioral principles you can use to negotiate skillfully and manage objections effectively.

The Hold-the-Line Axiom	Holding the line on price while addressing objections is more than a negotiation tactic; it's the key to capturing value.

Bringing a Method to the Madness: A Complete Commercial Transformation for a Global SaaS Player

Optimizing pricing and packaging can drive significant impact, but profitable growth often hinges on effective sales execution, especially in the B2B arena. Ultimately a negotiation comes down to a conversation, and without the ability to confidently defend your value and price, you risk conceding too much. Based on our experience with hundreds of projects training sales teams and developing tools to maximize deal value, we've consistently found that well-equipped sales teams are critical to extracting greater value from negotiations. How can you train your sales teams to excel in negotiations? Let's explore this with a practical example.

We worked with a global SaaS company on a complete overhaul of its commercial excellence strategy. This SaaS player had successfully cracked some major enterprise accounts and was poised for global expansion. It had a strong, hands-on leadership team and an ambitious sales force ready to scale worldwide. However, it faced a simple yet critical problem: It had never developed a value-selling strategy to sustain growth during the scale-up phase. Pricing and negotiations were handled on an ad hoc basis, which severely hurt the company's profitability. It needed a way to stop leaving money on the table in every deal and ensure their growth was both scalable and profitable.

To begin our work, we assessed the client's status quo and discovered a number of issues that needed addressing. A few of them were:

- *Trying to sell just one thing.* The sales team was too used to offering all customers the company's single best package; in fact, close to 90% of the deals the team closed were for their company's "best" Enterprise package, regardless of customer needs. The problem was that the sales team was eroding the value of the package by giving a lot more for a lot less. Putting just one single offer in front of clients meant that all negotiations came down to price, and there was no discussion about trade-offs on features and benefits across offers. Salespeople also were creating massive downstream problems, since, if you sell everything for a discounted price, you don't have anything to upsell on renewal.

- *Discounting all over the place.* To understand the client's discounting practices, we designed a simple analysis in which we mapped different customer sizes to the amount of discount provided. (See Figure 10.1.) The scatter plot we created showed no discernible discounting logic, with customers of the same size being offered all sorts of different prices. When asked to explain, salespeople gave us seemingly precise reasons to justify their pricing of different deals, but there was no overarching logic behind the seemingly random variations. This problem is a familiar one—when salespeople are given inadequate pricing guidance, they always come up with a reason to justify a poorly-priced deal.

Acing Big Deals: Mastering Negotiations and Handling Objections

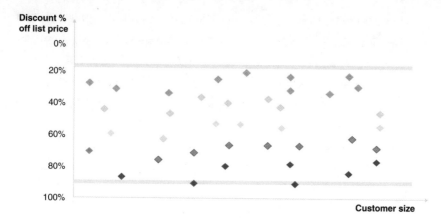

Figure 10.1 Customer Size versus Price Discount Offered

- *Failing to account for deal-specific situations.* As we analyzed the deals made by the client's sales force, we found that salespeople typically resorted to presenting customers with very similar price quotations, regardless of the type of customer they were selling to, the amount of competition vying for the same deal, the payment terms offered by the customer, and even the contract length. In a well-oiled system, salespeople have differentiated prices for each deal-specific situation.

To address these challenges, we introduced a suite of methods and tools designed to standardize discounting practices, reduce price erosion, and provide the sales team with deal-specific pricing guidance. The team members were trained to focus customer conversations on the value of their product rather than just its price. These improvements in the team's negotiation effectiveness ultimately led to our client increasing its annual recurring revenue by 30% within just six months. The sales force was able to sell *faster* (increase sales velocity), *better* (increase win rate), and *more* (get larger deals).

In the sections to come, we detail how we transformed our client's sales strategy and provide actionable insights to help you achieve similar success in your own organization.

Turbocharging Your Negotiations: What Best-in-Class Companies Do

Without well-crafted and formalized negotiation strategy and policies, salespeople are often left to fend for themselves in conversations with their clients. When every salesperson operates as they see fit, many will choose to discount as much as they can; only a handful will do their best to defend the value of their products.

To avoid this problem and equip your sales team to ace negotiations, you must be able to answer these five questions convincingly:

1. How do we prepare and employ value defense?
2. How do we come up with "the price" for a deal?
3. How do we quote price and provide discounts (if any)?
4. Which negotiation tactics should we use?
5. How can we best handle customer objections?

Let's explore the best ways to answer each of those five questions.

Question #1: How Do We Prepare and Employ Value Defense?

In the world of negotiation, achieving excellence means mastering the balance between defending value and making strategic concessions. Doing so involves understanding the technical aspects of negotiation and the psychological tactics that can influence outcomes.

The art of value defense is a key component of such negotiation excellence. It ensures that the worth of your offering is recognized and appreciated, solidifying your ability to charge. Value defense involves clearly communicating the unique benefits of your product or service and ensuring that discounts or concessions do not undermine its perceived value. Practicing value defense requires a deep understanding of your offering and the ability to effectively convey its benefits to your counterpart.

In addition to getting great at the three steps to mastering value communication and messaging (the value blueprint) as outlined in Chapter 6, value defense requires you *to master the ability to create customer needs, foster strong customer buy-in, and effectively communicate the return on investment (ROI) of your offering*. Let's examine these components of value defense one by one.

Don't Just Address Your Customer's Needs; Create Them

Any reasonable sales process involves a process of needs discovery, and you'll likely have given your sales reps a checklist of questions to ask that allow you to tailor an offer to meet the needs of your customers. Although this is a great start, most sales reps often miss the point of the needs discovery process entirely. It's not just about discovering the prospect's needs; it's also about *educating the prospect* about needs they didn't even realize they had.

Before your sales reps dive into their long list of questions, have them ask prospects about the major pain points they face across the business (focusing on the pain points that are relevant to your product, of course). An educated buyer is likely equipped with a list of pain points that will help to get the ball rolling. If buyers aren't aware of their pain points, however, this is your chance to *create* a need.

For example, the SaaS client we discussed earlier made it easy for its customers to measure the ROI of each marketing campaign on a real-time basis. To maximize the perceived value of this offering, we trained the client's sales team to educate prospects and "create the need." When the sales team met with prospects, the line of questioning went this way:

- "How much transparency do you have into the performance of your marketing campaigns and customer engagement activities today?"

- "Oh, I see. So, you do have great transparency, that's great. May I ask, how easy is it for you to calculate the ROI of your campaigns? Is your marketing team able to do this themselves, or are they reliant on your data science/engineering teams?"

- "I understand. So, your marketing team sends campaign data to your data science team weekly, and they produce a report that informs their subsequent initiatives. Wouldn't it be great if your marketing team could view campaign effectiveness results in real time and make changes on the fly?"

- "What would the extra time saved through a real-time solution mean to you? What value could you unlock with the time savings?"

Suddenly buyers are reflecting on inefficiencies that weren't top of mind initially and roughly estimating the costs associated with them. This mindset makes the next phase of the sales conversation much smoother, as buyers now understand the product's value and its potential impact. Better still, buyers feel as if they arrived at this realization on their own.

As you implement such tactics in your own organization, make sure that your sales reps are also able to highlight the *implications* of a client's failure to act. In the example we just discussed, this might involve saying "You know, one of the biggest players in your industry uses our product, and they were a lot like you. Within six months post-implementation, we found that they were saving over $1 million a month by eliminating their inefficient marketing activities more quickly than ever."

By creating a need, you've sold buyers on the value of your product (without having to do much traditional selling), you've made the value of your product highly specific to their situation, and you've made it incredibly difficult for them to walk away without giving you a shot at a sale. They're now dreaming wistfully about the cost savings you've highlighted, and you're one giant step closer to closing.

The Created-Need Axiom	Great sales teams don't just uncover needs; they create them. Creating need is how you elevate perceived value and command premium outcomes.

Foster Strong Customer Buy-in

Developing customer commitments during a sales pitch is critical to ensure great value defense. Doing so involves engaging customers in a dialogue where they verbally affirm the value of your product or service. The verbalization not only reinforces their interest but also helps solidify their commitment to the purchase. Now let's look at a few examples of how you can implement this tactic in practice.

Let's assume you're conducting a product demo in which you highlight the benefits of a product in a way that aligns with the needs of prospects. To foster customer buy-in, strategically pause to ask customers questions that elicit positive responses and affirmations. For instance, after demonstrating a feature, you might say, "I recall you mentioning that you had a very basic marketing effectiveness dashboard at the moment. Now that you've seen ours, what do you think?" If they respond positively, follow up with "Awesome, I'm glad to hear it. What specifically did you like about the demonstration?" This question encourages them to articulate the specific benefits they see, reinforcing their perception of value.

As the conversation progresses, continue to build on their affirmations. For example, if they mention that the user interface is intuitive and the usage alerts are helpful for managing costs, acknowledge their points: "As you said, our customers often say that the user interface is easy to use, and the usage alerts are helpful in managing costs." This comment not only shows that you're listening but also reinforces the positive aspects they've highlighted.

Where possible, compare your product to their current solution to further emphasize the value: "Now that you've seen our entire dashboard demo, how would you rate the ease of use against your current dashboard?" When they respond "I like it better!," you can reinforce their positive experience: "I'm glad that our dashboard checked all the boxes we'd previously discussed. I'm happy to walk you through some of our other features, or alternatively we can pivot the discussion to what I can offer you." This smooth transition from demonstration to discussion about the offer leverages customers' verbal commitments to pave the way for closing the deal.

In summary, fostering strong customer buy-in involves:

- Asking targeted questions that encourage positive affirmations and create a sense of ownership and commitment.
- Reinforcing customer responses to highlight the value they see.
- Comparing your product to the current solution to emphasize improvements.

Effectively Communicate the ROI of Your Offering

A critical component of value defense is effectively communicating the ROI of your offering. Doing so requires developing a credible model that clearly demonstrates the economic value your solution delivers, making the purchase decision an obvious choice for customers. To achieve such a model, it's essential to use reliable assumptions; to believe the ROI calculations, customers must trust the inputs.

Start by asking the right questions during discussions to gather data that informs these assumptions, effectively validating them in advance. For example, in the case of the SaaS company mentioned earlier, a fundamental assumption for the ROI model was the time and money saved by transitioning from manual processes to a real-time platform. By engaging the customer during the needs discovery phase and validating potential savings, our client established credible inputs for the model. Validating assumptions up front not only ensures trust but also creates a consistency trap—once customers agree to the assumptions, it becomes harder for them to argue against the model later. Without this step, customers may pick apart the model during negotiations, even if they fundamentally believe in its accuracy, purely as a tactic to lower your price.

A well-rounded ROI model should also account for opportunity costs. Consider what customers could achieve with the time and resources saved by using your product. For instance, if your solution saves two weeks of work, what is the financial value of the initiatives customers could pursue with that time? Additionally, the model should include tangible ROI, such as income generated by new initiatives enabled by your product. For example, if the AI feature in an SaaS platform recommends a marketing campaign a customer hadn't considered, the potential revenue from the campaign should be factored into the ROI.

To summarize, the components of a comprehensive ROI model are:

- *Savings.* Tangible reductions in time, headcount, materials, or resources
- *Opportunity cost.* The value of additional tasks or initiatives made possible by resources freed up through your solution
- *Incremental value.* Measurable improvements in metrics like conversion rates, engagement, or retention, directly tied to deploying your solution

The foundation of a successful ROI model lies in the data-gathering process. By asking insightful questions early, you can shape assumptions that resonate with customers. Once you've developed a believable model, guide customers through the potential value they can achieve by adopting your solution. Help them build a compelling business case that makes the ROI undeniable. The ultimate goal is to position your offering in a way that simplifies the decision-making process. After all, who wouldn't pay $1 to make $10?

The ROI Co-Creation Axiom	When customers agree to the inputs, they're less likely to argue with the output. Early assumption validation turns your ROI model into a closing tool, not a debate.

Question #2: How Do We Come Up with "the Price" for a Deal?

There are three price points that you need to keep in mind when negotiating a specific deal. The first is the *start price* or the going-in offer that you plan to make to begin the negotiations conversation. The next is the *target price* that you wish to achieve after the negotiations. The third is the *walkaway price*, which is the minimum price you can accept; anything lower is nonnegotiable.

These three price points define the *price range* for every deal. It's important to arrive at a price range for every deal before you begin negotiating. Doing so allows you to sound reasonable from the get-go (with a good start price), to aspire for more (more than the target price), and to avoid contaminating your own pricing (by knowing when to walk away).

But how do you come up with deal-specific pricing range guidance for your sales team? A highly effective approach is to use what we call the "target pricing methodology," which enables a company to dynamically define deal-specific pricing guidance. Let's explore the three steps needed to get this done.

Step 1: Define Pricing Drivers

No two deals are the same. Each is shaped by a unique combination of factors that define the deal. These factors, specific to the transaction, are

Acing Big Deals: Mastering Negotiations and Handling Objections

referred to as "pricing drivers" when they influence what you charge the customer. For instance, the client's industry sector may be a deal-specific factor. You might categorize deals as, for example, "negotiating with a retail client" or "negotiating with a hospitality client." If you observe that retail clients consistently pay more due to the added value your product offers them, then the industry sector becomes a pricing driver.

Each pricing driver can have different levels, representing various possible scenarios. For example, if you sell to clients in four sectors—hospitality, retail, travel, and industrial—then the industry sector pricing driver has four levels corresponding to these sectors.

To begin applying the target pricing methodology, identify three to five key pricing drivers that could impact your pricing decisions for deals. Some typical examples include:

- *Industry sector.* The sector in which your client operates. Certain industries might be willing to pay more than others because of the value your product provides.

- *Deal size.* Larger deals may qualify for volume discounts.

- *Billing frequency.* Offering better pricing for annual billing as opposed to monthly, as it increases customer retention and lifetime value.

- *Strategic value of the client.* Providing preferential pricing for clients identified as strategically important. Be clear and objective about what "strategic" means to avoid overusing this classification.

- *Term length.* Offering more favorable pricing for clients willing to commit to longer contract terms (e.g., a 24-month contract versus a 12-month contract).

- *Competitive intensity.* Offering competitive pricing when facing strong competition.

Next, define the levels for each pricing driver. Note that some of the drivers (e.g., competitive intensity) might need to be represented using subjective levels (e.g., high, medium, low), while other drivers (e.g., billing frequency) might have more concrete levels (e.g., 6 months, 12 months, and 24 months). It's essential to define clear criteria for subjective factors like low, medium, and high. Doing so will ensure that your sales team can apply the levels consistently, eliminating any ambiguity.

Step 2: Establish Discount Levels

In this step, you'll determine the appropriate discount for each level of the identified pricing drivers. For certain factors, you can leverage historical data to quantify the necessary discount. For example, a regression analysis might reveal the premium your sales team can achieve for monthly versus annual billing cycles. For other drivers, the decision may rely on management's judgment and strategic priorities. For instance, based on your strategic goals and financial constraints, you might determine that offering a 5% discount to customers committing to a 24-month contract instead of a 12-month contract aligns with your objectives.

Of course, you can also conduct willingness-to-pay studies (as described in our book *Monetizing Innovation*) and analyze the results across different segments—for example, retail versus hospitality clients—to determine the optimal discount levels. Regardless of the method you use to establish discount factors for each pricing driver, the key is to implement a systematic framework. Doing so provides clear, consistent guidance for your sales team while also allowing for ongoing adjustments, ensuring you can refine the factors later if you find that pricing adjustments could improve profitability.

Step 3: Calculate target price and price range. In this step, you will apply the discount levels assigned to each pricing driver and aggregate the relevant discounts or markups for a specific deal. By summing these values, you can determine the target price for that particular transaction. Note that it's also important to establish a *reference price* from which discounts for various pricing drivers will be applied. When analyzing past deals, the 95th percentile value is often used as the reference point, excluding any outliers and providing a solid foundation for developing target prices.

Acing Big Deals: Mastering Negotiations and Handling Objections

Figure 10.2 illustrates this process for a sample deal. In this example, based on the deal-specific parameters, the target price should be a 14% discount from the reference price.

Next, it's important to translate the target price into a price range for use in negotiation. Recall that, to do this, you'll need to define three key prices: the start price, the target price, and the walkaway price. The methodology outlined earlier helps you establish the target price. The start price for the negotiation should be set 30% to 40% higher than the target price. The objective during the negotiation is to aim for the highest possible price— ideally as close to the start price as possible—while still accepting the target price as an acceptable outcome.

If a customer pushes for additional discounts beyond the target price, an internal escalation process should be in place before Sales considers further concessions. Historical deal data can help you determine the walkaway price by identifying the lowest price previously accepted that was deemed minimally acceptable.

Deal-specific target discount

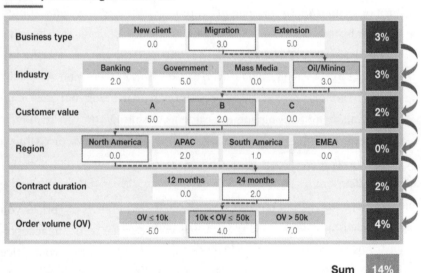

Figure 10.2 Deal-Specific Pricing

As you can see, the process of target pricing is straightforward: Identify your pricing drivers; establish discount levels for each; and use the deal-specific factors to calculate a target price for each transaction and then extrapolate that target price to a negotiation range. Experience has shown that training your sales team on this clear, intuitive framework not only eases their concerns about pricing but also enables them to focus on having value-driven discussions with clients rather than worrying about what price to quote and how the pricing was determined.

However, before you rush to implement target pricing in your own company, do consider these factors:

- *The risk of underselling based on historical precedents.* If it turns out that your historical pricing has always been too low, your historic best practices are meaningless. In this case, you cannot rely on actual transaction data. Then the pricing driver discounts will need to be defined either by management's expert judgment (based primarily on targets) or by external willingness-to-pay studies. If you rely on expert judgment, start by introducing a moderate markup over and above your historical best outcomes, test whether sales teams are able to hit these new prices, and then adjust them upward from there. Once you get a target pricing guidance system in place, you can always tweak the parameters based on sales performance. It is far more important to get the system in place as opposed to obsessing over getting it perfect from the get-go.

- *Best and worst practices evolve constantly.* As target pricing works its magic in your sales organization, you should see improvements in your pricing within the first three to six months. As the prices you attain shift upward, so should what you consider to be an acceptable price for the target. Therefore, make sure to revisit your price recommendations and pricing driver discount factors every six to 12 months.

Acing Big Deals: Mastering Negotiations and Handling Objections

The Target Pricing Axiom	The best negotiators never wing it. They use target pricing—a predefined range with a start price, a target price, and a walkaway price—to stay grounded and maximize value.

Question #3: How Do We Quote Price and Provide Discounts (If Any)?

Now that you have a way to come up with the pricing for a deal, how should you go about providing discounts (if any) while negotiating?

Always begin discussions at the starting price; avoid jumping straight to the target price you've determined. When quoting a price, there are three key factors to consider: *gives and gets, tapering concessions,* and *framing your price in relation to the value provided.* Let's briefly examine each of these concepts.

Gives and Gets

As outlined in detail in Chapter 7, mastering the art of making concessions while securing something in return is critical. Doing so not only ensures economic balance but also enhances your credibility in negotiations. To succeed, you need a well-defined concession matrix and a clear list of "gives" and "gets" to aim for. As highlighted in Chapter 7, when making concessions, prioritize non-price-related items first (e.g., extending payment terms from 30 to 45 days or offering value-added services) while maintaining the starting price. If a price concession is unavoidable, ensure that any discounts from the start price follow a structured approach of tapering your concessions.

Tapering Concessions

The principle behind tapering concessions is to offer progressively smaller concessions as negotiations advance. This method signals to buyers that you are approaching your lowest acceptable (walkaway) price and encourages them to conclude the negotiation. For instance, you might start with a 10% concession, followed by 5%, then 2.5%. This pattern signals that you are offering the best you can and that you are running out of room for further negotiation. By contrast, starting with 2.5%, then moving to 5%, and finally offering 10% would suggest to customers that they can keep pushing for more discounts, undermining your position.

Framing price in relation to value. Positioning the price relative to the value delivered helps contextualize the cost for customers and strengthens their internal business case. For example, in the case of the SaaS company we discussed, let's say the solution is expected to deliver a $10 million ROI. When asked for price, rather than saying "Our software will cost you $1 million," you can simply say "Based on a $10 million ROI, your investment in us would provide a 10× return."

The concept of framing price becomes even much more important if your pricing model is based on outcomes. For example, take the case of a med-tech company that makes lab equipment and software for hospitals and charges for the software based on the number of lab reports that it helps to generate. If the hospital on average is expected to have 1 million reports in a year, saying "Your price is $1 million" is less palatable than "We charge $1 for every report that we help you generate." The latter approach not only makes the price seem more acceptable but also allows customers to compare it more easily to alternatives, such as hiring manual labor.

Question #4: Which Negotiation Tactics Should We Use?

Although numerous books have been dedicated to the softer skills of negotiation, we believe that mastering just a *few key tactics* is sufficient to maximize the outcome of most negotiations.

First, you need to make sure you master the tactics already mentioned in the chapter, including the give and the get, tapering concessions, and framing price in relation to value. Next we discuss three additional tactics that are particularly useful: anchoring, the consistency trap, and forced trade-offs.

Acing Big Deals: Mastering Negotiations and Handling Objections

Anchoring

Anchoring occurs when the seller (yourself or your sales team) sets a higher reference point that influences subsequent offers, shifting the negotiation in the seller's favor. The principle is simple: If you aim high, you'll end up higher; if you aim low, you'll only go lower. Anchoring is especially effective in the early stages of negotiation as it shapes the buyer's perception of what is achievable right from the start.

For example, for the SaaS company, we trained sales teams to say something like "Companies like yours have typically paid us in the low seven figures, with a typical ROI of at least 10×" when asked about pricing early in the conversation. Such a comment not only sets a high reference point but also acts as a lead qualification tool; if a prospect reacts negatively to your pricing, it's better to know early on, allowing you to focus on more promising opportunities. In sales, time management is crucial. Knowing when to invest your efforts and when to move on is key, and early lead qualification through anchoring can save valuable time and resources.

Consistency Trap

A consistency trap is a negotiation technique in which the seller gets the buyer to agree to certain norms, principles, or priorities early in the conversation, which can then be leveraged later when presenting an offer. The trap works because individuals generally want to avoid appearing inconsistent and self-contradictory, which means they usually will adjust their current position to align with their previous statements. During initial discussions, such as the needs discovery phase, a buyer typically is not in a negotiation mindset and is more likely to agree to norms or principles.

For instance, a seller of an industrial part with the highest verifiable reliability rating uses this strategy to negotiate better outcomes. The needs discovery conversation might begin with questions like "Is minimizing downtime your main goal?" or "How much loss would you face if the line was down?" Buyers often provide candid answers, emphasizing the importance of minimizing costly downtimes and even quantifying the potential losses. Later in the negotiation, the seller can say, "Since we agreed that minimizing downtime is your primary goal and a production stoppage would lead to significant losses, our solution, while more expensive than alternatives, is the most reliable on the market. It is designed to ensure your lines run smoothly, eliminating the risk of costly downtime, which far outweighs any upfront savings you might get by choosing less reliable options from our competitors." This appeal to consistency creates a psychological advantage, making buyers less likely to resist the price premium.

Similarly, in the SaaS company example, we trained the sales teams to ask up-front questions that establish consistency and guide customers toward higher-value packages later in the negotiation. For example, if a customer agrees early on that "24/7 premium support is critical," the salesperson can later recommend a more expensive package by saying "Based on what we agreed earlier, that 24/7 support is essential, we recommend the advanced package." This strategy reinforces consistency, encouraging buyers to align their decisions with their earlier statements and often leading them to choose a premium option that also would be better suited for them based on their needs.

Forced Trade-offs

When a salesperson presents only one offer, the customer often faces two issues: The product may not fully resonate due to unwanted features, or the negotiation becomes solely about price. By offering multiple options to force trade-offs—say through a Good-Better-Best tiered packaging structure—you achieve two key objectives:

1. *You increase the likelihood of aligning with the customer's needs and preferences.* Price-sensitive customers are drawn to the entry-level offer, while quality-conscious customers naturally gravitate toward the premium package. For those who tend to avoid extremes, trade-offs encourage them to choose the middle option, striking a balance between cost and features.

2. *You shift the conversation from price to value.* For example, if a customer expresses interest in the Better package but raises budget concerns, the salesperson can respond with "What specifically appeals to you in the package, and how do you plan to use the package?" Such a response reframes the dialogue around the value and utility of the Better package rather than focusing on the cost.

There are also important psychological reasons behind the effectiveness of forcing trade-offs. Specifically, when customers are given choices and control over what they pick, they feel more invested in the decision, increasing the likelihood of long-term satisfaction and retention.

In the SaaS company case, before the sales transformation we did for them, the sales team typically asked for a budget and then tailored their offer to that figure. If a customer said they had a $100,000 budget, the salesperson would return with a $100,000 offer, which would often be negotiated down to $60,000. To change this dynamic, we introduced a simple technique: If the customer mentioned a $100,000 budget, the salesperson would present three options and force trade-offs: $100,000, $150,000, and $200,000. Although there was still an option that met the budget, if the salesperson did a good job on value defense, created the need for the features in the middle package, and effectively communicated the value, customers often ended up choosing the second option. This strategy allowed the salesperson to hold firm and close deals at $125,000 (providing a $25,000 discount from the $150,000 price but still getting an upside of $25,000 compared to the original stated budget).

Note that by offering three packages, the sales team also set clear boundaries around discount expectations, making the $125,000 option appear as a reasonable, meet-in-the-middle compromise between the $100,000 and $150,000 price points. This simple yet effective approach led to significant increases in annual recurring revenue, more than doubling deal sizes from $60,000 to $125,000 in many cases.

The Forced Trade-offs Axiom	Smart sales teams use multiple options (e.g., good/better/best packages) to force trade-offs, shifting the conversation from price to value and closing at higher price points.

Question #5: How Can We Best Handle Customer Objections?

What about when the conversation gets more challenging? How do you address customer objections in an effective way that makes you and your product shine? To round out our discussion on negotiations, let's look at what an ideal objection-handling framework looks like.

Objection handling is about turning concerns into confidence. Objections are not roadblocks but should be treated as opportunities to understand the buyer's perspective and provide further clarification. Mastering objection handling means having a framework to address concerns calmly and constructively, ultimately reinforcing the value of your product or service.

Objections typically arise from insufficient information, misunderstandings, or legitimate concerns. Your objective should be not only to address the specific objection but also to build trust and credibility with customers in the process. A robust framework for objection handling involves three main steps: *clarifying the objection, overcoming with value,* and *conceding wisely*. Let's dive in.

Step 1: Clarifying the Objection

When faced with an objection, the first step is to ask clarifying questions to understand the root of the concern. Hidden under the guise of a simple statement may lie multiple issues that need addressing, which means you can't afford to take a blanket approach to dealing with objections. Making the discussion more precise by asking the right clarifying questions shows customers that you are attentive to and considerate of their needs.

Acing Big Deals: Mastering Negotiations and Handling Objections

Let's look at what this could mean in the context of a very common objection: "Your product is just too expensive!" Here are some sample clarifying questions:

- "What are you comparing this price to that makes it seem expensive?" (This question checks if buyers have an existing offer at a lower price from a competitor.)

- "Are you referring to specific elements of the offer that are expensive, or are you referring to the package as a whole?" (If buyers mention specific elements, it's easier for you to have discussions based on their value without focusing exclusively on the overall price.)

- "What budget range were you expecting?" (Maybe they've had a budget in their heads all along but haven't communicated their ceiling yet.)

Step 2: Overcome with Value

Once the objection is clarified, provide a well-thought-out response that addresses the concern directly but returns the emphasis to the value of your product. Steer clear of any price-related conversations as a knee-jerk reaction to being put under pressure.

Let's look at what this might look like for the same "too expensive" objection. The next response addresses the concern but emphasizes value:

"I recall from our previous discussion that you had expressed a need for a dedicated customer success manager and our 24×7 capabilities—these fall under our Premium services offering. I'd be more than happy to match your price expectations and offer you our Core services. However, I just want to point out that the Core services package gives you only 8×5 support instead of 24×7, and you won't have a dedicated customer success manager."

In this example, you had identified that customers thought that the price was too expensive. The response demonstrates the *value* that they would be giving up if they decided to opt for an alternative package that met their budget. It is at this point where all your previous sales conversations can work together harmoniously. If you previously created a need for your Premium services offering and gained verbal commitments about the importance of these benefits and the ROI provided, you can start enforcing those consistency traps, selling on value, and forcing the right trade-offs.

Step 3: Conceding Wisely

In some situations, the value communication trade-off doesn't work, and you're forced to focus on price. At this stage, you should have exhausted all your arguments that aim at forcing customers to make value-based trade-offs. Don't be afraid to let customers sit with the offer for a while. If push comes to shove, never hesitate to protect your price integrity by walking away.

The Objection Opportunity Axiom	Handled well, objections aren't obstacles; they're opportunities to build trust through clarity, value, and wise concessions.

Beyond the Basics: Insights, Tips, and Tricks to Optimize Your Negotiation Strategies

Now you know how to address the five questions you need to answer to turbocharge your negotiations. To conclude this chapter, we leave you with some advanced tips and tricks to get the most out of your negotiation strategies.

- *Sales incentives*. It is critical to provide the right incentives and tools to steer the behavior of your sales team without adding bureaucracy and slowing down business decisions. Here are a few big insights that we have gathered from our work in setting sales incentives.

  o Revenue-based commission schemes are most common in many industries, but they don't provide sufficient incentive for salespeople to push for better-quality revenues (price increases versus cross-sell). To drive better outcomes, incentive plans should distinguish between different types of revenue and reward quality accordingly.

  o As discussed earlier, establishing a deal-specific price range (start, target, and walkaway) is critical. Sales should be incentivized to achieve prices above the target, with stronger rewards the closer they stay to the start price.

  o To further enhance your incentive system and motivate your team, consider incorporating gamification elements, such as contests, challenges, or leaderboards. The payouts of these components should never overshadow the primary incentive plan, but, when used correctly, these elements foster healthy competition and ambition among employees. You can also introduce time-limited boost factors for specific achievements to incentivize extra effort.

  o Don't overdo incentives. It's important to ensure incentive structures do not unintentionally encourage undesirable behavior. We see many cases where sales teams have sold products that customers never use, purely to game the system for higher incentives. Although these might look like good deals on paper, customers are most likely to churn, and the sales team has created a downstream problem. A well-designed incentive plan should guide salespeople toward the right behaviors, ensuring they secure deals that are well suited for customers (and your company) while leaving room for future expansion. Incentives ultimately should align sales behavior with long-term business objectives, driving both market share and wallet share.

- *Peer pricing.* Peer pricing is a way to turbocharge target pricing. The basic idea is that you layer in what the best sales peers have been able to achieve for similar deals as an additional guidance/cue for sales. Providing that extra bit of information on how successful peers have sold similar deals gives sales team members the extra confidence to ask for the deserved price—and strive to be the best pricing champions.

- *Negotiating with procurement.* When dealing with procurement teams, keep in mind that the people on the other side are incentivized to show that they got a discount. Consider bumping up the start price of negotiations in such cases so that you can showcase an even bigger discount and make it a win for procurement. In addition, always respond to requests for proposals with multiple offer options so that you can force trade-offs during procurement negotiations.

- *Escalations and approvals.* It's common for companies to implement escalation rules for sales that fall below the target price, with varying levels of approval required for larger discounts, often escalating to senior leadership. However, if your organization follows this model, we recommend conducting a simple analysis: Review how many deals go through the escalation process, how many are approved or rejected, and how the final approved price compares to the salesperson's initial request. We often see that companies invest significant time and effort in "approving" price requests, and the final approved price is identical to the initial ask. If this describes your process, it's likely functioning as little more than a glorified rubber stamp. A healthy approval process should result in a reasonable number of rejections and instances where the approved price is higher than the initial ask. Such a system ensures that the process is adding value, enforcing discipline, and encouraging sales teams to aim for better pricing outcomes.

Acing Big Deals: Mastering Negotiations and Handling Objections

Chapter Summary: How This Strategy Avoids the Single-Engine Trap

Many founders fall into the Disruptor trap of chasing customers at any cost—offering deep discounts, overcustomizing deals, or conceding too much just to land a logo. The strategies described in this chapter focus on helping leaders price large deals fairly, ensuring you're not undervaluing your offering or eroding your business model just to close. This is about acing big wins on the right terms. By negotiating with clarity and confidence, you broaden your reach (market share) while capturing full, fair value in return (wallet share). Profitable Growth Architects don't just win big deals; they win them on strong terms.

CEO Questions

- Do you have a good understanding of the best and worst negotiation practices in your sales organization? Have often do you perform deal postmortems to identify best practices and areas of opportunities? Do you listen in to any sales calls? How often?

- Do you provide deal-specific pricing guidance to sales? If not, why not?

- Are your sales teams able to effectively create needs when talking with customers, or are they too reliant on standard needs discovery questionnaires?

- Is your sales team able to communicate effectively the ROI provided by the investment in your product or service?

- Do you have a structured process for providing discounts? If you give discounts, what do you get back? Do you have a list of gives and gets that your team employs?

- Do your teams leverage anchoring, and do they force trade-offs systematically across all sales conversations?

- Are your sales teams equipped with a standard set of objections and effective means to address them?

Stopping Churn Before It Starts: The Big Missed Opportunity

W hen you stop a customer from departing, that's one fewer customer that must be acquired. The revenue attached to that customer is money you won't have to find elsewhere to pay your employees, cover fixed costs, and meet your other obligations. And a dollar lost through churn exactly offsets a dollar won in the marketplace; it sets you back from meeting your targets just as a lost sale would.

Everyone understands this in principle. It's roughly the same as "a dollar saved is a dollar earned." Yet even well-run companies do not give churn the attention—or the systematic approach—that they give to sales and marketing efforts. Companies that closely track bookings sometimes have only a vague idea about attrition. Executives think long and hard about how to compensate and motivate sales but have few good benchmarks for the team on the front lines against lost revenue. Sometimes that team doesn't even have a name.

This lack of focus should be a flashing red light. Studies show that existing customers, particularly longer-tenured ones, are worth more than new customers. They contribute far more to profits and are much more likely to provide a market for a company's new products. Stopping these valuable customers from walking out the door is, dollar for dollar, almost certainly more important to your business than attracting new ones.

Furthermore, companies with high churn are much more likely to be punished during economic downturns and other external shocks because they depend on new customers for growth. During financial uncertainty, customers tend to cling to the companies they know and trust, making new acquisition more challenging.[1] The converse is also true. If you have low churn—if *you* are the brand they know and trust—it will be harder for competitors to win customers away. Low churn makes it easier to weather economic storms.

Many companies say that they have a retention strategy, when in reality they merely intercept customers who are trying to cancel. That's just waiting for churn to happen. In this chapter, we'll show you exactly when and how to fight the problem, with an emphasis on attacking churn *before* it happens. Finally, we will teach you the single best trick for improving customer retention.

What's Not for Dinner: Churn at a "Meal in a Bag" Company

Blue Apron, one of the first meal kit delivery companies, rocketed to a $2 billion valuation on its initial public offering. It had around a million subscribers signed up to receive ingredients and recipes for weekly meals in their homes. Within two years, however, the company collapsed; its stock price tumbling a shocking 95%. Ultimately, the company was sold to Wonder Group for a mere $103 million. How could a company like this tumble and never recover?

Blue Apron's strategy focused on new customer acquisition instead of retention. Once generous introductory offers expired, more than 70% of customers canceled their subscriptions. The math worked when the cost of acquisition was a low $100, but as competitors like Hello Fresh and Plated entered the market, that number jumped from $150 to $400. With its economics flipped, Blue Apron's fall became inevitable.

Blue Apron's story is an important reminder that your model must be built to survive a changing market. Your best defense is ensuring you create durable customer loyalty in the scale-up phase, allowing you to retain the head start you won in the startup phase. Doing this begins with understanding the different threats to retention you will face.

Study Your Enemy: Not All Churn Is Equal

To fight an opponent, first know the opponent. There are four different types of churn, each requiring its own strategy. Understanding them allows you to better position your counterattack.

1. *Usage churn* is contraction from a shrinking footprint. This form of churn might mean that customers are placing smaller orders or buying less frequently, authorizing fewer licenses, consuming fewer hours, or requesting less of whatever you offer. It is the quietest form of attrition, often going undetected beneath the surface.

2. *Product churn* is a downshift, such as a Gold customer going to Silver or an account with your full suite going to an à la carte bundle. It may involve a partial cancelation, such as when a subscriber keeps Amazon Video but cancels Amazon Prime. Product churn is generally a more serious indication of loss than usage churn.

3. *Dollar churn* is when a customer pays less for the same thing, usually as the result of a discount, negotiation, or save action.

4. *Customer churn* is full cancelation—kiss them goodbye, they're gone. Generally, this type of churn is the most expensive and the most difficult to reverse.

Note that one sort of attrition tends to lead to another. For example, a customer downgrades her order, then bargains for a discounted price to stay, later canceling altogether. To paraphrase the famous quotation, churn happens slowly, then all at once. See Table 11.1 for a closer comparison of the four types of churn.

Stopping Churn Before It Starts: The Big Missed Opportunity

Table 11.1   The Four Types of Churn

Type	Typically Results from...	Category	Usually Originates with...	Typically Occurs...
Usage Churn	Order shrink, seat reduction, lower consumption	Contraction	Them	Continuously
Product Churn	Downgrading or removing add-on products	Contraction	Them or you	At renewal
Dollar Churn	Discounting or rebating	Contraction	You	At renewal
Customer Churn	Cancelation	Loss	Them	Continuously

What's Measured Gets Managed: Assessing Churn Like Best-in-Class Companies Do

Before you can fight churn, you need to understand your company's specific situation. Begin by measuring *overall* churn in the four categories just discussed. Then move on to assessing the risk that *specific customers* customers are likely to churn or contract.

Overall Churn

Few organizations have a truly accurate read of their own churn. One common error is to define churn as the number of customers lost in a year divided by the total number of customers overall. As the overall customer base grows, this churn percentage may appear to shrink—simply because the denominator is increasing—even if no real progress is being made in reducing attrition.

The correct way to analyze churn is to focus on a cohort, meaning a set of new customers who were all acquired at once. In a subscription context, it's standard to use the billing period to define the time period for a cohort, so if you are on quarterly billing, all members of a cohort should have been acquired in the same quarter. In a nonsubscription world, use the average period between purchases: A tax provider would use a full year, but a ride service like Uber might look at all new customers from a month or week.

For any cohort, this relationship must hold:

Overall Revenue Churn = Use Churn + Product Churn + Customer Churn + Dollar Churn

To be best in class, report regularly on all four types of attrition in a churn dashboard. Doing so is key to spotting leaks in your bucket. At one software company, sales teams went against management, retaining irate customers by switching them to cheaper, outdated packages. Customer count and even the number of individual units sold still looked good, but dollars were flying out the door. Had the company not been monitoring product churn, it might not have spotted the problem until it was splashed in red across their profit-and-loss statement.

Finally, keep in mind that some forms of churn are beneficial. For example, cutting the price of a sticky offer may generate short-term dollar churn but pay off in the long run; that's the principle behind offering an annual discount. A proper set of metrics, captured in a dashboard, will help distinguish these edge cases from the types of churn that will harm you financially.

The Churn Clarity Axiom	You can't reduce churn if you don't measure it precisely. Track churn by category and cohort to see what's really working.

Stopping Churn Before It Starts: The Big Missed Opportunity

Risky Customers

Before targeting account-level attrition, understand that customer satisfaction measures and net promoter scores are not churn risk indicators.

Wait: Aren't people who are happy likely to stay customers and those who are irritated prone to leaving? Not necessarily. Satisfied customers may decide they are "full" and push away from the table. By contrast, grumpy customers may find every bump in the road irritating precisely because they rely on you completely. Customers tapping their toes impatiently at the long returns line at Costco or Ikea are annoyed in part because they *know* they will be there again, frustrating though the experience may be. In fact, filling out a customer satisfaction survey often indicates a customer has a lower propensity to churn, even if their actual rating is not great (within reason).

A good churn propensity model should help you to predict contraction as well as account churn, meaning it should identify the factors that explain why customers pull back and ultimately leave.

You should also study the inverse of this metric, often called a "velocity score," which identifies customers who are at low risk of churn and likely to spend more with you.

But even the best churn propensity score is not a crystal ball, naming exactly which customers will leave and when. There is no model so sophisticated that it can tell you, *Jones & Company will cancel their account next Tuesday at 3 pm.* In the real world, most methods can do little more than indicate which customers are tilting toward attrition over a 12-month window: *These accounts are more likely than others to contract or churn in the next year.*

Attacking Churn: How and Where to Fight

You may have your dashboard, you may have your account-level risk and velocity scores. But none of that matters if you don't know how to actually make a difference. Attacking churn requires knowing both what to do and when to do it.

How to Fight: Creating Killer Retention Tactics

Here's a simple truth: Every customer who has ever left you has one thing in common. At one point, they all said "yes."

How did they go from yes to no? This simple question has profound implications. It may seem to you that there are many paths that switch might take. In fact, there are only a few, and they are easily identified with the right framework.

The first factor to consider is a question of price versus value. Someone becomes your customer when they believe that the benefit they will get is equal to, or better than, what you are charging relative to alternatives in the market. It follows that if customers do leave you, the balance between price and value is seriously off. With just two factors in play, you need only to ask: Was it the perceived benefit that changed? Or was it the price?

The only other factor you need to determine how things went wrong is to find out whether this change was internal to your customer—"It's not you, it's me"—or external, stemming from you or from your competitors.

These two factors lead to the framework shown in Figure 11.1. This straightforward model allows you to assess how your customers went from yes to no—and how you can restore balance. Locating your problem areas in this framework is the start of creating truly effective retention tactics. See Table 11.2.

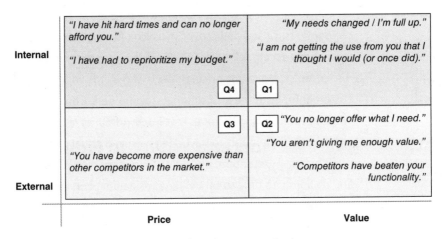

Figure 11.1 The Customer Churn Framework

225

Table 11.2 How to Apply the Customer Churn Framework

Quadrant in Figure 11.1	Tactics to Apply
I: Internal and Value	*Situation:* The customer's needs have shifted. Customers in this quadrant are not necessarily unhappy. They may have come to the realization that, like a regretful gym member, they just are not using you as often as they thought they would. Others may feel that they have gotten great use from your product or service but now their needs are satisfied— they're "done." Alternatively, it may be that customers have changed their plans; they will no longer be pursuing whatever brought them to your door. *You will be tempted to:* Accept the cancelation gracefully. *Instead you should:* Provide incentives to encourage such customers to explore your full range of offerings. After all, they already like your brand. They no longer need or want the specific product or service that brought them in, so what else do you have to offer them? For example, that hypothetical fitness club member who is leaning toward canceling may be pleasantly surprised to discover you also offer pickleball and will happily accept a free month of court access to try it out. *Also consider:* Move to a price model that rewards your customer for bringing in additional stakeholders. Consider Spotify's family plan: It's not as revenue-optimal as requiring all household members to have their own individual plan, but it improves retention, since it's a low per-person price, and deciding it's time to cancel requires gaining consensus among multiple people.

(continued)

Table 11.2 *(continued)*

Quadrant in Figure 11.1	Tactics to Apply
II: External and Value	*Situation:* The customer's perception of your value has dropped. Sometimes this is because promised benefits did not materialize, or customers may gradually decide that your quality has slipped. Some will arrive in this quadrant after a competitor claims it offers everything you do and more, making you seem weak by comparison. *You will be tempted to:* Offer credits to make up for product shortcomings and commit to costly custom development for larger customers. *Instead you should:* Focus on strategies to increase feature discovery. What's often missing is the *perception* of value, not actual value. Do not assume that customers understand everything you offer. Countless times, we've seen companies lose customers who are looking for a specific feature that is actually on offer—and, in many cases, it is a feature *that the customer is already paying for.* Consider providing a free trial of the next-size-up package, if there is one, paired with complimentary training to help them get more out of what you offer or, if this is early in the customer's life cycle, giving them a white-glove onboarding experience. One value-based retention tactic utilized by several Fortune 100 companies, as well as companies a fraction of their size, is to identify customers' overarching objectives with a jobs-to-be-done framework, then co-create an explicit program to help them reach their goals.

(continued)

Stopping Churn Before It Starts: The Big Missed Opportunity

Table 11.2 *(continued)*

Quadrant in Figure 11.1	Tactics to Apply
	Also consider: Adopt a packaging structure that in and of itself encourages feature awareness. The classic solve here is tiering, which invites direct comparison: "What does the Silver package have that Bronze does not?" However, even if customers are aware of your full product set and all its features at the time of purchase, that does not mean that they will continue to keep up with the new features and capabilities you've introduced. Avoid blasting them with a laundry list of capabilities. Instead, offer targeted information about product innovations that specifically tie to their goals, paired with free trials to increase exposure.
III: External and Price	*Situation:* Your customer finds your price unattractive. These customers may be anchored on what you originally charged them and upset about a recent price increase. Alternatively, price pressure may come from competitors who are trying to poach them. *You will be tempted to:* Drop your prices or discount. . .heavily. *But instead you should:* Focus on value communication before anything else. Price does not exist in a vacuum. Ensure that customers in this quadrant are fully aware of your key benefits. As with quadrant II, offer promotions that encourage customers to fully explore your value, such as upgrading them to a better package for a period at no additional cost or providing enhanced training that will allow them to unlock features they were not using.

(continued)

Scaling Innovation

Quadrant in Figure 11.1	Tactics to Apply
	If the issue is price comparison with a given competitor, first challenge whether the rival offers the same value you do, particularly regarding the differentiators you have identified. To highlight competitive advantages, we advised one client to construct a Basics package that simulated what a particularly aggressive competitor provided. When customers called, pointing out that the competitor was cheaper, our client offered to downgrade them to the Basics option. Very few took our client up on that offer.
	Another powerful tactic to turn a quadrant III conversation in your favor is to ensure there is a visible price tag on every retention offer you make. Think about the difference between offering 25 hours of training for free versus offering "a $5,000 voucher, redeemable for 25 hours of hands-on training." Customers likely will divide 5,000 by 25 to conclude that this training is worth $200 per hour, a strong signal of value. The "free" offer lacks this economic signal, meaning you won't get the same credit despite offering the same thing.
	There are times when a value concession will not be enough. A promise to provide "price protection," meaning a limit on future increases, or even a reduction in the current fee may be required. However, with proper feature awareness and the value substitution tactics just described, you can preserve your price as much as possible.

(continued)

229

Stopping Churn Before It Starts: The Big Missed Opportunity

Table 11.2 *(continued)*

Quadrant in Figure 11.1	Tactics to Apply
	Also consider: Evaluate whether your price increase program has been too aggressive. A temporary lack of churn may mask structural weakness in the loyalty of your base. Be sure to monitor your customers for a period after a major fee increase.
IV: Internal and Price	*Situation:* Customers are cutting expenses where possible. This may be because the customers are in financial distress. Or customers may be tightening their belts for other reasons. *You will be tempted to:* Discount to a price level they consider affordable. *But instead you should:* Determine whether customers are newly frugal or struggling to stay alive. In the former situation, you may consider offering them a less expensive alternative rather than a discount. As described in Chapter 8, this version of your product is not merely stripped of bells and whistles but brought down to a level of truly limited functionality—at a lower price. Whether customers opt for the less expensive alternative or not, the simple act of evaluating it may make them more aware of the value you provide, putting you in a better bargaining position for any negotiations that may follow. (And remember that the less expensive alternative should be reserved for dire circumstances, serving as a life raft; it never, ever should be part of your published product lineup.)

(continued)

Table 11.2 *(continued)*

Quadrant in Figure 11.1	Tactics to Apply
	If the customer is struggling to stay alive and facing true financial hardship, consider whether they are worth saving. The best path may be simply to part ways, if the risk of nonpayment or future insolvency is high. Also, recall from the start of this chapter that dollar churn is just as real as customer churn—and discounting can be contagious, if others learn that there is a lower price to be had.
	Finally, quadrant IV is rife with gaming, where cries for help often turn out to be simply customers hunting for lower prices. Ensure your policies are firm here, lest you be taken advantage of.
	Also consider: A powerful technique for this quadrant is introducing a loyalty plan or another way of building credits. Such methods can make your product or services effectively cheaper for your best customers without discounting heavily or lowering your price. Furthermore, a healthy set of credits tends to anchor customers, since the pain of walking away from an earned benefit is high.

The Broken-Balance Axiom	When customers churn, the price-value balance has failed. The fix starts by asking: Did the benefit change—or the price? And was the shift internal to them, or caused by you or a competitor? Churn is a symptom. Diagnosis is the unlock.

Stopping Churn Before It Starts: The Big Missed Opportunity

Where to Fight: Picking Your Battleground

With a framework for analyzing why customers go from yes to no, you now have a way to fight attrition. But you do not have an infinite number of employees or an unlimited budget to commit. You must position your valuable resources where they will create the greatest impact. Think carefully about the customer life cycle points shown in Figure 11.2.

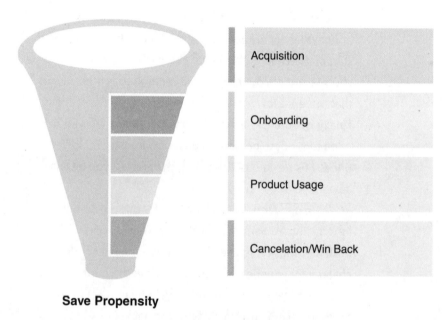

Save Propensity

Figure 11.2   Churn at Four Stages in the Customer Life Cycle

Saving at Cancelation: Popular and Painful

Businesses often start their fight by establishing a *save team*—a group brought together for the express role of changing the minds of customers who have firmly decided that they want to leave. This path is the most common popular way to address churn, and it is also the most painful.

It's also expensive and inefficient. By way of analogy, if you wait until your toothache is unbearable before seeing the dentist, you are likely going to need a root canal—if you can save the tooth at all.

Switching cost—specifically, the lack of it—is what makes cancelation the worst place in the customer journey to fight churn. As we mentioned earlier, people like to stick with what they know and dislike the pain of trying something unfamiliar: "If it ain't broke, don't fix it." This aversion to the unknown is like a natural, protective shield helping companies to retain their customers.

But by the time a customer contacts you to end your relationship, that barrier has been completely stripped away. If customers depended on you, if they relied on your product or service, they have almost certainly found an alternative before they picked up the phone. Most people would not fire their accountant until they had found some other way to file their taxes. In fact, your customer may have already signed a contract with a new provider, and in a B2B setting, that decision may have been made by a group of stakeholders, meaning you don't even know whom to plead with. That's why turning things around will mean a tough, protracted uphill battle waged at a severe competitive advantage.

But maybe you weren't that important to your customer. Your product was nice to have rather than fulfilling a need. The decision to cancel might have been emotional, a momentary fit of pique. This situation should give you some hope, since there's less effort required to reverse a decision that wasn't fully thought through. But when you win them back, what have you gained? Expect a short life span and repeated requests for discounts and concessions. These customers are also more likely to exhibit silent churn, lowering their usage or otherwise pulling back, so the revenue stream from this save is not only short but thin. In such a situation, it is critical to closely manage the save team so they don't offer concessions that will not be paid back in loyalty.

Finally, your save team may inadvertently expose you to customers who are just threatening to cancel in the hopes of getting a better deal, habitually asking for concessions to keep their loyalty, whether they actually plan on leaving or not. One well-known software company believed it had good governance over discounting, with smaller concessions going to

Stopping Churn Before It Starts: The Big Missed Opportunity

minor accounts and larger ones granted only to the majors. But on closer review, the company found that some small customers were asking for concessions so often that, in aggregate, they were granted as much or more than giant accounts 10 times their size.

The Final-Mile-Fallacy Axiom	Trying to save customers at the point of cancelation is the most common churn reduction strategy—and also the least effective, as it targets those who have already decided to leave—and may not be worth saving.

Saving During Product Usage: A More Effective Approach

Rather than focusing on customers who are ready to cancel, it is far better to address retention at strategic points during the customer life cycle.

The first reason for this is timing. At cancelation, your agents will have little time to save a cancelation—generally a single interaction, sometimes with mere minutes to turn the customer around. By contrast, if you focus on the customer journey, you massively expand the surface area, gaining multiple interaction points spread out over months or years. An additional dimension is the depth of interaction available to you. At cancelation, you can only speak with whomever is on the phone—and they might not even be the decision maker. During product usage, however, you can deepen the set of stakeholders to incorporate others in the company (or, in the case of B2C, household). Doing this will bolster your account, making it harder for any one individual to cancel.

The second reason is that, by properly positioning your efforts throughout the customer journey, you can go beyond stopping churn and start thinking about expansion. A good retention team should be working both sides of the net retention equation effort, both shoring up risky relationships and capitalizing on strong ones. That's not possible if you're speaking only with customers who are telling you goodbye.

Here is where your churn propensity score (and your velocity score) can be very powerful. Rather than blanketing your population with uniform communication, target your messaging to the right parties. Promotional dollars are expensive, and so are talented sales reps and customer care agents. Deliver them to the places where they are needed, guided by risk scores, and incorporate additional measures to ensure success. For example:

- Add a minimum number of contacts with risky accounts to your sales team's compensation plan.

- Group promotions by risk tier. Doing this means reserving certain offers for your riskier customers and allocating a specific budget to each tier, allowing you to target money where it's most useful.

Encourage front-line representatives to have open and honest conversations with unhappy customers. Doing so may uncover opportunities to show them the value they had been missing.

Saving During Onboarding: Seal the Deal

We use the term "onboarding" loosely; depending on your circumstances, this might be the final step of the purchase process, the first communication postsale, or even customer training and product implementation. During onboarding, customers' choices are fresh and, generally, so is their enthusiasm for you. That makes onboarding an opportunity to deepen their expectations for your relationship. It's a key moment to increase their perception of what you offer—a great time to ask, in effect, "Do you want fries with that?" It's also often the last point where you can expand their idea of what they want to accomplish, potentially altering their long-term plans and positioning you as a true partner.

By contrast, customers who are already well into their tenure tend to have a fixed idea of who you are and how they'll use you. If you are their favorite breakfast spot, they may not see you as a place to take a dinner date, no matter how many coupons you push at them. Try too hard, and you may alienate loyal customers who liked you the way you were.

Onboarding is an ideal time to learn about your customers' hopes and dreams. Gather information that will allow you to target your communication during the product usage phase.

If you can understand what they like about your product, or if you can identify goals they are trying to achieve with what you offer, then you can create more targeted messages in the future.

The Best-Kept Secret: Fight Churn Through Acquisition

It turns out that the best place to fight churn is not at cancelation, during usage, or at onboarding. It's prior to acquisition.

Understanding why this is so builds from a remarkably simple principle: *The customers who are most likely to churn are the first to quit, leaving behind a more loyal population.*

To illustrate this concept, imagine you are organizing a 10-mile foot race through difficult terrain. You start with 500 runners. In the first mile, 50 runners—10% of the population—drop out. How many will quit in the last mile? Intuitively, it should be far fewer than 50. Those who made it through nine miles are unlikely to drop out in the final stretch. These are the people who trained seriously, who have the grit to get through a challenge, or are just physically gifted athletes. The 50 who dropped out in the first mile lacked these qualities. What about the eighth mile—how many will drop out there? Again, far fewer than 50, although perhaps a bit more than in that final mile.

The runners in the ninth mile are more likely to finish than those in the eighth mile; the runners in the eighth mile are more likely to finish than those in the seventh mile; and on down. It's as if the group gets progressively "fitter" as the race goes on. A similar story is playing out in your business. Your customer base almost certainly develops a lower incidence of churn over time *because the "unfit" customers—those likely to churn—have already canceled.*

Returning to our story: Recall that you are the one organizing this race. If you're compensated by how many runners cross the finish line, what could you do to increase your payout?

You can see it's nearly useless to revive runners who, like a customer at cancelation, are refusing to take another step due to exhaustion. It is somewhat easier and more effective to motivate runners who seem to be struggling but haven't yet given up, perhaps handing water and energy bars to those who are falling behind—the equivalent of targeting retention tactics during usage. Better still, you might coach them during onboarding prior to the start of the race, identifying the ones who haven't tied their shoes, giving them a strategy to tackle the hills ahead. All of this will help, marginally.

But what if, instead of wasting your time and money signing up everyone who has running shorts, you focused on recruiting people who look like runners? Even if there aren't as many of them around, making them costlier to attract, you are almost certain to have more of your runners cross the finish line—and that may be worth the extra expense. You even know exactly what you're looking for: Just base recruitment on finding runners who look like those who finished the last race successfully.

We hope this analogy makes it clear why the single best retention tactic is *focusing on whom you acquire*. This cheat code literally lets you stop churn before it happens. You can optimize your search engine strategies to double down on the keywords that brought in long-lived customers in the past. You can narrow the criteria for market-qualified leads and allow sales greater discount latitude for prospects who look like "great runners." With some care and planning, you can also create a targeted promotional strategy to bring in more "natural athletes"—which involves both finding the best ways to engage them and discovering where they are likely to be found. The best plan combines a bottom-up and a top-down approach.

Bottom up means evaluating each source of paid acquisition—channel partners, individual salespeople, search engine keywords, and so on. Typically, you can assess these sources by metrics like win rate or conversion rate and average contract value or average revenue per user. Now factor in the expected duration of the relationship.[2] If you do not have enough data to determine duration, you can develop an estimate using the churn propensity risk score you developed earlier. The goal is to prune sources that bring in customers who are less likely to stay and reinvest the money in sources that will bring you better, more durable accounts.

To develop your top-down view, create a look-alike, meaning the customer profile you're hunting for. Base this look-alike on the profile of the long-lived customer accounts you already have or those in the lowest risk score bucket. If possible, enhance your look-alike profile with additional information to bring more detail to the profile and to help you determine where similar customers can be found.

These two views work together, with the bottom-up strategy providing a good stream of prospects and the top-down strategy working as a filter to ensure you are focused on the right targets. The combination gives you two key advantages:

1. *The green banana principle.* You will now have customer accounts that are highly likely to be more durable, yielding stronger and more reliable profits that can be invested in other areas, just as buying green fruit at the grocery will give you a longer shelf life in your kitchen.

2. *The land grab rule.* Since acquisition spend is usually a competitive process—bidding on a limited number of keywords, paying for a small set of commercial slot—performing a rigorous lifetime value assessment allows you to grab the best real estate, leaving rivals overpaying for terrain that is less fertile than what you acquired.

The Retention-Led Acquisition Axiom	The most effective way to reduce churn is to stop it before it starts—by acquiring the kind of customers who stay, not just the ones who buy.

Beyond the Basics: Insights, Tips, and Tricks to Optimize Your Churn Reductions Methods

Here are some additional tips you should consider to further strengthen your toolkit for minimizing the harm done by churn.

- *Encourage feature discovery.* One way to do this is by asking customers did-you-know questions: "Did you know we're not just a great place for a car wash, but we can also check your tire pressure while you wait?" This method is particularly powerful if the additional functionality allows you to reach other stakeholders: "Did you know that your monthly activity can be exported into a progress report for others in your company?" Another method is to use the moment of purchase, or shortly thereafter, as a great time to expand customers' ideas of how you can be useful to them—as when you bring an item home from the supermarket and find a great recipe for preparing it on the back of the package. Consider pairing this approach with a suggestion of how "other customers" are getting value from your product or service. One client of ours messaged new customers what their "Top 5 Requested Services" were, which had the effect of expanding the average footprint of newcomers' accounts.

- *Fix communication breakdowns to prevent churn from happening.* Weak relationships often are based in poor communication. You may have to rebuild pathways of conversation before you can do the work involved in saving a customer account. One of the factors that creates a spiral toward cancelation is a poor communication loop. For example, customers who feel they aren't seeing the value from your product or service may stop reading your messages. Then, because they are not listening to you, you cannot make them aware of additional value you have recently introduced in your product or service. To get out of this loop, you may need an exceptional offer to jolt the lines of communication back open. Such an offer could be something that plays on their fear, uncertainty, and doubt, or it could be a special offer that they have never seen before. If you are thinking about introducing a loyalty program, for example, telling your customer base that you are rewarding their loyalty by awarding them credit retroactively is a great way to jump-start a conversation.

- *Create new switching costs to strengthen your retention tactics.* Stopping customers during the actual moment of churn may require a "surprise," an unexpected offer too good for them to ignore: "Before you walk out that door, you should know, I was going to take you to Paris." By making canceling customers aware that they are leaving something behind and communicating the pain of loss, you can, in effect, introduce a new switching cost. Examples include loyalty points the customer would forfeit upon cancellation, or a discounted rate the customer "earned" by being an early adopter—one that wouldn't be available if they returned later. As New Yorkers know, no one leaves a rent-controlled apartment. Or it might simply involve highlighting a benefit customers have not yet used, which will be unavailable to them after cancelation. If you cannot easily complete the sentence "If you leave, you will lose X," you may need to give this approach greater focus.

- *Comparing the two sets of numbers can reveal* thrash, *where a group of expanding customers masks the impact of other customers contracting.* Once identified, the problem posed by this "weak" customer group can be addressed.

Chapter Summary: How This Strategy Avoids the Single-Engine Trap

It's easy to fall into the Disruptor trap of focusing only on landing new ones while ignoring those you've already acquired or the Money Maker trap of trying to squeeze too much from existing customers, making them shop around for a better deal. The strategies described in this chapter help you build proactive systems to spot and address churn before it becomes a problem. By keeping the customers you've worked hard to win (market share), and continuously growing their value over time (wallet share), you build a truly durable business. Profitable Growth Architects know that growth isn't just about what you add—it's about what you keep.

CEO Questions

- Has your company developed a system for measuring the four types of churn and determining which ones have the greatest impact on your efforts to scale?

- Have you created a save team focused on retaining customers who have announced their intention of departing? If so, are you training and evaluating this team so that they are equipped to expand and deepen your business relationships throughout customer life cycles rather than simply at the point of departure?

- Are your sales and customer service teams familiar with the Customer Retention Framework? Do they understand how to use

Stopping Churn Before It Starts: The Big Missed Opportunity

the framework to improve the effectiveness of their customer retention efforts?

- Have you begun to apply a deeper knowledge of customer loyalty characteristics to your acquisition process in order to improve your likelihood of attracting customers who will become long-term sources of revenue and profits?

Learning from the Best: Success Stories

Putting It All Together: From Playbook to Practice

You've made it through the playbook. You've seen the traps, learned the patterns, and studied the moves. Now comes the hard part—the part that separates companies with potential from companies that scale with purpose and endurance.

Reading strategies is one thing. Putting them into motion is another.

The goal of this book was never just to get you thinking. It was to get you *building*. To arm you with a repeatable, strategic approach that avoids a single-engine strategy to growth and enables you to balance both reach and revenue. Because that's what profitable growth truly is—not a burst of hype or a streak of lucky deals but a system. A system designed, architected, and executed by leaders who know how to drive both market share and wallet share.

Let's step back and connect the dots.

In Part I, we looked at why so many companies fail to scale. Not because they lacked vision, or talent, or even customers—but because they relied on a single engine: chasing acquisition without monetization, monetizing without expanding reach, or nurturing loyalty at the cost of long-term economics. We showed how these single-engine strategies often feel logical—at first. But over time, they trap businesses in a cycle of overreliance and underperformance. We introduced the three leadership archetypes:

Disruptor, Money Maker, Community Builder—and gave you a new target: the Profitable Growth Architect.

Then, in Part IIA, we laid out the strategies start-ups need to adopt early to avoid falling into those traps. From pricing models to value messaging to freemium plays with monetization paths built in, we showed how to start right—so you don't need to "fix" the business later. These aren't theory. They're the exact moves used by high-growth companies that knew how to land and expand from day one.

In Part IIB, we turned to scale-ups—companies already in motion, with real customer bases and real stakes. This is where many stumble, assuming what worked in the early days will work forever. But scale requires new disciplines: rethinking your packaging, learning to raise prices with confidence, negotiating for full value, and actively stopping churn before it starts. It's also where leaders must begin to see the whole system—where product, pricing, sales, success, and marketing must move in sync.

Making It Real: Institutionalizing the Playbook

So how do you make this real inside your company?

Here's what that takes:

1. Make Profitable Growth a Cross-Functional Mandate

First, you need to build cross-functional muscle. No strategy works in a silo. If you want to architect profitable growth, you cannot let your org chart dictate your growth model. Silos—between marketing and sales, product and customer success, finance and operations—are the enemy of scale. Great strategies fall flat when teams chase goals in isolation.

Rewire your leadership meetings so growth isn't a round robin of updates. It's a unified conversation about how acquisition, monetization, and retention are performing—*together*.

Every strategic planning cycle should ask two questions:

1. How will we grow market share this year?

2. How will we grow wallet share from what we already have?

Don't bury these in a 40-slide deck. Build them into your quarterly objectives and key results. Ensure every major initiative ties back to at least one lever—reach *or* revenue per customer—and preferably both.

Companies that do this well often assign dual owners to every big initiative: one focused on scale, the other on depth. That tension creates better design, clearer trade-offs, and more balanced bets.

2. Rebuild Your KPIs

Align your organization on shared outcomes, not departmental wins. Doing this means measuring acquisition *and* monetization *and* retention in a unified dashboard that everyone sees. It means making your pricing model and packaging structure visible beyond the finance team. It means treating value messaging as something owned by the whole org, not just marketing.

To do this, you need to rebuild your KPIs around the dual mandate of market share and wallet share. Every function should know how its work contributes to both. Your marketing team should be accountable not just for leads but for leads that convert and retain. Your sales team should be accountable not just on revenue won but on revenue that expands. Your customer success team should be measured not just on NPS but on renewals, upsells, and full customer lifetime value.

3. Run Cross-Functional Experiments, Not Isolated Optimizations

You must create space for iteration. No growth strategy survives first contact with the market unchanged. Teams must have the room to experiment—test

Putting It All Together: From Playbook to Practice

packaging variations, pricing models, discounting logic, churn triggers—and bring those learnings back into the system. Profitable growth isn't static. It evolves with the business, the buyer, and the competitive landscape.

When you test a new pricing model, loop in Sales, Product, and Finance from the beginning. When you launch a freemium tier, have your success team define the conversion triggers. Stop running experiments in functional bubbles. Every experiment should be designed with cross-functional learning in mind—and reviewed as a cross-functional team.

4. Design Incentive Systems that Reinforce the Playbook

If your sales comp plan only rewards closing new deals, don't be surprised when expansion suffers. If your product roadmap prioritizes feature velocity but not monetization potential, you're building in the wrong direction.

Adjust your incentives. Align bonuses, KPIs, and promotions to reflect the dual nature of growth. Reward people who help capture value, not just create volume. If you don't shape behavior, your strategy won't stick.

5. Make Growth Part of the Culture, Not Just the Strategy

Profitable growth doesn't live in a spreadsheet. It lives in daily decisions, hallway conversations, product debates, and customer interactions. That's why the best leaders narrate their strategy in real time. They share not just what decisions are made but *why*—and how those decisions tie back to the broader strategy.

Give your team a vocabulary for profitable growth. Talk about wallet share and market share explicitly. Name the traps. Use the terms. Language is the first step toward institutional memory.

Finally, you must give leaders permission to think like architects, not just executors. Doing that means equipping them to think in systems: how a change in offer structure impacts the sales cycle; how a price increase lands differently across segments; how value messaging drives both acquisition and expansion. This leadership skillset needs to be taught, reinforced, and rewarded.

In summary, profitable growth has to become a company-wide operating system. It's not a project. It's not a sprint. It's a mindset and a method, embedded in the way your company thinks, builds, sells, and scales.

The good news? Companies are doing this—and winning.

Segment grew from a single API tool to a $3.2 billion acquisition by balancing developer love with strong monetization discipline. Canva mastered the land-and-expand model by combining a beautiful freemium entry point with upsells that felt natural and empowering. ServiceChannel cracked a complex two-sided marketplace through packaging and pricing reinvention. Each company made a conscious choice not to chase one metric but to architect the whole.

In Part III, you'll see how these companies—and others—put the playbook into practice. These aren't vanity stories; they're blueprints. They show what it looks like when the strategies from this book come alive inside real businesses, with real constraints, real pivots, and real outcomes.

Let's see how it's done.

Chapter 13

Segment: From Idea to a $3.2 Billion Acquisition

Peter Reinhardt sat in a cramped Cambridge apartment, surrounded by three equally restless minds. Together with his cofounders—Calvin French-Owen, Ian Storm Taylor, and Ilya Volodarsky, Peter was chasing an idea they thought would change education forever. The year was 2011, and they had just dropped out of MIT to build ClassMetric, a revolutionary classroom analytics tool. But there was one problem: Nobody wanted it.

Despite the team's vision of professors using real-time engagement data to better connect with students, the feedback from users was clear. Professors didn't care for it. It was too intrusive, too unnecessary. Peter and his cofounders had bet everything on this concept, but the market wasn't biting. The energy in the apartment shifted from the excitement of creation to the grim reality of failure.

What now? They were tech-savvy MIT dropouts, and the clock was ticking. Every day without traction felt like a nail in the coffin of their dreams.

Then, on December 12, 2012 (12/12/12), a spark of hope came from the most unlikely of places—an open-source library. It was a small, internal tool they'd created to help developers manage multiple analytic tools. Initially, it wasn't meant to be a product; it was just something they used to solve a problem they faced while testing ClassMetric. They shared the library online, expecting it to fail. Then it blew up on Hacker News, a popular tech forum. Developers everywhere were downloading and using the tool, excited by how simple it made collecting and managing customer data.

It wasn't what they'd intended to build, but it was what the world wanted.

The sudden popularity of this simple library lit a fire under the team. They realized they had stumbled on a bigger opportunity than they had ever imagined. The opportunity wasn't about improving education anymore; it was about solving a universal pain point in data collection across businesses. Every company with a digital presence struggled with integrating data from countless touchpoints—Sales, Marketing, Customer Service—and Segment, as its creators named their software product, was about to become the connective tissue that brought it all together—a unified system to collect, manage, and route customer data across the business.

This was no grand, premeditated pivot. It was serendipity—a moment of recognition that, sometimes, the best ideas come when you aren't even looking for them. As the famous saying goes, It's better to be lucky than to be right.

Driven by their newfound purpose, the team transformed Segment into a customer data infrastructure platform that would revolutionize how businesses understood their customers. No longer confined to the vision of improving classrooms, they were building something far larger—something that could change how businesses operated at their core.

But success didn't come overnight. Segment's rise from that Cambridge apartment to a billion-dollar unicorn and a multi-billion-dollar exit involved relentless hard work, countless iterations, and the courage to pursue what worked rather than stubbornly holding onto what didn't. Peter, Calvin, Ian, and Ilya took the accidental success of their open-source tool and rode the wave, scaling the company to over 600 employees across the globe, with a robust client base of over 20,000 businesses, including Atlassian, GAP, IBM, Intuit, and *TIME*.

Segment's founding story is a testament to resilience, adaptability, and the strange alchemy of luck and timing. In the chaotic world of startups, sometimes the best ideas are the ones you stumble on by accident, and the secret to scaling the innovation often is recognizing when and how to double down on them. The journey was marked by numerous lessons, which we explore in the next sections.

Lessons Learned During the Startup Phase

Segment learned several important lessons during the startup phase.

Finding True Product-Market Fit Needs to Be a Deliberate Exercise

One of the most important lessons Segment learned during its startup phase was the critical value of achieving true product-market fit. As Peter puts it:

> *If you distill down our two failures and one accidental success, I'd say that the first two ideas we tested were very vision-driven. They were guided by an internal belief that the world would be better if it operated in a certain way—an inside-out perspective on what the world needed. Unsurprisingly, this approach failed to create a sustainable business. The world doesn't care how you think it should operate. What we found instead is that the world cares about its own problems, and you need to identify and solve those problems. We stumbled upon this insight by accident, but there are far more deliberate ways to discover a problem, solve it, and thus find product-market fit.*

Larger companies often become entangled in internal politics and organizational complexity, while smaller companies may pursue a vision disconnected from external reality. The key is to understand how and why customers derive value from your offering—this serves as the ultimate reality check. Peter's experience highlights that achieving product-market fit requires identifying a segment of customers who genuinely need your product and ultimately are willing to pay for it. Rather than building a product and then searching for a market, you first must identify a market segment

Segment: From Idea to a $3.2 Billion Acquisition

and then develop a product tailored to its needs and willingness to pay. Product-market fit is not something that happens by chance; it is a deliberate, focused effort.

Don't Be Afraid to Ask for More

You may be delivering far more value than you realize, and it's crucial to charge appropriately for that value. In its early days, Segment charged $120 per year, hesitantly asking customers for $10 a month. However, the team at Segment eventually discovered that they could increase their prices by over 1,000 times what they initially charged.

Segment brought on a sales advisor early in its journey, who firmly suggested, "You need to ask for $120,000 per year." Peter initially found this suggestion absurd, but the sales advisor insisted, "Either ask for it, or I quit." Reluctantly, in the next Sales meeting, they asked for $120,000 a year. Peter recalls:

> I turned beet red. The customer negotiated us down to $15,000 per year, which was an 85% discount—but to me, it was 150 times more than what we had been charging. That was a huge win and an eye-opening moment in understanding the value we were providing. In many ways, raising prices became a tool for Segment to discover the actual value customers were deriving from our product.

By the end of the following year, Segment's largest contract was over $200,000 per year, and, by the time Segment was acquired, its largest contract was in the millions per year. Average contract size was approaching $100,000 per year.

Raising prices can be daunting, but if you don't ask, you'll never know if customers are willing to pay more in line with the value you deliver. One effective strategy in the early days of a B2B company is to continually double your price with each deal until you're laughed out of the room. At that point, you've likely found the ceiling for customers' willingness to pay. Similarly, in B2C businesses, you must have the courage to experiment with different price points to find the optimal pricing during your startup phase. If you don't ask, you won't receive.

Changing the Pricing Model Can Unlock Amazing Value

Segment experienced rapid growth in its first two years of commercialization, scaling from zero to approximately $10 million in revenue. However, in its third year, the company faced a significant slowdown, with growth plateauing at $12.5 million during the first half. Peter and team recognized that something fundamental needed to change if they were going to get back on track. They understood that the issue wasn't with the product itself but with how they were pricing it and communicating its value. As Peter explained, "It was a very scary period. During those six months, we realized that our pricing model was misaligned with the value we were delivering."

The challenge, however, was that the team didn't have clarity on exactly where the misalignment was or how to fix it. Yet the company needed to act quickly. To address the problem, Segment commissioned a comprehensive study involving both customers and prospects to determine the most effective way to structure its pricing.

Through the study, Peter and his team discovered a key insight: The metric that most resonated with customers and prospects was monthly tracked users (MTUs). This metric captured the value Segment brought to clients—the more customers a business could track through Segment's platform, the greater the value derived from its data-driven insights. Armed with this information, Segment overhauled its pricing model, aligning it with MTUs to better reflect the value it delivered.

The results were transformative. During the year following the relaunch of the new pricing structure, Segment's revenue surged from $12.5 million to $20 million. This remarkable turnaround was driven by a deeper understanding of Segment's customer needs, the value proposition, and an effective alignment of the company's pricing strategy with the key value drivers.

Lessons Learned During the Scale-up Phase

Segment continued to grow at a fast clip but again hit a pivotal moment in the scale-up phase when it was around $70 million in annual recurring revenue. Even though the company still was growing new accounts, the growth rate was declining. The question of how long it would take to hit the magic $100 million annual recurring revenue number loomed. The issue was clear: The company was facing a very big retention problem. Renewals were getting tougher, especially with the big enterprise accounts. The blended retention rate was around 70%, with the retention among enterprises as low as 60%. Something had to be done to fix the leaky bucket.

To solve this issue, Peter hired Joe Morrissey as the chief revenue officer to lead Sales and Customer Success. Joe joined with a month to go in the second quarter and asked for time to observe and identify the core of the issue. He spent 30 days doing 100+ hours of interviews internally across the organization. His goal was to give a readout to the board of his assessment of the big challenges Segment was facing and how to deal with them through the rest of the year. The plan sounded good, but, as Mike Tyson says, everybody has a plan until they get punched in the mouth.

The quarter started to implode immediately. Three of the biggest enterprise deals that were coming up for renewal appeared set to churn. It was all hands on deck. Joe immediately jumped in to take the lead on all three of those deal renewals. Somehow he turned them around, getting the enterprise clients to renew. Otherwise Segment would have fallen way short of its quarter numbers.

The experience left Joe with mixed feelings. The outcome had been good, and his efforts had earned him currency with Peter. The reaction from the leadership was "This is exactly what we told you, Joe. We have a sales execution problem. If we just fix sales execution, we will do great!" But this was not what Joe was hearing from the assessment interviews he was conducting. His intuition was that Segment was suffering from both a product issue and a sales issue—specifically, the mistake of selling on features rather than on value. He realized that this was not a great way to scale a business.

Joe set out to get to the bottom of the issue. He tackled the combined problems along with Peter and Tido, the head of Engineering and Product. After a lot of struggling, they collectively identified the core issues and managed to achieve success, scaling handsomely all the way to their $3.2 billion buyout.

In the end, several lessons were learned during that scaling phase.

A Big Unlock Grew Out of Fixing the Sales/Product Tension

As Segment scaled, the company faced a growing tension between its sales and product teams—a common challenge for fast-growing organizations. Sales wanted more features to meet customer demands and close deals, while the product team struggled under the weight of one-off requests. This friction not only strained both teams but also caused growth to slow as product development became reactive rather than strategic.

Joe recalls his first conversation with Tido as a moment of realization:

> When I joined the company, we had a meeting, and Tido said, "The product is great, but the problem is the sales team. They don't know how to sell it anymore. They could when we were smaller, but now that we're bigger, we can't train every single salesperson on the product." His advice to me was "Put everyone through product training." But that immediately set off alarm bells in my head because I believed Sales shouldn't be focused on selling product features. It should be selling value.

The key challenge was a profound difference in perspectives. Joe believed the sales team was too focused on product details rather than communicating the broader value of Segment to customers, while Tido saw the sales team's lack of deep product knowledge as a barrier to effective selling. To get to the bottom of the issue, Joe conducted interviews with key executives across the company. "I asked everyone the same three questions: What problems do we solve for our customers? How specifically do we solve them? And how do we do it better than the competition?" Joe recalls. "We had six people in the room, and we got six different answers. It was clear that while we had built a great product, we weren't aligned on what exactly we were selling or who we should be selling to."

This lack of alignment came to a head during Segment's annual planning process, which Joe describes as a low point in the Sales/Product tension. Reflecting on the frustration of that period, Tido said, "I remember being halfway on vacation in Tahoe, trying to do annual planning, and just feeling so frustrated. Joe had this impossible set of priorities. The key piece was that we had no alignment around value drivers."

This situation led to a pivotal moment during the planning meeting. Over 48 hours, Joe, Tido, and Peter, along with top-performing sales engineers, account executives, product managers, and Segment's cofounders, locked themselves in a room to address the tough questions: What value does Segment provide? What are customers really paying for? What can we do better than anyone else?

Through this intense session, they found clarity. The team narrowed down their priorities and agreed on three core value drivers for the year. For Joe, the shift in priorities was monumental. He said:

Historically, Segment's growth came from building new products. Before I arrived, the company was launching products all the time. But now I had to tell Tido, "Let's focus on just three things: nail product quality, make the platform extensible, and support multiregion." I thought I was being reasonable, but Tido pushed back hard on some of those things. It was frustrating, but it forced us to really define what mattered.

This focus on a few key initiatives allowed the product team to streamline its efforts, freeing members from the constant pressure of customer-driven feature requests. "We had to stop the madness of trying to do everything at once," Tido explained. "The big unlock for me was realizing that Joe wasn't just another sales leader who would say yes to everything. He was committed to enforcing boundaries and keeping us focused on what really mattered."

This shift in focus led to clearer goals and better execution. "For the first time, we were saying no to things that didn't align with our core value drivers," Joe said. "If a feature request didn't fit, we'd tell the customer, 'We don't do that.' And instead of losing customers, we built trust by being transparent about what we could and couldn't deliver."

Looking back, both Joe and Tido acknowledged that the tension between Sales and Product was a necessary part of the process. As Joe put it, "The learning is always in the struggle. You've got to embrace the tension, have the hard conversations, and find a way to resolve it on both sides. That's how you create the platform for real growth." Tido agreed, adding "We had to get out of the mindset of building for everyone. Once we defined our value drivers and committed to them, it was like a weight was lifted. We could finally see the path forward."

The experience at Segment serves as a compelling example of how sales and product teams can overcome friction and align around shared objectives. The sales and product teams at Segment made deliberate choices about which customers to target and which revenue opportunities to pursue or decline. By concentrating on selling value rather than features, setting clear product priorities, and maintaining discipline in decision making, Segment successfully navigated the challenges of scaling and architected for profitable growth.

Blow Up Packaging and Start with Segmentation

In Segment's early startup days, a shift in the pricing model had unlocked significant growth. However, as the company began signing larger enterprise

Segment: From Idea to a $3.2 Billion Acquisition

deals during its scale-up phase, the existing pricing model created challenges, particularly in renewal discussions. The primary issue stemmed from large enterprise customers being required to forecast their MTUs at the time of signing. Doing this proved difficult and often led to overforecasting in an attempt to secure the best per-unit pricing, with internal incentives driving customers to appear as though they'd negotiated a favorable deal.

Although this forecasting strategy led to large up-front contracts for Segment, it presented several issues over time. There were three possible outcomes: Customers (a) hit their forecast exactly (which was highly unlikely), (b) underconsumed and received no credit for the unused portion, or (c) overconsumed and faced overage charges—often at a higher, punitive rate. Both underconsuming and overconsuming led to dissatisfaction, resulting in poor customer experiences and a higher risk of churn. Recognizing the urgency of the situation, Joe, Peter, and their team realized they needed to do something fast to fix the situation. *It was time to blow up the packaging and pricing and revisit the structure for the growth stage.*

The solution was to introduce tiered packages for enterprise customers, organized as Good, Better, and Best offerings. Each package provided a set allocation of MTU consumption, offering transparency and eliminating the need for precise forecasting. The Good package came with a modest consumption allocation, and customers were also provided with a clear discount schedule for any usage that exceeded their allocation. The more the product was used, the better the per-unit price. There were no more hidden overage fees. This transparency simplified the pricing model and removed surprises during renewal discussions.

The Better and Best packages followed the same logic but offered larger allocations and deeper discounts, allowing larger customers to gravitate toward higher-tier packages with the assurance that they would receive the best possible price based on their actual consumption. This approach not only allowed Segment to secure large deals but also helped maintain long-term customer relationships by fostering trust through clear, predictable pricing structures. Renewal conversations became easier, as customers appreciated the lack of unexpected costs and the clarity of the value they received.

Another key shift in Segment's approach to packaging was the introduction of service packages. Before this change, custom requests for product enhancements often were entertained and provided for free to close deals, leading to product development inefficiencies. However, with the new focus on prioritizing the three key product initiatives, custom requests had to be managed differently. Instead of saying no outright, Segment began offering paid service packages that included a set number of service hours and clearly defined outcomes.

Because customers paid, Segment could provide higher-quality services. Customers, in turn, were willing to pay for these tailored services because the outcomes were clear and valuable. A virtuous cycle was created: Because Segment delivered exceptional service, customers requested and paid for even more services. This new model had a profound impact, with some of Segment's largest customers signing contracts worth millions of dollars for services alone.

Stop Churn Before It Happens

Although the changes to the packaging helped with renewal conversations, the team at Segment had to do much more to stop churn before it happened.

The first thing Joe decided was to overhaul the customer success (CS) team and hire Steve Davito as the chief customer success officer. The singular goal of the CS team was to ensure customers attained the business outcomes that were promised during the sales cycle.

Prior to this change, customers were spending a lot of dollars with Segment but were unsure about value delivery. The CS team was working really hard, but it was primarily firefighting renewals and chasing late payments.

Often the team's efforts were already too late and too tactical. Joe and Steve had to take a step back and redesign the CS process.

1. They tasked the CS team with clear responsibilities during the onboarding phase. The CS team had to clearly capture customer pain points and positive business outcomes that customers were trying to achieve. The team also needed to align with the customers up front on the KPIs and metrics that would judge success. Ultimately, the team needed to make sure customers knew why they bought Segment, what value delivery and outcome to expect, and how the value should be tracked and measured. This approach enabled the client "champion" to showcase the value to their leadership and thereby close the loop on the ROI from investing in Segment.

2. They assigned a dedicated CS lead, called the "customer success manager" (CSM), for each of their top 50 accounts. This manager was tasked with helping customers get to the required, positive business outcomes that were promised during the sales cycle.

3. They retrained the CSM teams to focus on what Joe refers to as the "customer needs hierarchy."[1] Activities not connected to these needs were deprioritized. The customer needs hierarchy as defined by Joe in brief are:

   - *Technical health: Does your product work?* CSMs should identify both aggregated and specific customer signals to determine what's not functioning, why, and its impact on customers. If technical issues arise, CSMs should involve the services team to scope solutions and sales to close any relevant deals.

   - *Feature completeness: Does your product have the right features?* While addressing technical health means asking "Is this feature broken?," ensuring feature completeness asks "Is this feature missing?" CSMs should identify gaps between current and expected product performance and communicate this to the product team.

- *Key relationships: Are you nurturing champions and economic buyers?* Even the best product is at risk if relationships sour. Account executives should build champion relationships, while CSMs nurture them. Regular business reviews are critical for maintaining expansion opportunities and renewals. If a champion is lost, CSMs should reengage account executives to rebuild relationships.

- *Customer sentiment: Are you aligned on problem-solving?* Customers need assurance that you're aligned on addressing their pain points. CSMs should help organize executive briefings and customer advisory boards to align your strategic vision with customers' needs and report on insights from these sessions.

- *Outcomes: Are you delivering business value?* At this stage, CSMs should report on how your company is delivering on agreed business outcomes. If there's a gap, the managers should sound the alarm and develop a success plan to guide customers toward improvement.

- *Commercial health: Are customers set to renew or expand?* CSMs should assess whether customers will churn, renew, or expand, considering both business outcomes and external factors. If expansion is likely, CSMs can generate customer success–qualified leads to feed into the sales funnel. If contraction is forecasted, the Sales team should engage to mitigate risk.

4. They tasked CSMs not just to report on customer health but also to actively build systems to improve it. When customers stalled at a certain point, CSMs were required to create processes to relay feedback to the appropriate teams to ensure positive business outcomes.

5. As a final step to operationalize these steps, a customer health scorecard was created for the top 50 accounts and an initiative called the "Lighthouse Program" was launched. Joe recalls this step as the most

263

important one: "If you don't have a data-driven approach to measure the implementation of this hierarchy—like a customer health scorecard—you'll likely have a very difficult time getting your CS organization to actively improve customer health." For each need from the hierarchy of needs, the CSM would score a red, a yellow, or a green and indicate whether Segment is underperforming, meeting expectations, or overperforming. The scorecard would get discussed in detail in the weekly Lighthouse meetings, which lasted about an hour, and two accounts would be discussed each week. The participants would be cross-functional—Sales, Product, CSM, and C-Level (Joe and Tido). Each scorecard would be jointly presented by the account team—the salesperson and the CSM in charge for the account. The goal of the discussions was to ensure customers achieved the business outcomes they were promised.

Over time, Segment also was able to replicate and automate this process for a broader set of accounts. The overhauling of the CS team and the continued focus on not just selling on value but also showcasing the value on an ongoing basis ensured that Segment could stop churn before it happened. Over a two-year period after implementing these changes, the enterprise retention percentages improved from the low 60s to the high 80s.

The End Result

In October 2020, after nearly a decade of growth, Segment was acquired by Twilio, the cloud communications giant, for a staggering $3.2 billion. It was one of the largest acquisitions in Twilio's history and marked a monumental success for Peter and his team. For Segment, the acquisition meant more than just an exit; it was the culmination of years of strategic growth, product-market fit, and, of course, the ability to adapt and capitalize on the market's needs. The buyout validated the founders' hard work, vision, and perseverance.

Peter Reinhardt and his cofounders had built something extraordinary. Their journey from failure to unicorn status—and beyond—serves as an inspiring blueprint for entrepreneurs everywhere to scale their innovations by architecting to profitable growth.

Chapter 14

Canva: The Master Class of Landing and Expanding

When David Burson joined Canva in 2017, he was given a unique challenge. Canva had been in the market for four years and had built a strong and rapidly growing following in its mission to democratize design. As with many startups, most of the Canva team remained focused on product development during the initial years. However, David was brought on as the first product manager Canva hired, with a different mission. Canva had already proven it could build a product that people loved. It was already gaining strong momentum in the market. Melanie Perkins's vision to "empower the world to design" had attracted over 10 million users and showed no signs of slowing down. Now the goal was to turn that product into a successful business—and David's team would be central to making that happen.

In an interview, David stated: "Our goal was to take the entire design ecosystem, integrate it into one page, and then make it accessible to the whole world."[1] Canva's easy-to-use online platform was rapidly replacing the clunky, slow, and hard-to-learn offline tools of the past. And, for many users, it wasn't just about how simple Canva was to use; it was also hard to beat the fact that it was free.

The key question for Canva now was: How do you drive paid growth around a core free experience?

"I firmly believe free is a double-edged sword," David reflected on Canva's early growth phase. "It is incredibly powerful because it removes barriers to entry and can really help a business grow. But it also puts pressure on you as a business to demonstrate immediate and continuous value to users and make them want to come back, or you risk churning them forever."

David and his team set out to tackle the challenge to drive growth around the two pillars of freemium and product-led growth (PLG).[2] They have achieved astounding success. Canva skyrocketed from 10 million users and $23 million in revenue in 2017 to over 200 million users and $2.5 billion revenue by 2024.

Along the way, David and his team picked up invaluable lessons about scaling innovation and navigating evolving challenges as the business grew. In the sections to come, we explore some of the key insights from both the startup and growth phases of Canva's journey.

Lessons Learned During the Startup Phase

Canva learned several important lessons during the startup phase.

Product-Led Growth Lives and Dies by Value Delivery and Communication

From the get-go, Canva knew the value it aimed to deliver was a product that helped people create designs and digital graphics in an increasingly visual world faster, easier, and cheaper than ever before. Even in its early days, the team understood that its success depended on clearly and consistently delivering and communicating this value to win over users.

David and the Canva team saw PLG as a mutual and symmetrical exchange of value between Canva and its customers. As David puts it: "PLG lives or dies at any stage of the business by how much value you offer the end user. And I think the very definition of PLG is getting yourself pulled into your customer's world by being the best at delivering and meeting the specific needs of your end users, in a scalable way."

But how do you effectively demonstrate and communicate value in a PLG approach?

When you've built a great product, it's easy to get wrapped up in the excitement of all its bells and whistles. Every new feature addition Canva was launching came from hard work and innovation, and there's the temptation to showcase everything. But the key to success for Canva wasn't to highlight features; it was to communicate the value those features bring.

When reviewing feedback from Canva's customers, David noticed a trend. The happiest and most loyal customers weren't talking about features. They were focused on how Canva helps them achieve their goals and what benefits they received from using Canva. Very few mentioned specific features.

As David observed, "We can be deep in our product, in all our ideas, but most customers just don't think about what they need in terms of features. They want to know how the product solves their problems." This realization sparked a shift in communication strategy. David's team revised Canva's upgrade flows, replacing feature-heavy descriptions with benefit-driven language that reflected what those happy customers actually were saying. The result? A 7% to 8% increase in trial conversion, simply by changing communication focus from features to benefits.

Canva also had another key strategy for demonstrating value: *contextual conversion*.

One of Canva's key insights was that customers are more likely to upgrade from free to paid when the value of a paid feature is communicated at a contextually relevant moment—right when they're trying to accomplish something within the platform that a paid feature can help them achieve.

Driven by this insight, Canva decided to make all its paid features visible within the free experience. When users search for templates or images, premium assets are displayed alongside free ones. In the download menu, the option to download images with background removed (a premium feature) appeared right next to the regular download button. By embedding

Canva: The Master Class of Landing and Expanding

paid features into moments when users needed them most, Canva was able to maximize their conversion potential.

Offer a Simple Conversion Path

Sometimes the simplest solutions yield powerful results. As freemium PLG became more common, David noticed a surprising oversight among many companies: "A lot of these companies overlook the powerful simplicity of just having a button that says 'upgrade to paid.'"

As Canva gained traction, many users were ready to upgrade from free to paid on their own terms. These users may have already done their research or gained confidence through word-of-mouth referrals from their connections. Forcing them to dig around for a pricing page or pushing them through an unnecessary trial creates friction and risks losing potential paying customers who just want to dive into the paid product. Offering a quick, easy-to-find path to upgrade is key to capturing these users without delay.

Placing clear, accessible upgrade buttons in Canva's highest-traffic product areas accounted for 10% to 20% of all paid conversions. When combined with contextual conversion strategies, these approaches formed a powerful conversion toolkit that accelerated time-to-value for users and built a loyal, paid customer base.

Churn Is Driven by Lack of Value Realization

David observed:

> A lot of PLG companies say "we've got a churn problem" or "we've got a leaky bucket problem." But I actually think it's a value realization problem rather than a churn problem. If you've done the work to build a good product and you're confident you have a good product, that's how you can get users to actually engage

*frequently and deeply with that value. When I look into churn
at Canva, it's when we fail to get users to realize the value of
the product.*

A great example of Canva's focus on value communication is in its cancelation process. Many PLG companies make it difficult to cancel subscriptions, often forcing users through multiple steps and hurdles. In response to these policies, California passed a state law in September 2024 mandating a click-to-cancel rule aimed at simplifying cancelations through regulation.[3]

Canva, however, takes a different approach from other companies. Instead of hiding the cancelation option, Canva uses the cancelation moment to communicate to customers the value they have been receiving. On a single page, Canva reminds users of the paid features they used most frequently and how these features have supported their key use cases. If relevant, users are also shown any discounts or benefits they're receiving, such as preferred pricing for long-term customers versus new signups. This approach encourages users to reconsider the value Canva provides before making a decision to cancel.

When assessing churn, Canva looked beyond the typical churn causes and understood how often and deeply customers were engaging with Canva's platform and features. Were customers realizing Canva's value? Were there enough resources in place to help communicate and reinforce that value? And were churned customers returning to the paid version of Canva when their need arises again? Answering these questions helped David and his team address churn more effectively, better retain customers, and continuously improve value delivery.

Finding the Right Pricing and Packaging Strategy Is an Iterative Process

Finding the right strategy was not a one-and-done process for Canva, especially during the startup phase. "There's a lot of experimentation to get the

Canva: The Master Class of Landing and Expanding

pricing and value communication strategy right," David noted. "In fact, the seventh version is often many orders of magnitude more effective than the first."

Here are two key learnings David picked up along the way:

1. *Cheaper isn't always better, and it doesn't always drive growth.* For freemium products like Canva, there is a constant balancing act between expanding the paid subscriber base and maximizing revenue from individual paid users. Once Canva built a large free user base, David admitted the company was tempted to lower prices to convert more price-sensitive free users to paid. However, David found that lowering prices works only up to a point. "There's actually a point where, by lowering prices, you're leaving a lot of revenue on the table without driving more upgrades. People expect to pay a certain amount for high-quality software. If you price it like a throwaway app, it devalues the perceived value of your product." Instead of reducing prices, make sure your price is aligned with the value you are delivering and with your broader go-to-market strategy.

2. *More choice doesn't always equal better.* There's also a balance between offering enough options to meet differentiated needs and overwhelming users with too many choices. "Many customers come with a general sense of what they want to achieve with your product, but they do not come to you wanting to make a series of complex subdecisions about exactly what features they need to achieve that," David explained. Especially in a self-service freemium PLG model, David found that simplicity is key. Having a clear, strong opinion about what the paid experience should be for different types of users and putting those offers in front of relevant users was far more effective than allowing options to proliferate. Too many choices can create friction in the decision-making process and lead to missed opportunities to convert customers who might be ready to upgrade if the decision was made easier for them.

Lessons Learned During the Growth Phase

Canva's subsequent growth can only be described as explosive. When David joined in 2017, Canva had 10 million users. Since then, Canva more than doubled its user base roughly every two years, skyrocketing to over 200 million users by late 2024. Canva found particular success with the digital-savvy user, who increasingly used the platform for professional and collaboration purposes. By all measures, Canva had cracked the customer acquisition side of the PLG formula.

As Canva's user base grew, David's team shifted focus to the next set of challenges and opportunities. Two key priorities rose to the top: How could Canva better retain its hard-earned paid users, and how could Canva start expanding into new customer segments and use cases?

Success (and Retention) Requires Continuously Delivering and Onboarding Users to New Value

"Driving ongoing retention is a job that's never finished at any PLG SaaS company," David emphasized:

> Once we were confident in our free-to-trial and trial-to-paid motions, our focus shifted to driving more paid value and refining life cycle education—what we refer to as the continuous onboarding of new value. You might onboard a user right at the start of their journey as a paid subscriber, but as you add more value over time, you have to continuously onboard users to that new value so they see the product is getting deeper, richer, and solving more of their problems.

An effective onboarding experience ensures Canva users can realize the value of the paid offer as quickly as possible. During a free trial period, quick value realization boosts the likelihood that users will choose to stick around after their 30-day trial ends. For paid users, the onboarding experience incentivizes them to stay engaged and keep returning to Canva.

Canva has consistently excelled at introducing new, value-adding features since its initial launch. The Canva you see today is significantly more feature-rich than it was just one year ago, as the platform continues to evolve and the team continues to innovate. But all this innovation would be wasted if the new features didn't address real use needs—or if users weren't even aware of their existence.

A critical part of understanding value delivery comes from listening to your customers directly, especially those considering cancelation. One of the most valuable tools Canva has for driving improvements is its churn survey.

"I would highly recommend all companies to conduct churn surveys if they don't already," David advised.

> *Ask your users on the way out why they are canceling and obsess about that feedback, because it's some of the most priceless feedback you can get. It told us where users were not realizing value quickly, where onboarding and product education were needed, where product depth and quality were not met, and where additional needs were being articulated but not delivered.*

Canva's relentless focus on delivering and onboarding users to new value has paid off.[4] Its personalized onboarding process is consistently recognized as best-in-class for PLG SaaS companies and is a key driver of retention. When users see the product continuously becoming more useful and feature-rich, they're more likely to feel their money is well spent and stick with the product.

Overcoming the PLG Trap

The other priority for David's team was to help expand Canva into new customer segments. Up until around 2018, when Canva was being positioned for explosive growth, its user base was primarily made up of individual users purchasing through its website or platform. "Team and multiplayer were always part of the Canva vision, but we were only really starting to get to the early stages of a team experience by that time," David explained. "We always believed that Canva is a tool that would empower teams and businesses, as much as it empowered individuals."

Moving into intentionally serving businesses and even enterprises seemed like a natural next step. Millions of users were already using Canva for professional purchases, and teams across various businesses had organically adopted the platform for the same reasons independent users discovered and fell in love with the product. There was optimism that a groundswell of organic adoption would naturally translate into enterprise deals—after all, users within those companies were already using Canva.

However, going upmarket was not as simple as it seemed. Canva has been rooted firmly in the PLG go-to-market motion. Reaching enterprise customers required significant investments, both in product development and in rethinking Canva's go-to-market approach and team structure.

David and his team soon encountered what is known as the PLG trap, a concept coined in 2023 by Oliver Jay, former chief revenue officer of productivity software Asana, to describe common challenges PLG companies face when moving upmarket.[5] Companies like Canva, Asana, and Dropbox succeed by perfecting the PLG motion. Canva built a great product that users love and optimized it to serve individuals and small teams. However, when the opportunity to serve enterprises came up, Canva needed to evolve significantly to meet the needs of enterprise decision makers; Canva's existing product and team structure even were obstacles to going upmarket.

"The process of discovering pain points and attributing value to those pain points was incredibly different between our existing customers and enterprise buyers," David recalled. "In Canva's context, the buyer we need to sell to in an enterprise sale is often a [chief marketing officer] who has never and may never use the product."

In other words, in an enterprise context, the product no longer sells itself.

Canva initially struggled with this shift. "We probably applied our PLG-first approach to enterprise a little too long early on," David admitted. "It took us time to learn that there were major differences between the two and that we needed to adjust both our product and go-to-market processes to meet the needs of end users and enterprises, at the same time."

One of the key lessons was that, to succeed in the enterprise segment, Canva needed to build a top-down, sales-led motion that is supported by having different versions of the Canva product tailored specifically for large organizations. The value proposition for enterprise buyers had to address the unique pain points of decision makers, such as chief marketing officers and chief information officers, who often were removed from day-to-day product use.

"We needed to build a product strategy that mapped to the enterprise segment," David explained. "That meant a lot of intentional structural changes to make sure we had teams that were focused on the use cases for both individuals and for enterprise decision makers, like the [chief information officer]."

Another important lesson Canva learned when going upmarket may be counterintuitive for PLG companies—namely, that additional steps and human assistance can be a very good thing. While self-serve onboarding is key for individual users, enterprises require a different approach. Onboarding for enterprise customers often is more effective when delivered through a sales team and customer success partners who act as subject-matter experts.

Fortunately, Canva didn't have to start from scratch. It can leverage the organic adoption of its self-serve product to create champions within customer organizations—individuals who can influence the purchasing decision at the enterprise level. Additionally, Canva introduced a product-led sales motion, an evolution of the PLG model for businesses. With product-led sales, Canva lands in companies via its self-serve product. Once enough internal usage builds up, this organic groundswell can be leveraged to initiate a sales conversation with a buyer. From there, Canva consolidates the usage into a single enterprise contract, expanding its footprint within the company.

As David explained:

> *The beauty of starting with a PLG motion is that, if you're doing it well, you have a lot of people who really love your product and believe it adds an incredible amount of value. They believe it would benefit their organization as a whole if more people were using your product the way they are.*

In May 2024, Canva launched Canva Enterprise, a product specifically designed to support large organizations and enable the sales-led motion.[6] "The ideal scenario," David noted, "is where you have a PLG self-serve model driving bottom-up adoption, which is then accelerated and consolidated by a sales-led growth...motion, targeting lower-volume but higher-value customers."

Looking Ahead

Canva's journey from a startup to a design giant offers valuable lessons in scaling innovation and navigating the complexities of growth. By maintaining a relentless focus on value delivery, user-centric design, and adaptability, Canva successfully transitioned from a PLG model to incorporate a robust enterprise offering.

To sustain a strong growth trajectory, Canva will need to continue iterating on its product offerings, expanding its ecosystem of integrations and partnerships, and exploring emerging technologies. By staying ahead of the curve and anticipating the evolving needs of its users, Canva can ensure that it remains a driving force in the design and productivity space.

Chapter 15

ServiceChannel: Cracking the Code to Two-Sided Marketplace Success

Tom Buiocchi, Dan Leff, Brent Pearson, and Cameron O'Reilly huddled in the New York City office of their latest investment: facilities management software platform ServiceChannel. In 2014, they had invested in majority control of the company, which they regarded as a potential hidden gem. ServiceChannel operated a two-sided marketplace business service for retail facility management teams that wanted nationwide access to contingent contractor labor and a platform that allowed them to match skill sets to jobs needed as well as to transact smoothly from job request to close-out payment. Over the previous 15 years, ServiceChannel had been bootstrapped and grown to $9 million in annual recurring revenue, largely driven by annual contracts with the country's top restaurant chains and retailers, ranging from Apple Stores to Applebee's.

Now ServiceChannel faced a challenge common to businesses in the process of achieving scale: how to accelerate its revenue growth while continuing to expand its share of the marketplace.

As is typical of many early-stage startups, customer contracts had been crafted mostly through founder-led negotiations aimed at meeting the demands of an initial existing budget. As a result, there was no clear logic behind the pricing applied to ServiceChannel's various customers. Some retail chains were paying $1 per site per month while others were paying $10 per site per month, all independent of any recent data regarding willingness to pay and devoid of contractual mechanisms to adjust price over time.

In an initial brainstorming workshop, the group came up with three possible strategies for revenue acceleration:

1. Charge the existing chain customers a more value-based amount per site.

2. Begin charging the other side of the labor market (the contractors) for each job completed.

3. Begin building out an array of value-added services for both the chains and contractors, such as tools to help contractors stand out on the platform via enhanced work histories and certifications, or a parts and supplies portal to help both customers and contractors handle complex jobs quicker and more reliably.

With these three concepts on the table, the team set about engaging both enterprise customers and service providers in discussions to gauge how easy these changes would be to make. Team members spoke to 27 of ServiceChannel's 200 enterprise customers. It quickly became clear that willingness to pay had been vastly underestimated historically. Team members heard comments about ServiceChannel's offerings like: "I can't live without it," "It would take multiple full-time employees to replace the automated workflows," and "There is no competitive alternative."

However, the most eye-opening comment came from one very large customer for whom ServiceChannel had built out multiple workflows based on the customer portal. The customer agreed that the company's service was invaluable—but he also pointed out that the user experience was still rickety and that the company was not investing in improving it. He summed up his thinking about the company by cynically asking the ServiceChannel executives "Y'all in business or not?"

Taking all this feedback into account, the overall message was clear. ServiceChannel was offering a valuable service for which customers would be willing to pay significantly more. But the flipside of asking for more from customers would be that ServiceChannel had to take those proceeds and reinvest them in the core product to make it truly enterprise grade. If the hidden gem was to realize its full value, it needed to be burnished and presented accordingly.

The interviews with customers provided other valuable insights. For example, it became clear that there were key differences between restaurants and retail chains. In a retail setting, when a display case breaks or an electrical outlet fails, it reflects poorly on the shopping experience, but employees tend to find ways to work around the issue. By contrast, in a restaurant environment, if an oven breaks down or a workstation is inoperable, it has the potential to shut down the entire kitchen and grind all revenue-generating activity at the site to a halt. Differences like these needed to be reflected in the value offerings of ServiceChannel as well as the prices charged for those offerings.

The team also picked up on the fact that, even within industry verticals, opportunities for value-based pricing also existed based on the varying use cases and strategies of different retail and restaurant chains. For example, the brand image of a Louis Vuitton retail outlet makes a pristine store presentation absolutely essential; the same importance may not apply to a small GameStop location.

Based on these insights, the team created a simple target pricing mechanism based on retail versus restaurant segmentation and varying end-customer business models to ensure similar like-for-like customer pricing. It also aggressively raised target pricing across the board, with many customers seeing a 3× price increase. Given the magnitude of the changes envisioned and the relatively small universe of customers, every account got a call from a ServiceChannel executive to explain the changes. As a concession to the reality of budgeting processes, ServiceChannel also offered a multiyear ramp approach that would get the customers to the new highwater mark after two to three years.

Communicating the new pricing system wasn't free of challenges. The executive team members "got yelled at a lot." But because they understood the rationale for the price increases and the solid value being provided to their customers, team members accepted the bumpy moments. Over time, they even started to look at the price renegotiations as a competitive challenge and an opportunity to show their individual fortitude. Ultimately, after implementing the complete contractual overhaul with enterprise customers over a six-month period, ServiceChannel's committed annual recurring income increased from $14 million to $40 million, including a very minimal amount of churn, mostly from very small and financially insignificant customers.

Having reset the enterprise customer pricing, the team turned its attention to the second revenue-increasing option: charging the other side of the labor market for the value provided by the platform.

With billions of dollars in maintenance and repair activity already flowing through the platform, it wasn't necessary to go big on this front right away. Instead, the initial strategy was to establish a modest $1-per-invoice fee to the service provider. This fee ensured that only completed and paid jobs were charged, while it encouraged providers to recognize and acknowledge the value that they were getting from ServiceChannel.

The sales team developed a value message it shared consistently with providers, like a mantra: "You conveniently receive the work orders on your phone, with the explicit approval of chains, and you get paid faster than in an offline world." Some providers protested loudly, and a few even had to be shut off from platform access for refusing to go along with the new fee. But after a few weeks, and with the recognition that the $1 fee was a very small fraction of the average $600 invoice on the platform, the protests died down. ServiceChannel was now operating as a two-sided paid marketplace, changing the trajectory of the business. And with well over 1 million invoices processed per month, the aggregate total of the $1 fees provided a significant boost to the top line.

The two initial revenue-enhancing steps taken by the ServiceChannel team proved sufficient to gain the attention of additional investors, including

Accel at Series B. The team also established a foundation for further efforts to address the needs of service providers. In the years to come, Service-Channel launched a parts and supplies marketplace, third-party matching services, and other profile enhancements to help its provider customers enhance their own success and encourage them to increase their usage of and, ultimately, dependence on the platform.

Cracking the Code at ServiceChannel: Lessons for Every Founder

ServiceChannel's experience provides several important lessons that every founder should know:

- *Customer segmentation drives value pricing and revenue growth.* When it's time to scale, many customers discover that the pricing model that worked for the first few deals to establish product-market fit is no longer appropriate. In the ServiceChannel case, the company needed to examine the differentiated value it was offering to various customer segments and cohorts, including how the product affected downstream use cases in order to optimize pricing. It also needed to recognize the natural inflection point at which the provider side of the business, which had been participating for free, was ready to pay for access.

- *Price increases shouldn't be artificially limited.* Research and communication with customers made it clear that ServiceChannel was drastically undercharging for the value created for customers. If the company simply had targeted increases of 5% to 10% annually, its trajectory as a slow-growth company would not have changed materially. By biting the bullet and accepting the necessity of major price increases, ServiceChannel shifted into a sustainable, high-growth channel with the potential to achieve real scale.

- *A thoughtful negotiation and communication process can minimize the risk of churn.* The ServiceChannel team approached the challenge of negotiating new, high pricing with existing customers with some trepidation. However, once the process began, allowing team members' natural competitiveness to take over yielded surprisingly positive results. In addition, they found that a willingness to take a long-term view with concessions such as multiyear price increase ramps went a long way to maintaining strong relationships with customers.

- *Some churn is desirable.* The goal of your sales and customer teams should not necessarily be to achieve zero churn. When provider invoices were launched, a handful of former customers ended up being shut out of the system. This approach sent an important signal to the rest of the market that ServiceChannel was serious about establishing a true two-sided market and unwilling to back down from its strategic vision.

- *Keeping your give/get promises is powerful.* ServiceChannel's promise to reinvest the higher contract fees into the business through improvements to the platform was a highly compelling story that the product team was able to fulfill. The front-end user interface was overhauled and the back end became more scalable. As a result, over time, credibility was built into the system, and each successive price increase was easier to justify.

The End Result

By the time the founders of ServiceChannel were ready to look for an exit for their early investors, the company's business model had been dramatically improved. What's more, the business had developed multiple ancillary revenue streams adding up to $125 million in revenue—a tenfold increase over just five years. These developments made it possible for the business to be sold in 2021 to Fortive for $1.2 billion.[1]

Chapter 16

CoCounsel: Scaling the AI that Passed the Bar

Back in 2013, Jake Heller was an associate at Ropes & Gray, a prestigious law firm based in Boston. Despite being part of a top-tier legal practice, he couldn't shake the feeling that the tools lawyers relied on were woefully outdated. While his iPhone could instantly tell him which Thai restaurant near his Boston office was open late, finding the case law that might determine the outcome of a billion-dollar lawsuit often required nights of painstaking research. He knew something had to change.

As both a lawyer and a lifelong programmer, Jake saw an opportunity. If modern technology could revolutionize industries like retail and healthcare, why couldn't it do the same for legal practice? What if lawyers could rely on tools that streamlined research, drafting, and analysis—saving them time and improving outcomes? Armed with this vision, Jake cofounded Casetext together with Pablo Arredondo (chief innovation officer) and Laura Safdie (chief operating officer and general counsel) with the aim of bringing the legal profession into the 21st century.

But building Casetext wouldn't be easy. Incumbent giants like Westlaw and LexisNexis dominated the legal research space, boasting vast databases and decades of institutional trust. Jake and his cofounders knew they couldn't compete head-on. Instead, they leaned into the power of community and accessibility. Inspired by platforms like GitHub and Stack Overflow, Casetext's initial product was a free, collaborative search engine for federal cases. It was a bold bet to democratize legal research, allowing anyone—not just lawyers—to find the legal insights they needed.

Casetext's early traction proved the founders' instincts right. Lawyers across the country flocked to the platform, drawn by its simplicity and speed. However, scaling a free product in a capital-intensive industry came with its own challenges. As venture capital sentiment shifted in the mid-2010s (with venture capitalists focused more than ever on earnings over potential), Casetext was forced to pivot. The company began building premium tools powered by ML and natural-language processing (NLP), including CARA (Case Analysis Research Assistant), an advanced research assistant that could instantly analyze briefs and surface overlooked insights. This pivot marked a turning point in Casetext's journey, transforming it from a research tool to a serious enterprise solution for law firms.

Fast forward to 2022, and Casetext was once again redefining the legal tech landscape with CoCounsel, an AI-powered assistant capable of drafting, analyzing, and reviewing documents at speeds no human associate could match. From its modest beginnings in a Boston law office to becoming a pioneer in AI-driven legal solutions, Casetext's story is one of relentless innovation and adaptability.

In the following sections, we dive into the defining moments of Casetext's monetization journey—how it built a community, pivoted to AI, and found a way to thrive in an industry often resistant to change. This isn't just a story about building a company; it's a story about transforming an entire profession.

Lessons Learned During the Startup Phase

Casetext learned several important lessons during the startup phase.

Product-Market Fit: A Spectrum, Not a Destination

In the early days of Casetext, Jake and his team believed they had achieved product-market fit (PMF). Their free legal research platform was gaining traction, with lawyers discovering it organically, engaging with its tools, and even recommending it to peers. By traditional metrics, it seemed like the product was resonating with its target audience. But in hindsight, Jake realized this initial success wasn't PMF in its truest sense; it was merely the first step on a spectrum.

"Product-market fit isn't a switch you flip—it's a spectrum," Jake reflected, citing Marc Andreessen's famous essay "The Only Thing That Matters." Andreessen describes PMF as an unmistakable moment when the servers are constantly going down because you have too many users and sales teams can't keep up with the demand. In the essay, Andreessen writes:

> *You can always feel when product/market fit isn't happening.* The customers aren't quite getting value out of the product, word of mouth isn't spreading, usage isn't growing that fast, press reviews are kind of "blah," the sales cycle takes too long, and lots of deals never close.[1]

For Casetext, that moment didn't come until nearly a decade later, with the launch of CoCounsel. "In the beginning, we thought we had PMF because people were using the product," Jake admitted. In reality, the company hadn't fully solved the deeper problems their customers were facing—or reached the point where customers were clamoring to pay for it.

The lessons the team learned along the way reshaped their understanding of PMF. Casetext's initial product—a free legal research tool—addressed a surface-level need: giving lawyers faster access to case law. However, Jake notes that Casetext's early traction had lacked the telltale signs of PMF: the overwhelming demand, the viral growth, the inability to keep up with customer demands. Those came later, during the explosive adoption of CoCounsel, which was the company's moment of unquestionable, true product-market fit. It was a stark contrast to the team's early days, where engagement was encouraging but inconsistent and monetization remained an ongoing challenge.

Pivoting Away from a Growth-at-All-Costs Mindset

In its early days, Casetext, like many startups of its time, operated under a growth-first philosophy. Encouraged by venture capitalists, the team was told not to worry about monetization and instead focus on building a user base. The strategy seemed sound: Platforms like Facebook and Google had achieved massive success by scaling first and figuring out monetization later. Casetext's free legal research tool followed this playbook, attracting users through organic search and community-driven content contributions.

However, by 2015, the tide had turned. Investor sentiment had shifted, and venture capitalists began prioritizing sustainable business models over user acquisition. The market went from celebrating growth at all costs to demanding profitability. This shift forced Casetext to confront a hard truth: Although its free tool had drawn users, it wasn't enough to sustain the business. Relying on free access and community contributions could take the company only so far, and the team realized they needed a revenue model that aligned with their long-term vision.

The solution came in the form of CARA, a machine-learning-powered tool that analyzed legal briefs and provided actionable insights. CARA was a clear value-add for lawyers, saving them time and improving the quality of their work. Law firms quickly recognized its potential, and many were willing to pay $50,000 to $200,000 annually to equip their teams with the tool. This point in time marked a critical pivot for Casetext—from a growth-focused company dependent on free users to a revenue-driven business with a premium enterprise offering.

For founders, the lesson here is twofold. First, growth at all costs can sustain you for only so long; at some point, monetization becomes essential. Second, pivoting to a revenue-driven model doesn't mean abandoning your original vision; it means aligning that vision with the realities of the market. Casetext's ability to build on its free platform and create premium tools allowed it to transition seamlessly into monetization while retaining its core mission of empowering legal professionals.

Lessons Learned During the Scale-up Phase

After successfully pivoting from a free legal research platform to a revenue-generating business with tools like CARA, Casetext had established a strong foundation. These early years were defined by adaptation—listening to the market, identifying the gaps in the company's initial model, and building solutions that resonated with both enterprise clients and smaller law firms. By introducing a premium tier of features and embracing a freemium model, Casetext not only diversified its revenue streams but also created a natural pathway for user upgrades.

Armed with this momentum, the company was ready to enter its next phase—a period defined by exponential growth, deeper market penetration, and the rollout of game-changing innovations like CoCounsel. Casetext was no longer just a legal research tool; it was becoming a transformative force in the legal tech industry, reshaping how lawyers approached their work and setting a new standard for AI-powered solutions.

Unlocking Unexpected Markets

As Casetext entered its scale-up phase, the team focused on refining its business model to scale effectively. Initially, the company assumed that its primary market would be large law firms, given the team's own experience in these environments and the significant budgets such firms could allocate for technology. However, Casetext was in for a surprise: The small and mid-size law firm (SMB) segment, which had not been a focus for the founders, emerged as a critical driver of growth.

The discovery came somewhat unexpectedly. While Casetext had initially designed its entire go-to-market motion for large firms, it also made its tools available for self-service purchase through a simple Stripe payment page, primarily as an experiment. When the team at Casetext checked the numbers, they found that hundreds of small firms had subscribed—many at price points considered high for this segment. These firms were signing up without any sales conversations or support, driven solely by the value of the tools Casetext offered.

This discovery shattered several assumptions. Unlike large firms, which have extensive resources and established workflows, smaller firms often operate under tighter constraints. For these firms, Casetext's tools represented a cost-effective way to gain capabilities they couldn't otherwise afford—essentially acting as a "force multiplier" for small teams. In fact, surprisingly, many SMBs saw greater urgency in adopting technology than their larger counterparts.

Data-Driven Growth in Packaging and Pricing

In the scale-up phase, Casetext's approach to pricing and packaging evolved significantly. Early on, the strategy was largely organic, shaped by years of conversations with customers and firsthand experience in selling the product. The team maintained a culture of constant engagement with users, with Jake personally speaking to 10 to 20 customers a week, ranging from solo practitioners to enterprise law firms. Over time, this relentless focus on customer feedback created a wealth of qualitative data—insights into what customers valued most, how they preferred to pay, and what pricing felt right to them.

This organic approach worked well in the early days because it gave Casetext an intuitive understanding of the market. The team knew, for example, that large law firms cared deeply about predictability in pricing, preferring subscription models that offered certainty over pay per use or other variable structures. They also learned that complexity in packaging could be a deterrent. Simplifying the number of options available and bundling features into straightforward plans ensured that customers didn't feel overwhelmed when choosing a package.

For the SMB segment, they took this learning further. Although the initial traction with SMBs came as a surprise, it also presented an opportunity to refine Casetext's approach in a more systematic way. Unlike enterprise sales, which involved long negotiation cycles and bespoke contracts, the SMB market required simplicity, speed, and scalability. These learnings led to a shift from intuition-driven pricing to more data-driven decision making.

The high volume of SMB customers subscribing to Casetext's tools through self-service provided a goldmine of data. With thousands of users adopting the platform, Casetext could test different price points, trial lengths, and feature bundles to understand what resonated most with this segment. For instance, the company experimented with shorter free trials to drive quicker conversions and tested tiered pricing to gauge customers' willingness to pay for advanced features.

Although the data wasn't always statistically perfect, patterns emerged that were too clear to ignore. SMBs gravitated toward simple, all-inclusive plans over complex feature-based pricing. They preferred affordable monthly subscriptions that mirrored the cost of hiring an additional employee at a fraction of the price. Using these insights, Casetext tailored its packaging for SMBs, offering plans that struck the right balance between affordability and value.

Being Proactive About Churn

For Casetext, minimizing churn was not just a matter of protecting revenue; it was central to sustaining growth in a competitive legal tech market. The company's approach to churn reflected a deep understanding of customer behavior across its two core segments: enterprise clients and SMBs. Each segment required distinct strategies, but the common thread was a proactive and product-led approach to retention.

Among enterprise clients, churn was almost nonexistent. These large firms typically signed multiyear contracts and relied heavily on Casetext's tools to maintain their competitive edge. For these customers, Casetext prioritized high-touch engagement through dedicated account management and customer success teams. The enterprise team's focus was twofold: ensuring clients derived maximum value from the tools and identifying opportunities for upselling. Regular check-ins, personalized training sessions, and tailored feature updates kept enterprise clients engaged and satisfied. By addressing issues proactively, Casetext ensured that enterprise relationships deepened over time, leading to high net revenue retention and long-term loyalty.

Retention among SMBs, however, was a more complex challenge. Many small law firms operated on tighter budgets and shorter planning horizons, making them more susceptible to churn. Some churned due to external factors, such as unstable businesses, unpredictable revenue, or even the winding down of operations. Others subscribed for short-term needs, such as a specific case, and left once the immediate demand was met. Casetext addressed this situation in several ways:

- *Proactive customer success.* Instead of waiting for problems to arise, the customer success team actively monitored usage data to identify customers at risk of churn. If usage dropped or critical features weren't being leveraged, the team reached out to offer support, suggest workflows, or highlight underused features.

- *Continuous engagement.* Live events, community webinars, and regular updates kept customers informed and engaged. These touchpoints not only showcased Casetext's commitment to its users but also reinforced the value of the platform.

- *Retention through product.* A key pillar of Casetext's retention strategy was its ability to iterate quickly based on customer feedback. If churn was driven by missing features, those features were prioritized in product development. Casetext also focused on delighting users with incremental improvements and new capabilities that made the platform indispensable.

Building for the Future

Casetext's journey to sustained growth and market leadership culminated in one of its most transformative innovations: CoCounsel, an AI-powered legal assistant designed to fundamentally reshape how lawyers approach their work. By the time CoCounsel launched, Casetext had already established itself as a leader in legal tech, but the development and release of this product reinforced the company's commitment to staying ahead of the curve through relentless innovation.

The idea for CoCounsel wasn't born overnight. For years, Casetext had been engaging deeply with its customers, gathering insights not only about what they loved but also about what was missing. Lawyers consistently expressed a desire for tools that didn't just help them find information but actively assisted in completing the work itself: drafting, reviewing, and analyzing legal documents with the precision and efficiency of an associate.

The technological leap that made this vision possible came in the form of advanced AI. Casetext's early investment in ML and NLP paid off when it became one of the first companies to experiment with OpenAI's GPT-3 and later GPT-4. Unlike traditional legal research tools, CoCounsel leveraged this cutting-edge AI to perform complex legal tasks with human-level nuance and superhuman speed.

Having seen what these new GPT models (which at the time were not publicly available) were capable of, Jake, Laura, and Pablo decided to pivot the entire company's focus. Although the sales team continued to sell the existing product, the majority of the company's resources were reallocated to developing CoCounsel.

The response to CoCounsel was overwhelming. Early beta testers, many of whom were seeing GPT-4 capabilities for the first time, were astounded by what the product could do. Tasks that previously took hours or even days were now completed in minutes, with a level of precision and depth that rivaled that of human associates.

For Casetext, CoCounsel wasn't just about launching a new product; it was about redefining the boundaries of what legal tech could achieve. The release marked a new chapter in the company's history, one characterized by explosive growth and true product-market fit. Within months of its launch, CoCounsel became the fastest-growing product in Casetext's portfolio, nearly tripling the company's revenue and positioning it as a trailblazer in AI-driven legal solutions.

Casetext's Blueprint: Lessons Every Founder Should Know

Casetext provides invaluable lessons for founders, particularly in building, scaling, and sustaining an SaaS business in competitive markets. From mastering product-market fit to innovating continuously, Casetext's journey is rich with insights on growth, retention, and monetization. Let's dive in:

- *Product-market fit is a journey, not a destination.* Casetext's early traction gave it the illusion of product-market fit, but true PMF only came years later with the launch of CoCounsel. Early adoption metrics were encouraging but didn't reflect whether the product deeply solved customer problems or drove a willingness to pay.

  The Lesson: PMF is a spectrum. Early traction is a starting point, not the finish line. Keep iterating to solve deeper pain points and align with customers' willingness to pay.

- *Pivoting to monetization with purpose.* Casetext initially followed the growth-first philosophy, prioritizing user acquisition over revenue. But as investor sentiment shifted, the team pivoted to monetization by introducing CARA, an AI-powered tool that customers valued enough to pay for. This pivot allowed Casetext to transition to a revenue-driven business while staying true to its mission.

  The Lesson: Don't delay monetization indefinitely. Growth is critical, but sustainable success requires aligning your product's value with what customers are willing to pay.

- *Unlocking unexpected markets through data.* Although Casetext initially targeted large law firms, its self-service subscription experiment revealed an untapped SMB market. Smaller firms valued Casetext as a cost-effective alternative to hiring more staff. The Casetext team used data from SMB sign-ups to refine pricing and tailor offerings for this high-velocity segment.

  The Lesson: Look for unexpected traction and use data to refine your strategy. Adjacent or overlooked markets can become critical growth drivers.

- *Proactive retention through engagement.* Casetext's retention strategy combined proactive customer success with product-driven improvements. For enterprises, the team focused on high-touch account management and upselling. For SMBs, it invested in regular updates and feature rollouts that addressed churn drivers.

  The Lesson: Retention starts early. Proactively engage customers and improve your product to address pain points before they churn.

- *Continuous innovation that addresses core customer needs keeps you competitive.* The launch of CoCounsel demonstrated Casetext's commitment to staying ahead through innovation. By leveraging cutting-edge AI and addressing customer demands for deeper functionality, Casetext created a transformative product that redefined the legal tech market.

  The Lesson: Innovation isn't optional. Stay ahead of competitors by continuously improving your product and addressing evolving customer needs.

The End Result

Casetext's journey came full circle in 2023 when it was acquired by Thomson Reuters for $650 million. The deal marked a major milestone, validating Casetext's relentless focus on innovation and its transformative impact on the legal tech industry. Thomson Reuters, a dominant force in professional information services, recognized the immense value of Casetext's AI-powered solutions, particularly CoCounsel, which redefined legal workflows with unprecedented speed and precision. This acquisition not only rewarded Casetext's visionaries but also underscored how aligning product innovation with market needs can create lasting value and industry leadership.

Chapter 17

Airbnb: The Blueprint for Turning Community into Cash Flow

San Francisco was bustling with visitors arriving for a major design conference in 2008. Lodging options were stretched thin, and hotel prices soared. Brian Chesky and Joe Gebbia—both design graduates eager to experiment—saw an opportunity. They decided to offer air mattresses in their apartment's living room to a few out-of-town guests, sweetening the deal with simple breakfasts. This improvised "air bed and breakfast" was a humble, almost accidental prototype of what would soon become Airbnb: a global travel marketplace built on trust, personal connection, and community.

However, in those early days, skepticism ran high. Many investors balked at the idea of strangers sleeping in each other's homes; some early users wondered if the concept would even scale. The company pressed on, though, opting first to establish market share and nurture the community rather than squeeze out maximum revenue. The company carefully recruited hosts, refined trust mechanisms—such as user reviews and secure payment platforms—and expanded across continents, amassing millions of listings.

Over time, as the platform's global network solidified, Airbnb began turning its enormous reach into robust streams of revenue. By combining broad market share with well-targeted "wallet share" strategies, it introduced services like Airbnb Experiences and premium categories such as Airbnb Luxe. The company refined pricing models and offered hosts better tools to manage their listings and operations, reducing churn and enhancing satisfaction. By 2023, Airbnb had secured over 6 million active listings in 220+ countries and regions, posted $650 million in net income in Q2 of that year, and generated $3.9 billion in free cash flow over the trailing 12 months—testimony that a trust-based marketplace could be both beloved by users and profitable at scale.

Crucially, Airbnb didn't stop at simple transactions. The company made strategic moves to retain hosts and guests alike, experimenting with loyalty features, flexible booking options, and a whole suite of ancillary solutions that encouraged repeat usage. By balancing community with monetization, Airbnb became a modern paragon of profitable growth, proof that strong marketplace fundamentals can pave the way for innovative, high-margin revenue streams.

In the pages ahead, we dissect Airbnb's journey from a quirky idea born out of a local conference crunch to a multinational platform architected for profitable growth. We explore how it navigated early skepticism and balanced market expansion with revenue optimization—lessons that can guide entrepreneurs as they transform ambitious visions into enduring business models.

Lessons Learned During the Startup Phase

Airbnb learned several important lessons during the startup phase.

The Importance of Community and Trust

From the very beginning, Airbnb was asking people to do something that ran counter to most established norms: open the doors of their homes to complete strangers. Unlike many traditional marketplaces—where transactions revolve around commodities or products—Airbnb's platform centered on personal spaces and shared experiences. When the product you're offering is someone's home, the stakes are inherently higher. Safety, security, and comfort are not just nice-to-haves; they are absolute necessities. If either side of the marketplace—hosts or guests—harbored lingering doubts about the reliability or honesty of the other, the entire system could collapse before it ever got off the ground.

It's precisely because of this delicate proposition that Airbnb's founders chose to prioritize community and trust over quick revenue grabs. Charging more fees or introducing premium features too early might have scared away fledgling users. Instead, the team doubled down on creating an environment where potential guests felt confident booking a stranger's spare bedroom and where potential hosts felt secure inviting unknown travelers into their homes. The team rolled out verified IDs, dedicated customer support, and user review systems, all of which signaled to their community "We hear you, and we care about your peace of mind." By showcasing these efforts, Airbnb demonstrated that the platform was built for people, not just profit.

This approach was critical for another reason: A stable, thriving community increases the long-term value of the marketplace. If the earliest adopters had a poor experience—maybe a suspicious listing, a confusing transaction, or an unresponsive host—no amount of monetization would retain them. Negative word of mouth could have spread quickly, and the platform might never have reached critical mass. By contrast, building trust from the ground up allowed Airbnb to steadily accumulate positive reviews, loyal hosts, and satisfied guests. Each good experience became a mini test case proving that home-sharing could be safe and enjoyable. In due course, this meticulous approach created a powerful, self-reinforcing cycle: As more trustworthy hosts and happy guests joined, the marketplace grew more robust, more appealing, and, ultimately, more profitable.

In essence, for a model as personal and sensitive as home-sharing, trust couldn't be an afterthought. For Airbnb, prioritizing community was not only the ethical choice, it was a strategic imperative. By focusing on the user experience, safety, and authenticity first, the company created fertile ground for revenue streams to bloom naturally.

Focusing on Customer Centricity

From the outset, Airbnb faced a formidable challenge: It was building a marketplace that served two distinct sets of customers, each with its own priorities. On one side were the hosts, individuals willing to list their homes and personal spaces for travelers. On the other side were the guests, people eager to find reliable, comfortable, and affordable accommodations. The tightrope walk was in ensuring that both parties felt seen, supported, and valued. If either side's needs were overlooked, the entire system would fail. Trust and safety, as we just discussed, were only the first steps. Long-term success would hinge on Airbnb's ability to learn from their users—both hosts and guests—and continuously refine the product based on that feedback. This approach set the tone for a customer-centric culture that was never complacent.

For hosts, the company understood that making it easy to join and succeed on the platform was paramount. That's why Airbnb invested in professional photography services, helping hosts showcase their spaces in the best possible light. It introduced intuitive dashboards and pricing recommendations, allowing hosts to manage their listings more effectively. These tools weren't arbitrary; they directly addressed hosts' expressed pain points, whether it was difficulty standing out to potential guests or uncertainty about how to price their rooms. By delivering meaningful support, Airbnb helped ensure that hosts felt confident and cared for—a sentiment that kept them engaged, producing a steady supply of quality listings.

On the guest side, the approach was similarly customer-centric. Guests needed to find what they were looking for quickly and feel certain that their chosen space would match their expectations. Airbnb refined its search algorithms, bolstered its filtering options, and made reviews and ratings a central component of the booking experience. Guests could read about past stays, gain insights into their hosts, and form an informed opinion before ever stepping through the door. All of these enhancements flowed naturally from what customers requested: more clarity, greater transparency, and a smoother path to discovery. By demonstrating that it was listening and acting on customer input, Airbnb built loyalty and trust that extended well beyond a single transaction.

Critically, these customer-centric moves were not made in isolation. Airbnb didn't simply implement a feature and assume it would work forever. Instead, it adopted a test-and-learn mentality. New features, pricing models, and host support initiatives were rolled out, measured, and refined. If something didn't resonate with users—say, a particular fee structure or a new premium listing category—Airbnb didn't double down blindly. It reevaluated, talked to users, and adjusted course. This iterative approach, always anchored in user feedback, ensured that the product evolved in lockstep with the real-world needs of the community it served.

By relentlessly focusing on what both hosts and guests needed rather than on what might maximize immediate revenue, Airbnb built a marketplace that not only flourished but endured. Entrepreneurs who adopt this customer-centric mindset will find that monetization becomes less about convincing people to pay and more about earning their willingness to invest in the value you've created together.

Lessons Learned During the Growth Phase

After solidifying its early footing by prioritizing trust and cultivating a flourishing two-sided community, Airbnb was no longer just a promising startup trying to prove the home-sharing concept—it had established itself as a credible, global platform. In the startup phase, the company learned to balance host and guest interests and continuously refined its user experience. With these foundational lessons internalized, Airbnb was ready to move beyond the question of whether people would share their homes with strangers. The focus now shifted toward unlocking exponential growth, exploring new markets, and introducing diversified offerings that went well beyond spare rooms and couches.

This next stage was not merely about scaling the business; it was about reimagining travel, expanding what customers could do within the Airbnb ecosystem, and translating a community-driven ethos into sustainable, wide-reaching financial success. Armed with hard-earned insights, strong brand recognition, and a loyal global base, Airbnb was set to transform from a clever startup into a true hospitality powerhouse, shaping how people thought about lodging, culture, and experiences around the world.

Expanding Your Customer Value Proposition

As Airbnb moved beyond its startup roots, the company realized that simply relying on room rentals wouldn't guarantee long-term resilience. Although its core marketplace model—connecting guests to hosts—was performing well, Airbnb understood that a platform is at its strongest when it offers multiple paths for users to engage and spend. To achieve this goal, Airbnb systematically broadened its portfolio, creating offerings tailored to different travel tastes and price points.

One of the most notable moves in this direction was the introduction of Airbnb Experiences in 2016. No longer confined to providing a place to sleep, Airbnb began curating local activities and cultural excursions hosted by knowledgeable locals. These offerings ranged from pasta-making classes in Rome to surfing lessons in Bali. This shift redefined Airbnb as more than just an accommodations platform; it became a brand synonymous with immersive travel experiences. Guests could now craft an entire vacation through Airbnb, which boosted loyalty, repeat usage, and ultimately revenue.

Going further, Airbnb introduced Airbnb Luxe, a premium category aimed at travelers seeking higher-end, verified listings that met stringent quality and design criteria. While the initial home-sharing marketplace brought affordability and uniqueness to the forefront, Plus and Luxe appealed to a demographic willing to pay more for comfort, reliability, and premium amenities. This approach allowed Airbnb to capture a greater share of a traveler's budget by offering something that traditional hotels had long excelled at: consistent quality and upscale service. The evolution into higher-end products also demonstrated that Airbnb could compete at multiple levels of the market—from budget travelers to affluent globetrotters—without diluting its brand identity.

These diversification efforts worked because they aligned closely with user needs. Gradually, Airbnb's customers had grown to trust the platform for lodging; now customers could extend that trust to other parts of their trips. By owning more components of the travel journey, Airbnb secured a larger wallet share from existing guests, who no longer needed to look elsewhere for activities, luxury stays, or curated experiences. Instead of extracting more value from users through aggressive pricing on its core product, Airbnb provided genuinely enhanced offerings that justified higher spending. This approach not only increased immediate revenue but also created stronger customer loyalty and reduced the likelihood of users drifting to competing platforms for other aspects of their trip.

For entrepreneurs, Airbnb's strategy offers a key insight: *Sustainable growth often emerges from delivering more value, not just charging more for the same service.* By thoughtfully layering new products and segments onto a successful core proposition, companies can lock in customers for a longer portion of their journey, providing them with reasons to stay engaged and continue spending. Rather than risk commodification by standing still, Airbnb kept evolving its brand into a full-fledged travel ecosystem, converting guests into repeat users and advocates. This holistic approach to product diversification and value enhancement allowed Airbnb to weather market fluctuations, strengthen its competitive advantage, and raise the overall lifetime value of its customer base.

Continuous Refinement Drives Sustainable Monetization

As Airbnb entered its growth phase, one of its most complex and finely tuned challenges was monetization: determining how to charge both hosts and guests in a way that felt fair, transparent, and valuable. Doing this wasn't a simple calculation. Like many marketplaces, Airbnb faced a delicate equilibrium: Hosts needed to feel they were getting a fair shake for sharing their homes, while guests needed confidence that they weren't being squeezed by opaque fees or unpredictable price hikes. The company's evolving approach to monetization, spanning everything from service fees to dynamic pricing tools, offers a masterclass in how to build sustainable revenue models that remain rooted in customer needs and feedback.

From the host perspective, Airbnb's fee structure initially required some balancing acts. Today, many hosts choose between a split-fee model (where guests pay the bulk of service charges and hosts pay a smaller percentage) or a host-only fee model (around 15%), depending on their preference and business setup. This flexibility allows hosts to select a structure that aligns with their revenue goals and local market conditions. Beyond these fees, Airbnb introduced Smart Pricing, a feature powered by algorithms that adjust nightly rates based on factors like demand, seasonality, and local market trends. By giving hosts data-driven recommendations, Airbnb ensures that prices remain competitive without requiring constant manual adjustments. This system rewards responsive hosts who trust Airbnb's analytics, creating a smoother earnings journey for property owners.

On the guest side, the monetization puzzle proved equally intricate. With time, travelers grew vocal about feeling blindsided by cleaning fees, taxes, and other add-ons that surfaced late in the booking process. Airbnb's response demonstrated its commitment to iterative improvement and customer-centricity. In 2022, the company introduced "Total Price Display," showing the entire cost up front—rent, fees, and taxes—so guests wouldn't be surprised at checkout. CEO Brian Chesky openly acknowledged these criticisms, pledging to make pricing more transparent and fair. He spoke publicly about initiatives to help customers quickly identify the best overall value, reflecting a willingness to reshape longstanding policies in response to user input.

This ongoing dialogue between Airbnb and its users—hosts and guests alike—illustrates the company's understanding that monetization is never a set-it-and-forget-it proposition. Airbnb has straddled a line between complexity and clarity for years, learning that while fees and dynamic pricing can help align supply and demand, these tools must be wielded with empathy and guided by robust user feedback. When complaints arise or markets shift, Airbnb adjusts. When data shows that certain fees undermine the trust the company has worked so hard to build, the platform reconsiders its approach.

For entrepreneurs, Airbnb's pricing evolution conveys an essential lesson: Your monetization strategy must be as agile as your product development. It's not enough simply to charge what the market will bear. Instead, you must demonstrate value at every step, ensuring that those who pay (guests) and those who earn (hosts) both recognize the fairness and purpose behind the numbers on the screen. By continuously listening, experimenting, and revising fees and pricing models, Airbnb keeps its community at the heart of its profitability strategy, proving that a marketplace can grow its bottom line without sacrificing the trust and satisfaction of the people who fuel its success.

Anchoring Growth in Host Loyalty

In a marketplace like Airbnb's, quality and consistency hinge on the reliability of its supply: hosts who consistently provide welcoming, well-maintained, and appealing accommodations. To strengthen this supply side, Airbnb invested heavily in host loyalty mechanisms. By forging durable relationships with top-performing hosts, the platform improved the overall guest experience while creating a stable, self-reinforcing network where satisfied guests are more likely to return.

At the heart of Airbnb's host loyalty strategy is the Superhost program, designed to celebrate and encourage top-tier hospitality. Achieving

Superhost status requires meeting high standards—maintaining at least a 4.8 average rating (from guests), providing fast response times, honoring confirmed reservations, and hosting frequently. In return, Superhosts earn elevated search rankings, a distinctive badge that signals trustworthiness to guests, and early access to new platform features. By tying meaningful rewards directly to hosting excellence, Airbnb creates strong incentives for hosts to invest more effort and care in their listings. This approach, in turn, ensures that guests frequently encounter polished, dependable accommodations, which reduces friction, improves reviews, and makes the platform more enticing for repeat visits.

Airbnb's host loyalty efforts extend beyond recognition programs. The company offers a suite of resources and protections that position hosts as valued partners. The AirCover for Hosts program provides comprehensive damage and liability protection, easing common anxieties around property rental. Free professional photography services, Smart Pricing tools, and performance analytics dashboards help hosts optimize their listings and maintain competitive rates. These measures reduce the operational burden on hosts, making it easier and more enjoyable for them to stay on the platform long term. By lowering barriers and mitigating risks, Airbnb ensures that motivated, reliable hosts continue to enrich the marketplace.

When Airbnb locks in its best hosts—those who deliver consistently high-quality experiences—it indirectly locks in guests, too. Happy guests who stay with vetted, engaged hosts are more likely to leave positive reviews and recommend the platform to others. They are also more inclined to rebook on Airbnb for future trips, knowing that the platform's host loyalty initiatives encourage excellence. This positive feedback loop is powerful: Reliable hosts attract satisfied guests, satisfied guests create stronger demand, and stronger demand encourages even more hosts to invest time and care into their listings. Over time, this synergy forms a stable base of both supply and demand, anchoring Airbnb's marketplace and cultivating enduring loyalty across the board.

Airbnb's Blueprint: Lessons Every Founder Should Know

Airbnb's journey from air mattresses in San Francisco to a global hospitality powerhouse offers invaluable lessons. From building community trust first to refining monetization and growth strategies, its story highlights the importance of evolving along with your customers.

- *Earning trust before monetization.* Before Airbnb could dream of becoming a household name, it had to convince people to open their homes to strangers. By prioritizing community and safety features—like user reviews, verified IDs, and secure payments—over early revenue, Airbnb built a foundation of trust.

  The Lesson: In businesses driven by network effect, trust is imperative. Prove your value, and your customers will be far more open to paying when the time is right.

- *Balancing a two-sided marketplace.* Hosts needed to feel supported and fairly compensated while guests needed a reliable, straightforward booking experience. Airbnb's continuous attention to both sides—through tools like Smart Pricing for hosts and transparent total price displays for guests—ensured that everyone felt valued.

  The Lesson: When you're building a platform, understand and serve every stakeholder. Happy suppliers breed happy customers, creating a self-reinforcing cycle of growth.

- *Monetization with transparency and flexibility.* Airbnb tested and refined its fee structures, learning the hard way that poorly communicated or opaque charges erode goodwill. Listening to user feedback, it introduced clearer pricing, giving hosts the choice of how fees are split and ensuring guests understand all costs up front.

  The Lesson: Monetization should be fair, easy to understand, and adaptable. When customers feel in control and see the value behind your fees, they're more willing to pay.

Airbnb: The Blueprint for Turning Community into Cash Flow

- Continuous improvements to the core product: Since 2021, Airbnb has made 500+ updates to the platform. This includes:

  o Updates to become more competitive on pricing, with upgrades like total pricing transparency, host education tools around pricing, and more.

  o Major reliability initiatives, like Guest Favorites, that make it easy for guests to find the best listings, as well as new tools and policies to deter host cancellations and remove low quality listings.

  o Simplified the booking journey to make it more fun, with shared wishlists, trip invitations and messages.

  o Overhauled the suite of host tools and support services, like the listings tab and earnings dashboard, to give hosts a clear view of what they make.

  The Lesson: Continuous improvement isn't just about adding features—it's about sharpening your competitive edge and reinforcing trust. By consistently refining pricing, reliability, and the user experience, you signal to both sides of the marketplace that you're committed to excellence. Every small upgrade compounds into a stronger, more resilient platform.

- *Diversifying offerings to capture more value.* Airbnb moved beyond basic room rentals, introducing Airbnb Luxe, and branching into Experiences. By offering guests more ways to engage with the platform, Airbnb increased its share of travelers' spending and cemented its place in the entire travel journey. Since the pandemic Airbnb has operated on a single roadmap, oriented around two product launches a year.

  The Lesson: Don't rely on a single offering. Expand your product or service line to meet evolving customer needs, stay focused on product roadmap, address different segments, and increase your wallet share in the process.

- *Locking in supply with host loyalty programs.* Recognizing that reliable, high-quality hosts attract loyal guests, Airbnb rewarded top performers with Superhost status, better visibility, and early access to new features. This approach created a virtuous cycle: Happy hosts delivered outstanding experiences, encouraging guests to come back.

  The Lesson: Invest in the success and retention of your supply-side partners. Their consistency and dedication drive guest loyalty, fueling sustainable, long-term growth.

- *Adapting through customer feedback.* Whether hosts wanted simpler pricing tools or guests demanded more transparent fees, Airbnb listened and adjusted. A willingness to acknowledge shortcomings and course-correct bolstered the brand's credibility and rapport with users.

  The Lesson: Stay humble and responsive. Show customers you're listening, and they'll reward you with trust, loyalty, and ongoing engagement.

Looking Ahead

As Airbnb continues to shape and be shaped by global travel trends, its future is poised to be as inventive and impactful as its past. Having proven its capacity to evolve—from scrappy startup to sophisticated hospitality marketplace—Airbnb now stands at the intersection of traditional lodging, experiential tourism, and community-driven innovation. With ongoing enhancements to its pricing models, fresh approaches to capturing long-term travelers, and new services designed to deepen user engagement, the platform shows no signs of slowing down. (You can now stay at Shrek's house!) As technology advances and consumer expectations shift, Airbnb's ability to listen, learn, and adapt will remain its most powerful asset.

Notes

Chapter 1

1. Felix Richter, "WeWork's Share Price Drops More than 99% in Two Years," *Statista*, November 5, 2023; https://www.statista.com/chart/30583/share-price-of-wework/.
2. David Gelles, "A $700 Juicer for the Kitchen That Caught Silicon Valley's Eye," *New York Times*, March 31, 2016.
3. "Silicon Valley's $400 Juicer May Be Feeling the Squeeze," *Bloomberg News*, April 19, 2017.
4. AvE, "BOLTR: Juicero, Cold Press Juicer for Rich Weirdos," https://www.youtube.com/watch?v=_Cp-BGQfpHQ&list=LLFLi6zngEFmmrWgAuwBOjdw&index=1239.
5. Frederick F. Reichheld, "The One Number You Need to Grow," *Harvard Business Review*, December 2003.
6. Stephanie Schomer, "How This Startup Succeeded by Ignoring Its Most Important Customers," *Entrepreneur*, June 21, 2017.
7. Harry McCracken, "How Shyp Sank: The Rise and Fall of an On-Demand Startup," *Fast Company*, March 27, 2018.
8. Ibid.

Chapter 2

1. From the Wynn Las Vegas website, https://www.wynnlasvegas.com/dining/casual-dining/the-buffet, retrieved October 16, 2024.
2. Read Bobby's own account, "How Freemium Almost Killed My Business," *Every*, November 1, 2023; https://every.to/p/how-freemium-almost-killed-my-business.

3. Clayton M. Christensen, *The Innovator's Dilemma* (Boston: Harvard Business Review Press, 2016).
4. Google, "How Our Business Works," https://about.google/how-our-business-works.

Chapter 3

1. Vineet Kumar, "Making 'Freemium' Work," *Harvard Business Review,* May 2014; https://hbr.org/2014/05/making-freemium-work.
2. Daniel Kahneman, *Thinking, Fast and Slow* (New York: Farrar, Straus & Giroux, 2013).
3. Lisa Tei, "Price Changes the Way People Experience Wine, Study Finds," *Stanford Report,* January 16, 2008; www.sciencedaily.com/releases/2008/01/080126101053.htm.

Chapter 4

1. Zocdoc, "Zocdoc's Turnaround: From an Unsustainable Path to Profitable Growth," October 15, 2020; www.zocdoc.com/about/news/zocdocs-turnaround-from-an-unsustainable-path-to-profitable-growth/.

Chapter 5

1. David Ulevitch and Rahul Vohra, "Building Products for Power Users," [Podcast], episode 567, posted June 23, 2020; https://a16z.com/podcast/a16z-podcast-building-products-for-power-users/?utm_source=chatgpt.com.

Chapter 7

1. Progressive Corporation, "Snapshot–Safe Driver Discounts;" Progressive.com; Insurance Information Institute, "Usage-Based Insurance (UBI)," iii.org; Telematics .com, "How Telematics Is Changing Insurance"; https://insidebe.com/articles/make-customers-earn-their-discounts/.
2. Jennifer L. Aaker, "Dimensions of Brand Personality," *Journal of Marketing Research* (August 1997), pp. 347–356; https://gsb-courses.stanford.edu/building-innovative-brands/wp-content/uploads/sites/25/2022/04/dimensions_of_brand_personality.pdf.

3. Morgan Sung, "Build-A-Bear's 'Pay Your Age' Day Was an Absolute Disaster," *Yahoo News*, July 12, 2018; Taylor Seely, "Build-a-Bear CEO Apologizes for 'Pay Your Age' Sale Fail," *USA Today*, July 13, 2018; https://www.yahoo.com/news/build-bear-apos-apos-pay-222416058.html.

4. Daniel Kahneman, "Thinking, Fast and Slow," *Washington* Post, December 16, 2011; https://www.washingtonpost.com/entertainment/books/thinking-fast-and-slow-by-daniel-kahneman/2011/12/08/gIQAmyh4yO_story.html?noredirect=on.

Chapter 9

1. "84 Warren Buffett Quotes on Investment, Success and Life," *Quotes Journal*; https://quotesjournal.com/warren-buffett-quotes/.

2. Arun Gupta, "Grailed Commission Fee Change FAQs," https://web.archive.org/web/20230209074127/https:/help.grailed.com/hc/en-us/articles/360051919514.

3. "Unity Software Rolls Back Parts of New Pricing Policy After Backlash," Reuters, September 22, 2023; www.reuters.com/technology/unity-software-rolls-back-parts-new-pricing-policy-after-backlash-2023-09-22/.

Chapter 11

1. Scott R. Baker, Brian Baugh, and Lorenz Kueng, "Income Fluctuations and Firm Choice," *Journal of Financial and Quantitative Analysis*, December 19, 2021, Swiss Finance Institute Research Paper No. 20-29; available at SSRN: https://ssrn.com/abstract=3533766 or http://dx.doi.org/10.2139/ssrn.3533766.

2. Customer lifetime value can be useful here as well but is properly a profit metric (e.g., after sales costs are taken out).

Chapter 13

1. Mark Regan, Joe Morrissey, and Abbas Haider Ali, "Customer Success Is Broken. Here's How to Fix It," Andreessen Horowitz, July 11, 2023; https://a16z.com/customer-success-is-broken-heres-how-to-fix-it/.

Chapter 14

1. Karen Gilchrist, "How a 32-Year-Old Turned a High School Yearbook Idea into a $3.2 Billion Business," Make It, January 9, 2024; www.cnbc.com/2020/01/09/canva-how-melanie-perkins-built-a-3point2-billion-dollar-design-start-up.html?msockid=202f1226047c6a6123fa00c505a36be1.

2. Product-led growth (PLG), a strategy where the product itself drives revenues, is a term coined in 2016. In PLG, users experience the value of the product directly through features like free trials, freemium models, and self-service onboarding.

3. Jon Healey, "Canceling Subscriptions Will Be a 'One-Click' Snap in California Under New Law," *Los Angeles Times*, September 24, 2024; www.latimes.com/california/story/2024-09-24/easy-to-cancel-subscriptions-new-state-law.

4. Rosie Hoggmascall, "Onboarding Personalisation Lessons from Canva," *Medium*, March 22, 2024; uxdesign.cc/onboarding-personalisation-lessons-from-canva-b65e83f06cae.

5. Ibid.

6. David Burson, "Introducing Canva Enterprise," May 24, 2024; www.canva.com/newsroom/news/canva-enterprise/.

Chapter 15

1. Fortive, "Fortive to Acquire ServiceChannel for Approximately $1.2 Billion and Provides Preliminary Financial Information for the Second Quarter 2021" [Press release], July 12, 2021; https://investors.fortive.com/news-events/press-releases/detail/80/fortive-to-acquire-servicechannel-for-approximately-1-2-billion-and-provides-preliminary-financial-information-for-the-second-quarter-2021?utm_source=chatgpt.com.

Chapter 16

1. Marc Andreesen, "Part 4: The Only Thing that Matters," Pmarchive, posted June 25, 2007; pmarchive.com/guide_to_startups_part4.html.

Index

Page numbers followed by *f*, *t*, and *e* refer to figures, tables, and exhibits, respectively.

315

317

and churn, 239–240, 284
of packages/bundles, 161–162
of price increases, 176, 183–186, 187
of pricing, 99–100
of value (*see* Value messaging)
Community, building, 298–299
Community Builders, 25–28, 30*f*
neglect of emerging needs by, 26–28
as people pleasers, 28
strategies for avoiding traps, 34*t*, 35*t*
Competence, as brand identity in
promotions, 128*f*, 129
Competition:
differentiating yourself from the,
114–115
and locking in customers, 65
and outcome-based pricing model,
67–69
using price metrics to differentiate
from the, 72, 73
Competitive advantages, highlighting,
111, 112*f*, 113
Competitive intensity, identifying
pricing drivers by, 202
Complex magazine, 172
Concession matrix, 135–138, 137*f*, 206
Consistency trap, 208–209
Consistent pricing, 97–98, 174
Consumer goods sector, 45
Consumption, synchronizing payment
with, 72
Consumption limit, fencing by, 52
Context, of price increases, 99–100,
174–175
Contextual conversion, 269
Continuous engagement, 292

Continuous innovation, 295
Continuous onboarding of new value,
273–274
Continuous refinement, 303–305
Contracts, 62, 86, 98, 106,
177–179, 279
Controlled-Narrative axiom, 184
Conversion, contextual, 269–270. *See
also* Free-to-paid conversion
Core customer groups, identifying, 96
Core value proposition, 49, 55, 258, 259
Cost(s):
initial high-cost products and
services, 46–47
opportunity, 200
and price metrics, 72
of serving free users, 48
switching, 240
Costco, 224
Counterconcessions, 135
COVID-19 pandemic, 10, 116
Created-Need axiom, 198
Credits, customer, 139, 142*f*
Cross-functional experiments, running,
247–248
Cross-selling, 26, 46, 103, 131, 134, 177
CSMs (customer success managers),
262–264
CTA (call to action), 132
Culture, making growth part of the,
248
Customers:
analyzing impact of price increases
on, 179–181
asking, to describe your product,
115–117

321

Index

322

Index

323

Index

325

Index

326

329

Index